How to
BUY STOCKS

SEVENTH REVISED EDITION # How to BUY STOCKS

by LOUIS ENGEL
and BRENDAN BOYD

Little, Brown and Company   Boston   Toronto

SEVENTH EDITION, REVISED

Sixth Printing

LIBRARY OF CONGRESS CATALOGING IN PUBLICATION DATA

Engel, Louis, 1909-
    How to buy stocks.
    Includes index.
    1. Securities.   2. Investments.   I. Boyd, Brendan.
II. Title.
HG4521.E6   1982   332.63′2   82-16230
ISBN 0-316-10439-6

MV

Published simultaneously in Canada
by Little, Brown & Company (Canada) Limited

PRINTED IN THE UNITED STATES OF AMERICA

Acknowledgments

SUCH is the process of learning that it is never possible for anyone to say exactly how he acquired any given body of knowledge. And that circumstance I now find somewhat consoling, because in a very real sense this book is not my book, but it is the product of hundreds of different people who over the years have taught me what I have written down here.

Obviously, I cannot acknowledge my indebtedness to all these people and so I must necessarily limit my thanks to those who helped me directly in the preparation and checking of the material in this book through all its seven versions from 1952 to 1982. Some are no longer associated with the institutions whose names are used to identify them here. Some are no longer even alive. But all of them are people to whom I owe a debt beyond repayment.

These include Alger B. Chapman, Jr., Cecil MacCoy, Willard K. Vanderbeck, Stanley West, F. W. Reiniger, Richard I. Callanan, Aileen Lyons, Thomas T. Murphy, Charles Storer, and George Christopoulos, all of the New York Stock Exchange; John W. Sheehan and Victoria Kelly of the American Stock Exchange; James H. Lorie and Lawrence Fisher of the University of Chicago; John McKenzie, Russell Morrison, George Olsen, and Donald A. Moser of Standard & Poor's Corporation; Max Fromkin of Fromkin & Fromkin; J. Scott Rattray and Huntly W. F. McKay of the Toronto Stock Exchange; Leah Cartabruno, Joseph H. Cooper, and Eno Hobbing of the National Association of Securities Dealers; and a score of individuals actively engaged in the securities business: Kenneth R. Williams, Robert L. Stott, Victor B. Cook, Edward A. Pierce, Milija Rubezanin, James E. Thomson, Donald T. Regan, Howard T. Sprow, Peter F. McCourt, James Albee, Cecil C. Burgin, John J. Cahill, Rudolph J. Chval, James D. Corbett, Dwight H. Emanuelson, John F. Ferguson, John A. Fitzgerald, Richard P. Gillette, Calvin Gogolin, Allan D. Gulliver, Gilbert Hammer, Stephen B. Kagan, Arthur L. Kerrigan, George T. Lee, George J. Leness, Josiah O. Low, Gillette K. Martin, Michael W. McCarthy, Anthony G. Meyer, Harvey L. Miller, John H. Moller, Samuel Mothner, Joseph C. Quinn, Walter A. Scholl, Julius H. Sedlmayr, Thomas B. Shearman, George L. Shinn, John W. Adams, Jr., David Western, Jay Robinson-Duff, Wallace Sellers, John Anderson, Thomas J. Christie, Robert E. Cleary, Francis J. Ripepi, Robert Rittereiser, Martin Portnoy, Nancy K. Hartley, Thomas E. Engel, and — most important — Robert L. Tebeau, Frederick P. Groll, and Robert C. Kavee.

Last, but certainly not least, let me list Muriel D. Nutzel, Ann Scourby, Loretta A. Gigante, Elizabeth J. Gibson, Loretta D. Hanley, Zita Millet, Agnes Rother, Janet K. Low, Lorraine M. Hanley, Gloria Duck, Barbara Lee, Gloria Wiener, Jane Keen, and Glea Humez.

And, of course, my long-suffering editor, Richard P. McDonough of Little, Brown and Company.

Foreword to the Original Edition

THIS book is based on a very simple premise: that the stock market is going up.

Tomorrow? Next month? Next year?

Maybe yes, maybe no. Maybe the market will be a lot lower than it is today.

But over any long period of time — 10 years, 20 years, 50 years — this book assumes that the market is bound to go up.

Why?

Because it always has.

Because the market is a measure of the vigor of American business, and unless something drastic happens to America, business is going to go on growing.

Because prices of food and clothing and almost everything else in this country — including stocks — have steadily gone up as the buying power of the dollar has gone down. That's a trend that isn't likely to be reversed.

And so these are the reasons why the author is sold on the value of investing, of buying stocks for the long pull — and not for a quick profit tomorrow.

There's nothing hidden about this prejudice. You'll see it when you read the book. And you will find other prejudices, other opinions, despite an earnest effort to focus this book strictly on facts — the facts about investing that have been obscured all too long by double talk, by financial jargon, and by unnecessary mystery.

Of course it can be said that here are no facts when you get beyond the simple business of adding one and one. That's true. So let's say that here are the facts as the author sees them — and as plainly as he can state them.

He has only one hope: that they will add up to good common sense in your own mind.

LOUIS ENGEL

Introduction to the Seventh Edition

TWENTY years ago I worked in a bookstore in Boston. We sold hundreds of copies of *How to Buy Stocks* every year.

A few years later, after opening my first brokerage account, I had a chance to read Mr. Engel's incisive primer and discover for myself the reason for its continued popularity.

I have since reread it on several occasions, never failing to marvel at the logic and clarity with which it makes seemingly forbidding investment procedures seem like the common, everyday undertakings they, in fact, can, and should, be.

But all too often are not.

Several months ago I was browsing through another Boston bookstore when a clerk asked me to recommend a book that would explain the intricacies of investing to him in the most comprehensive and least painful manner. My eyes scanned the hundreds of screaming titles: *How to Make a Million Dollars in Twenty Minutes with This Theory, How to Avoid the Coming Cataclysm with That Theory*. Then my eyes settled serenely on *How to Buy Stocks*. I handed it to the clerk without a word. Just as I would have twenty years ago.

Every investment book needs to be revised periodically to keep pace with changing market conditions. *How to Buy Stocks* is one of the handful of investment books that require, during this revision process, incidental updating rather than fundamental change. This is the mark of a true classic.

In undertaking this seventh revision, therefore, I have made it my primary objective to retain the full thrust of Mr. Engel's basic ideas. I have updated the main body of the text to conform to current regulatory conditions and shifting market moods. I have added new chapters on computerized stock selection, related stock market reading, and the many alternative investment vehicles that have emerged in the past five years. Otherwise I have sought neither to tinker with Mr. Engel's thesis nor to intrude on his methods of explication.

The extent to which I have succeeded in revising *How to Buy Stocks*, then, is the extent to which I have stayed out of its way in updating it.

I am grateful for the opportunity of ushering this indispensable volume into its fourth decade.

BRENDAN BOYD
May, 1982

A Note on the Gender of Pronouns

WHEN the first edition of *How to Buy Stocks* was published in 1953, there were very few women actively engaged in trading stocks, either as customers, brokers, or employees of the various exchanges. In the intervening 29 years most of the ludicrous prejudices that caused these exclusionary conditions have disappeared. As a result, women have finally begun to take their rightful places in the world of American finance. Whenever possible, therefore, we have replaced the masculine pronouns used exclusively in the earlier editions of this book to refer to both brokers and customers with more specific and appropriate words. We have retained the use of the masculine pronoun only when the clarity of the text absolutely necessitated it.

Contents

How to
BUY STOCKS

A Note on How to Read This Book

MANY people are afraid to buy stocks because they think investing is a complicated business.

If it were really complicated, more than 32.6 million Americans (14.4% of the country's population) wouldn't own stocks, as they did at the beginning of 1982.

Actually, investing only *sounds* complicated, and that is because it uses a lot of unfamiliar words. The words themselves stand for very simple things.

Winston Churchill once said, "Old words are best, and old words when short are best of all." This book tries to use old, short words instead of Wall Street jargon. It seeks to explain the technical words of the securities business by explaining the things they stand for. In other words, each term is explained in *context* as the story of investing unfolds. You won't find a glossary or any long list of definitions anywhere in this book.

In telling the investment story, the book begins with the common words in the business — *stock, share, capital* — and just to be sure that the reader realizes he has encountered a technical term, possibly new to him, the word is italicized the first time it is used. And to be further sure there is no misunderstanding or confusion, no technical term is used until the reader comes logically upon it in the development of the whole thesis.

If the reader has by any chance forgotten the meaning of a particular word, all he has to do is refer to the index and look back in the book to that page on which the word is first used.

Here, then, is the story of investing told in terms that the author believes everyone can understand — himself included.

CHAPTER 1

What Investment Means to You

THIS is a book about how to make your money earn more money for you by investing it.

It is not a book about how to make a million in the stock market. If there were any certain way to do that, all the brokers in the world, the men who are supposed to know more than most people about the market, would be millionaires. Needless to say, they're not.

This is a book about investing. Specifically, it's a book about investing in stocks and bonds, which is one way of putting your extra money to work so that in the long run it will earn a good return for you — either in the form of a regular income from dividends or in the form of a profit resulting from growth in value or a combination of both.

Most people, if they have anything left at all after paying their bills, will think first of putting that extra money into a savings bank or into life insurance. Nobody could possibly quarrel with such a prudent course. These forms of saving are essential if people are going to protect themselves properly against the always unpredictable emergencies of life.

But today millions of people have come to regard *securities* — stocks and bonds in all their varied forms — as an equally good form of investment.

Of course, there's a risk in buying stocks and bonds — and for most people it's a far bigger risk than it needs to be, because they've never taken the time to study securities or find out how to invest in them wisely.

But it should never be forgotten that there's some risk in any form of investment. There's a risk in just having money. Actually, having money is a double-barreled risk. The one risk — the risk that you might lose some of your money regardless of what you do with it — is always evident. The other risk is never so apparent. And that's the risk that the money you save today may not buy as much at some future time if prices of food and clothing and almost everything else continue to go up, as indeed they have, more or less steadily, since this country began. The person who simply hoards extra dollars — puts them in a vault or buries them in the ground — may avoid that first evident risk, the risk of losing any of them. But such a person can never sidestep the unseen risk, the risk of *inflation*.

So every decision you make about what to do with your extra money should take into consideration those two kinds of risk: the evident and the unseen.

Naturally, you must also consider the return you hope to realize on your money. In most forms of investment the greater the return you try to get, the greater the risk, the *evident* risk, you must be prepared to take.

If you put your money in a savings account, it's almost impossible to lose any of it because your savings are insured by the Federal Deposit Insurance Corporation for up to $100,000 in one bank. But you have to be willing to accept a return of only 5½% a year and you have to realize that a savings account provides no protection against the *unseen* risk of inflation. Your money, or capital, won't grow except by the redeposit of the interest you get, and then only slowly.

You can also put your money in various bank time deposits that offer markedly higher rates of interest than simple savings accounts (ranging up to 20% p.d. for $100,000 for 30 days during the credit squeeze of 1981, for example). Rates earned on these certificates depend on the amount of money you deposit and the length of time you agree to leave it with the bank. But even with these more generous yields you are still earning on your invested capital a return that barely keeps you even with the spiraling inflation rate and that remains largely exposed to the crippling taxing powers of federal, state, and local governments. Additionally, these types of deposit come equipped with another subtle drawback. They tie your money up completely for the length of time specified in the deposit contract, tie it up where you can't get at it, either for emergencies or to take advantage of other developing investment opportunities, without running the risk of incurring the "loss of interest" penalties that most of these time deposits stipulate for premature withdrawal.

Investing your spare cash in one of the new, and enormously popular, money market funds allows you to enjoy yields equal to, or slightly greater than, those available on time deposits of similar amounts. These funds are nothing more than a pooling of enormous amounts of money from thousands of individual investors for investing in a wide range of short-term money market instruments with various maturity dates. Thus, there is always a steady stream of cash flowing into, and back through, these funds to guarantee that individual investors can get any or all of their money out anytime they want to. Still, most money market fund yields are subject to the same rigors of taxation as bank interest (although there are money market funds that invest in municipal securities, and are therefore tax-exempt). The 15% they generated in 1981–1982 looks like a lot less when stacked against the double-digit rises in the cost-of-living index this country has been experiencing each of the past several years. Fifteen percent in. And then 15% back out almost before you can count it.

Life insurance is also virtually 100% safe, thanks to state and federal laws. But there's more sense in buying a standard life insurance policy to protect your family than there is in buying it as an investment. Over a long period of years, the usual life insurance policy may yield a return somewhat better than that of a savings account. But it too fails to protect you against the *unseen* risk of inflation. The money you may get on such a policy when you retire is not likely to buy as much as you could have bought with all the money you paid out in premiums over the years.

What else might you do with your money? Well, you might put it into a savings and loan association, which makes a business of lending money on home mortgages. Thanks again to government supervision, this kind of investment will be relatively safe as far as the *evident* risk is concerned. But it will pay you very little more interest than you would get on a savings account. And it will not protect you against the *unseen* risk of inflation.

You can invest in real estate. And as a general rule real estate prices are likely to rise if the prices of other things do. So there, you say, you *can* find protection against that *unseen* risk. Yes, there you can — provided you buy the right piece of property at the right time and at the right price, and provided you're just as lucky when you sell it. Provided, too, that all the taxes you pay while you own the property don't eat up your potential profit. And provided you cope with all the unpredictable actions of local zoning and assessment boards. Here the *evident* risks are so great, even for those who work full time at buying, developing, managing and selling properties, that real estate must be classified not as an investment, but as a speculation for the average man with only a little extra money.

Then too you can invest in some of the "hard asset" areas that recently have become so popular as inflation hedges. You can buy gold or silver. But they, and all other investment metals, strategic and nonstrategic, are very expensive to store and earn no dividends at all to help pay for their keep. You could buy gems or coins or stamps. But they require a great deal of expertise to traffic in and are characterized by exorbitant retail markups, which discount a significant percentage of their potential appreciation right off the bat. You could buy art or antiques. But they're not the most portable of assets for apocalypse-minded investors. And they're very difficult to liquidate in times of down markets.

Finally, you can invest in stocks and bonds. That's what banks do with at least part of the money you deposit with them, in order to earn the interest they pay you and to earn a profit for themselves. The same thing is true of insurance companies. Both kinds of institution have always invested heavily in bonds. But today they are buying more and more stocks, even to the limits permitted by the various state laws. Furthermore, commercial banks and trust companies, which are responsible for funds left with them to invest for various beneficiaries, are putting a greater proportion of those funds into stocks.

Why?

Because over the years, the record shows that the average stock has paid a better return and provided a better balance of protection against the evident and unseen financial risk than any other form of investment.

The stockholders of America are the people who own much of America's business — virtually all its more important business. As that business has grown, stockowners have prospered. As it continues to grow, they will continue to prosper.

Not all of them have prospered all the time. Of course not. But most of them have prospered most of the time. Some have made millions, and some have gone broke. Just as some companies have succeeded and some have failed. But over the years, the average investor has generally earned a significant return on his money. Most important of all, he has seen his stockholdings go up in value as prices generally have risen. He has been able most times to sell his stocks at a profit, especially if he has held them a long time. And he has thus protected his money against the unseen risk of inflation.

A study completed in early 1982 by Computer Directions Advisors of Silver Spring, Maryland, showed that over the entire 56-year period from 1926 to 1982, total returns on common stocks exceeded the rise in the consumer price index by a ratio of three to one. And during the 47 possible ten-year holding periods over those 56 years, common shares outpaced consumer prices in 41 of the 47.

These are the reasons why more people are buying stocks today who never gave them a thought until a few years ago. And all of these people are finding that it pays to know something about the fundamentals of the business. So . . .

CHAPTER 2

What You Should Know
about Common Stocks

THERE'S nothing commonplace about *common stock*. It's the number one security in our system, basic to all corporate business and to our whole free enterprise system. If you own a *share* of stock in a company, you own part of that company. You and the other shareholders own the company in common.

How does common stock come into being?

Assume for the moment that you've invented a fine new collapsible metal fishing rod. You've got your patents, and you're convinced there is a splendid market for your pocket fishing pole.

You're all ready to begin production, except for that one essential: *capital*. You haven't got the money to rent a small factory, buy the necessary machinery, and hire labor and salesmen. You could get your business under way for $20,000, but you haven't got $20,000. The bank won't lend it to you simply on the strength of your patents, and you can't find an "angel" with that kind of cash to put in your business.

So you decide to form a company and sell shares in the venture. You file the necessary incorporation papers as required by your state law, and the Pocket Pole Company, Incorporated, comes into being.

In setting up that company, you might find twenty people, each of whom was willing to put up an even $1,000 of *venture capital*. In that case, you'd have to issue and sell only twenty shares of stock at $1,000 apiece. Then every person who bought such a share would own 1/20 of the company.

But one person might be willing to put $2,000 into your Pocket Pole Company, while another person could only afford to invest $200. So instead of issuing twenty shares of stock at $1,000 each, you decide it's better to put a lower price on every share of stock and sell more shares. Such a plan would be more attractive to the people who might be interested in buying the stock, because if they ever had to sell it, they would probably find it easier to dispose of lower-priced shares. After all, more people can spare $10 or $100 than can afford to invest in $1,000 units.

So you finally decide to issue 2,000 shares at $10 apiece. Taken collectively, those shares would represent the common stock issue of the Pocket Pole Company. The $10 price you place on it would represent its *par value*.

You sell the 2,000 shares at $10 apiece, and by this means you raise the $20,000 capital you need. The Pocket Pole Company is in business. Actually, of course, you might well think of Pocket Pole as *your* business. So that when the company was set up, you might bargain with the other stockholders so you could acquire a stock interest in the company at little or no cost to yourself. But for purposes of simplicity it can be assumed here that you simply buy your stock like any other stockholder.

Every person who owns a share of Pocket Pole stock is a stockholder in the company. They are shareowners, part owners. How big a part of the company they own depends on how many shares they buy in relation to the 2,000 that are sold, or *outstanding*. If they buy one share, they own $\frac{1}{2000}$ of the company. If they buy twenty shares, they own $\frac{1}{100}$, or 1%, of the company. As evidence of their ownership, a *stock certificate* is issued to each stockholder showing the number of shares he owns.

When the stock is all sold, let's assume the company finds that it has 50 stockholders on its books. Now, it would be difficult to operate Pocket Pole if all 50 of them had to be consulted about every major decision — whether to buy this lathe or that one, whether to price the product at $40 or $50.

So the stockholders elect a *board of directors* to oversee the operations of the company. How is the board picked? By the stockholders on the basis of the number of shares of stock each one owns. If there are five shareholders to be elected to the board, each for a set term, the one who owns one share of stock will, as a matter of general practice, be allowed one vote for each of the five vacancies, and the one who owns ten shares will have ten votes for each vacancy.

This five-member board of directors elects its own *chairman*, and, once organized, is responsible for managing the affairs of the Pocket Pole Company. Since in most instances the board members can't give their full time to the job of running the company, they pick a president to be the actual operating head. They also name the other major officers. Such officers may or may not be members of the board. But they are responsible to the full board, and periodically — perhaps once a month or once a quarter — the officers report to the board on the progress of the company and their conduct of its affairs.

Then once a year the Pocket Pole Company board of directors will conduct a meeting open to all the stockholders: at this meeting the management makes its *annual report* to the owners. Furthermore, the board supplies all stockholders, those present and those absent, with a copy of the report.

If any stockholder is dissatisfied with the way things are going for the company, he can speak his mind at the meeting. He may even make a motion that the board adopt some policy or procedure that he thinks is an improvement on present practice. If the motion is in order, it will be submitted to the stockholders for a vote. In most instances, such issues are decided by simple majority vote, with each stockholder being allowed as many votes as he has shares.

If an action that requires a vote of the shareowners is scheduled to come before a meeting, such as the election of new directors, each stockholder is notified. If he cannot attend the *annual meeting* and vote, he is usually asked to sign a paper that authorizes one or more of the officers or directors to act as his *proxy*, or representative, and vote for him. That's why these papers are called *proxies*. Sometimes when new directors are to be elected, a dissident group of stockholders will propose a rival slate in opposition to those picked by the management. In such a fight, each side will try to get signed proxies from the stockholders favoring its slate. This is called a *proxy fight*.

In addition to the regular meetings of the board or the annual meeting of the stockholders, special meetings of either group may be called to deal with special problems.

Why should people invest money in the Pocket Pole Company? Because they think it has a good product and one that is likely to make money. If it does, they as part owners stand to make money. This can happen in two ways: first, through the payment of *dividends*, and second, through an increase in the value of Pocket Pole stock.

Let's look at the dividend picture first. Suppose in the first year, after paying all bills and taxes, the company has *earnings*, or profits, of $2,000, or 10%, on its $20,000 *capitalization*, the money that it raised by selling 2,000 shares of common stock. That would be a handsome profit for a new company, but not impossible.

It would then be up to the board of directors to decide what to do with that profit. It could pay it all out to the stockholders in dividends. Or it could vote to keep every penny of it in the company treasury and use it to buy more machinery to make more pocket poles and earn more profits the following year. Since all stockholders like dividends and all boards of directors know that, Pocket Pole's board might very properly decide on a middle course. It might vote to pay out $1,000 in dividends and plow the other $1,000 back into the business as *retained earnings*.

Now if the board has $1,000 for dividends and 2,000 shares of stock outstanding, the dividend per share is going to be $0.50.

That's what the shareholder with one share of stock gets, while the shareholder with ten shares gets $5, and the shareholder with 100 shares gets $50. For all of them this would represent a 5% return on their investment, regardless of the number of shares they own, since they each paid $10 a share.

But there's another intangible return that they would get on their money. Presumably that $1,000, which the board decided to retain and plow back into the business, will serve to increase the value of every person's share in the company — their *equity* in the company, as it's called.

If an original share of stock in Pocket Pole was fairly valued at $10, each of the 2,000 shares might now be considered to be worth $10.50, since the company now has an extra $1,000 in the business besides the original capital of $20,000.

Already that par value figure of $10 has been made slightly fictitious. As the years roll by, it will have less and less relation to the value of the stock, especially if the company continues to earn good money and if the directors continue, year after year, to put a portion of those earnings back into the company. In comparatively few years, the total *assets* of the company — everything it owns: its plant, machinery, and inventory of products — might well have doubled without a corresponding increase in its *liabilities:* the sum total of what the company owes. In that case, the *book value* of each share of stock — assets, less liabilities, divided by the number of shares outstanding — would be increased.

Par value is a term so generally misunderstood and so completely without significance that many companies today either do not set any value on their stock, in which case it is known as *no-par stock,* or they fix the value at $1 or $5, a figure so low that it could not possibly be misinterpreted as an index of its real value.

Even book value is a term with little real meaning today, although it had a real significance in the last century when *watered stock* was all too often sold to an unsuspecting public. That graphic expression, watered stock, is supposed to have had its origin in the practice of feeding cattle large quantities of salt on their way to market and then giving them a big drink of water just before they went on the weighing scales.

As applied to securities, the phrase describes the kind of company stock that was issued with an inflated value. For instance, an unscrupulous operator might pay only half a million dollars for some company, then issue a million dollars' worth of stock in it. He might sell all that stock to others and pocket a half-million dollars' profit. Or, after he sold half the stock and got his cost back, he might keep the remaining shares and thus own a half-interest in the company at no cost to himself. Such stock issues are now virtually nonexistent, thanks to improved government regulation.

Most stockholders have come to realize that book value frequently doesn't mean very much. What really counts is the earning power of a company and its growth prospects, not the total value of its plants and machinery. Frequently, the stocks of many big companies sell at a price considerably more than their book value — sometimes double or triple the book value. In contrast, other stocks, like those of the railroads, which have gigantic investments in equipment, sell for much less than book value. Book value is frequently thought of as representing what the owner of a share of stock could expect to get if the company were *liquidated* — if it went out of business and sold off all its property. This is often a misconception, because when a company is in liquidation it can rarely get full value for the property it must dispose of.

So how do you know what a share of stock is really worth — Pocket Pole stock or any other?

There's only one answer to that. Bluntly, a share of stock is worth only what somebody else is willing to pay for it when you want to sell it.

If the product isn't popular and sales suffer, if the cost of wages and raw materials is too high, if the management is inefficient, Pocket Pole or any other company can fail. And if it goes into bankruptcy, your stock can become worthless.

That's the black side of the picture. That's what can happen if the risk you assumed in buying a stock proves to be a bad one.

But if Pocket Pole proves to be successful company, if it has a consistent record of good earnings, if part of those earnings is paid out regularly in dividends and another part of them wisely used to expand the company — then your stock is likely to be worth more than the $10 you paid for it. Perhaps a good deal more.

And that is the second way in which a stockholder expects to make money on an investment. First, through dividends. Second, through an increase in the value of the stock — or, rather, an increase in the price that somebody else will pay for it. This is known as *price appreciation*.

The price of a stock, like the price of almost everything else in this world, is determined by supply and demand: what one person is willing to pay for a stock and what another one is willing to sell it for, what one person bids and another asks. That's why stocks always have a *bid* and an *asked* price. And don't forget that that price is not necessarily a reliable guide to good investing. Some people think that a low-priced stock is a good buy because it is cheap, and they shy away from a high-priced stock because they think it is expensive. That just isn't so. The stock of one company may sell at a low price simply because it has a large number of shares outstanding — because the whole pie has been cut up into lots and lots of little pieces — while the stock of another equally good company may sell at a high price because it hasn't been cut up into so many pieces and there are relatively fewer shares outstanding. The price of a stock takes on meaning only as you consider it in relation to earnings and dividends per share.

Here, in brief, is the story of common stock — what it is, how it comes into being, what it means to own it.

American Telephone & Telegraph, General Motors, and U.S. Steel may have millions of shares of stock outstanding, and they may even count their shareholders in the millions. But in these giant corporations, each share of stock plays precisely the same role as a share of stock in our Pocket Pole Company. And each stockholder has the same rights, privileges, and responsibilities.

There is only one significant difference between buying a share of Pocket Pole and investing in a share of American Telephone & Telegraph, General Motors, or U.S. Steel. These big companies have been in business for many years. You know something about them and the reputations they enjoy. You know how good their products or services are. You can examine their financial history, see for yourself how the prices of their stocks have moved over the years and what kind of record they have made as far as earnings and dividends are concerned. And on the basis of such information you can form a more reliable judgment about whether the stocks of these companies are overpriced or underpriced.

In contrast, the person who buys stock in our Pocket Pole Company has nothing to go on other than his own estimate of how good a product the company has and how big its sales are likely to be. There are no benchmarks to guide him, no past records on which to base an appraisal of the future.

As a matter of literal truth, the Pocket Pole stockholder cannot properly be called an investor. Most times, when a person buys a stock in a brand-new company, he isn't investing in it; he's speculating in it. An *investor* is a person who is willing to take a moderate risk with his money for the sake of earning a moderate return. A *speculator* is a person who takes a big risk in the hope of making a big profit as a result of an increase in the price of a stock. An investor usually has an eye on long-term values to be realized over a period of years. A speculator usually hopes to make a big profit in a relatively short period of time.

American business needs both kinds of risk takers. Without the speculator, new business wouldn't be born, nor would many an old business be tided over a rough spot. Without the investor, a company would not have the capital to carry on, much less grow and expand.

CHAPTER 3

How and Why New Stock Is Sold

LET'S assume that the years are good to our Pocket Pole Company. It continues to grow. The original collapsible fishing pole has proved a best-seller, and the company now has a full line of models. Good earnings year after year have enabled the management to put the stock on a regular annual dividend basis. It now pays $1 a year per share — $0.25 a quarter — and in several good years the directors even declared *extra dividends,* one of $0.25 and two of $0.50 a share.

Now the company feels that the time has come for it to expand. It could sell twice as many pocket poles, make twice as much profit, if only it had a bigger factory. So the board of directors decides to expand the plant. That means it will need more machinery, a larger workforce, and, above all, more money — a lot more money than it has in the company treasury. Problem: how to get $40,000.

A bank might advance the money. Maybe two or three banks would each put up part of the loan. But some of Pocket Pole's directors don't like the idea of being in hock to the banks. They worry not only about paying interest on the loan every year, but also about paying the money back in installments. That kind of steady long-term drain on the company treasury could eat into earnings and result in few, if any, dividends. Furthermore, banks don't usually like to make such long-term loans, and even if they are willing to, they might — to protect their loans — insist on having their representatives sit on the board of directors. That is a prospect some of Pocket Pole's directors don't relish.

Isn't there some other way to raise the money?

Yes, there is.

Maybe the present stockholders would like to put more money into the company. Maybe there are other people who would like to invest in a nice thriving little business like Pocket Pole. There's an idea.

And so the board of directors proposes to the stockholders that they authorize the company to issue 3,000 additional shares of stock — 2,000 shares to be sold at once, and the remaining 1,000 to be held against the day when the company may want to raise more money by selling more stock. Each of the new shares of stock will carry with it the same rights and privileges as an original share.

This proposal is approved by a substantial majority of the stockholders, but not without some disagreement. One stockholder objected to the plan. She thought the company should have two classes of common stock: a *Class A stock,* which would consist of the original issue, enjoying full rights and privileges, and a new *Class B stock,* on which the same dividends would be paid but which would not carry any voting privileges. In other words, she wanted control of the company kept in the hands of the original stockholders.

The board chairman replied to this suggestion by pointing out that such *classified-stock* setups, A stock and B stock, are no longer popular with investors. True, some companies still have two issues of common stock outstanding, but few companies have followed such a practice in recent years.

Furthermore, the chairman explained, the old stockholders would properly still retain about the same measure of control, since they could be expected to buy most of the new issue anyway. This appeared likely, because it would be offered to them first and on especially favorable terms. This is the usual procedure for companies that have a *new issue* of stock to sell.

In this instance, the board recommended that old stockholders be permitted to buy the new stock at $20 a share — a figure about $2 less than the price at which the original stock was then being bought or sold — while others who might buy any of the new issue that was left over would have to pay whatever the going price might be at the time.

After the stockholders approved the plan, each was given *rights* that entitled them to buy new shares in the company at a discount from the market price. This right was clearly set forth on a certificate mailed to each shareholder. Everyone who owned one of the 2,000 original shares was permitted to buy one of the 2,000 new shares at $20. And the owner of ten old shares could buy ten new ones if he chose to exercise his rights. But such rights had to be exercised within two weeks — for rights are relatively short-lived. If the right was good for a long time, perhaps for years or even perpetually, it would be called not a right but a *warrant:* a certificate that gives the holder the right to buy a specific number of shares of a company's stock at a stipulated price within a certain time limit or, in some cases, perpetually.

Some Pocket Pole shareholders, unable or unwilling to purchase additional stock, sold their rights. Often the market in such rights is a brisk one, even when they entitle the holder to buy only a part of a share — a tenth, a fifth, or a quarter of a share of new stock for each old share that he owns.

In the case of Pocket Pole each right was worth $1. Here is the way the value would have been arrived at: if you owned one share of Pocket Pole worth $22 and you exercised your right to buy an additional share at $20, you would then own two shares at an average of $21 apiece, or just $1 less than the going price per share. Hence, the right could be figured to have a value of just $1. Actually, some stockholders might sell their rights for a fraction of that, while others might get more than $1 apiece, if the price of

Pocket Pole advanced while the rights were still on the market. And, of course, some careless stockholders would ignore their rights, forgetting either to sell or to exercise them, in which case the rights would become worthless after the expiration date.

The standard formula for figuring the value of rights works this way: first, take the prevailing market price of the stock (in this case $22), then subtract the subscription price (here $20); divide this difference ($2) by the number of old shares it is necessary to own in order to buy one new share (1) *plus* an additional one (1 plus 1 is 2, and $2 divided by 2 is $1).

When the rights expired, Pocket Pole discovered that all of them had been exercised except for 50 shares of the new issue. These were readily sold at a price of $22. The company had raised $40,100 of new capital and had 4,000 shares of common stock outstanding.

Pocket Pole's plan for expanding the plant was put into effect. But because of delays in getting the machinery needed, it was two years before the new factory was in full operation. That situation raised for the board the awkward problem of how to continue paying dividends to the stockholders. In the first year of the transition period, the board felt obligated to continue paying the customary $1 dividend. But that put a serious dent in the company treasury. The second year, the directors decided it would be foolhardy to do that again. They concluded that the only prudent thing they could do was to *pass the dividend* and keep the full year's earnings in the treasury until the new plant was operating efficiently.

But if the company paid no dividend, what would the stockholders say? Omission of the dividend would certainly mean that the price of the stock would go down. It would be interpreted as a sign of trouble by those who might be interested in buying the stock.

The board found an answer to that problem in the 1,000 shares of new stock that had been authorized but not issued. With the approval of the stockholders, it took those 1,000 shares and distributed them without any charge among the owners of the 4,000 outstanding shares on the basis of one quarter of a share of free stock for every single share that a stockholder owned.

Actually, this *stock dividend* did nothing to improve the lot of any individual stockholders. They were not one penny richer, nor did they actually own any greater proportion of the company. The stockholder who had one share before the stock dividend owned 1/4000 of the company. Now with 1¼ shares out of the 5,000 outstanding, that stockholder still owns exactly 1/4000.

Yet in terms of future prospects, that extra quarter of a share had real potential value. When the company got rolling again, that extra quarter share could represent a real profit — and extra dividends, too.

That, happily, is exactly what happened. Pocket Pole prospered. The next year it earned $2 a share. And the directors felt they could prudently restore the old $1 dividend on each share. To the stockholder who held 1¼ shares, that meant a return of $1.25.

CHAPTER 4

What You Should Know
about Preferred Stocks

WITH its new plant and its new machinery, the Pocket Pole Company forged rapidly ahead. Earnings doubled. Then they doubled again. And most of those earnings, by decision of the directors, were reinvested in the business to expand production and improve operations. Dividends were modest. But the company was growing. Now its assets totaled almost $200,000

Then another problem — and another opportunity — presented itself. The Rapid Reel Company, a well-known competitor owned and operated by a single family, could be acquired for $75,000. It was, the Pocket Pole directors agreed, a good buy at that price. But where could they get the $75,000?

Negotiations with the president of Rapid Reel revealed that he was anxious to retire from business. He planned to invest whatever he got from the sale of the company so that it would yield him and his family a safe, reasonable income. Further, it was evident that he had a high regard for the management of Pocket Pole and was favorably impressed with the company's prospects. Here was the basis of a deal.

So the directors of Pocket Pole proposed that they take over Rapid Reel as a going concern and merge it into their company. How would they pay for it? By issuing *preferred* stock in the Pocket Pole Company — an issue of 750 shares with a par value of $100 per share — and giving it to the owners of Rapid Reel in exchange for their company.

Like most preferred stock, this issue would assure the owners a first claim on the assets of Pocket Pole, after all debts had been taken care of, should it ever be necessary to liquidate the company. Further, it was provided that this particular preferred stock would carry a specific dividend payable every year on every share before any dividends could be paid to common-stock holders. To make the deal as attractive as possible for the owners of Rapid Reel, the company was willing to pay a good dividend — $10 on every share, or 10%.

Sometimes such a preferred dividend is not paid in a given year because the company did not earn enough that year to cover it. But the most common type of preferred stock is *cumulative preferred*. That is the kind Pocket Pole issued to the owners of Rapid Reel. Pocket Pole's cumulative preferred stock provided that if Pocket Pole could not pay the $10 dividend in any year, the amount due for that year would accrue to the preferred-stock holders and would be paid the following year or whenever the company had sufficient earnings to pay it. If the company could not make the payments on the preferred for a period of years, the payments would continue to accrue during all that time and would have to be paid in full before the common-stock holders got as much as a dime in dividend payments.

On the other hand, it was agreed that this would not be an issue of *participating preferred*. This meant that the holders of the preferred would not participate, beyond the stipulated dividend payment, in any of the extra profits the company might earn in good years. Even if earnings were so good that dividends on the common stock doubled or trebled, the holders of the preferred would still get just their $10 a share and no more. Furthermore, they would have no participation in company affairs and no voting rights except on matters that might adversely affect the rights guaranteed them as preferred-stock holders. They were also guaranteed the right to elect two directors to the board if the company should ever pass, or fail to pay, the preferred dividend for eight consecutive quarters.

Although the terms of this issue might be regarded as fairly typical, there is no such thing as a standard preferred stock. About the only common denominator of all such issues is the guarantee that the owner will be accorded a preferential treatment, ahead of the common-stock holder, in the payment of dividends and in the distribution of any assets that might remain if the company was liquidated. That's why it is called preferred stock. And that's why its price usually doesn't fluctuate, either up or down, as much as the price of the company's common stock.

Besides their preferential status, specifications for preferred stocks vary widely. Most preferreds have a $100 par value. But some are no-par stocks. Dividends vary according to interest rate conditions at the time. Most preferreds are *nonparticipating*. But there are many exceptions.

Many preferreds are issued, as in the case of Pocket Pole, to acquire another company. But most are issued simply to acquire more capital for expansion or improvements at a time when the company's circumstances are such that its stockholders and the public at large might not be willing to invest in more of its common stock.

Cumulative preferreds are by all odds the most common. But there are some *noncumulative* issues on the market as well — principally those of railroads. Occasionally, in the case of cumulative preferreds, *accrued dividends* pile up in bad years to a point where it becomes impossible for a company to pay them. In such a situation the company may attempt to negotiate a settlement with the preferred holders on the basis of a partial payment. However, some companies have paid off more than $100 a share in accumulated back dividends due on a given preferred stock issue that cost the owners just $100 a share, originally.

Another kind of preferred stock that has become increasingly popular in recent years is the *convertible preferred*. Such a stock carries a provision permitting the owner to convert it into a specified number of shares of common stock at a specified time. Suppose, for instance, that a company sold a new issue of convertible preferred at a time when its common stock was quoted at $17 or $18 a share. In such a situation, the conversion clause might provide that every share of the new $100 preferred could be exchanged for five shares of the company's common stock at any time during the next five years. Obviously, there would be no advantage to the preferred-stock holders making such a swap unless the common stock advanced in price to more than $20 a share.

The price of a convertible is apt to fluctuate more than the price of other preferreds because a convertible is always tied to the price of the common stock of the company. This has its good and bad points. If the company is successful and the price of its common stock rises, the holder of a convertible preferred will find that the stock has had a corresponding increase in value, since it can be exchanged for the common. On the other hand, if the price of the common declines, the convertible preferred is apt to suffer too. This is because one of the features that was counted on to make it attractive has suddenly lost something of its value, and the other features of the issue, such as its dividend rate, may not prove as attractive or substantial as those of orthodox preferreds. Convertibles are always especially popular when stock prices are rising generally.

Most preferreds carry a provision that permits the company to *call* in the issue and pay it off at full value, plus a premium of perhaps 5%. A company will usually exercise this right to call in its preferred stock if it thinks it can replace the outstanding issue with one that carries a lower dividend rate.

From the point of view of the owners of Rapid Reel, the plan which Pocket Pole proposed looked attractive. So they accepted it — after the common-stock holders of Pocket Pole had approved the plan and authorized issuance of 750 shares of 10% cumulative preferred stock with 100% par value in exchange for the Rapid Reel Company.

With this acquisition, Pocket Pole was on its way to becoming a big business. And in the next ten years, with booming sales, it strode forward along that path with seven-league boots.

It bought the little Nylon Line Company for cash.

It acquired the Fishing Supplies Corporation with another issue of preferred stock. This issue it called *second-preferred*, because it had to recognize the prior claim to assets and earnings that had been granted the owners of Rapid Reel. To make this issue more attractive to the owners of Fishing Supplies, a conversion privilege was included in it. In other words, it was a convertible preferred.

It bought the Sure-Fire Rifle Company by authorizing an additional issue of common stock and arranging to trade the Sure-Fire stockowners one share of Pocket Pole for every three shares of Sure-Fire that they owned.

Finally, it acquired control of Camping Supplies, Incorporated, on a similar *stock-swapping* basis.

Now, with a full, well-rounded line of fishing, hunting, and camping supplies, backed by an aggressive advertising and merchandising campaign, the company decided to experiment with its own retail outlets. In a few years, these grew into a small chain of 30 sporting-goods stores, known as the Rod & Reel Centers.

Sales multiplied, and so did earnings — up to $10 and $12 a share. Dividends were boosted correspondingly, and with the adoption of a regular $6 annual dividend, Pocket Pole stock was frequently quoted at $120 a share and higher. Stockholders complained that it was too high-priced, that it couldn't be sold easily if they wanted to dispose of their holdings.

So the company decided to *split* the stock on a ten-for-one basis and simultaneously to change its corporate name to Rod & Reel, Incorporated — a much more appropriate name, since most fishermen consider the fishing "pole" passé. Hence, it issued new certificates for ten shares of Rod & Reel common stock for every single share of the old Pocket Pole stock. Theoretically, each of the new shares should have been worth about $12. But since stock splits frequently excite unusual investor interest, it wasn't long before the new shares were being bought and sold at prices a dollar or two higher, even though there had been substantially no change in the outlook for the company.

In companies with larger numbers of shares of stock outstanding than Rod and Reel, such a split can often have a negative effect on the stock's price. Increasing the number of shares outstanding by 500%, a larger company runs the risk of creating such an oversupply of stock in the marketplace that it requires substantial buying demand from the public to drive its price up.

Along its road to success, Rod & Reel encountered only one misadventure. Eyeing its growth, its sales and earnings record, and its general financial strength, the Double-X Sporting Goods Company proposed to Rod & Reel that they *merge* their two businesses. After many joint meetings and careful examination of the pluses and minuses of the proposal, the directors of Rod & Reel decided that the interests of their stockholders would best be served if the company continued to row its own boat, and so it declined the offer to merge.

But Double-X wasn't prepared to take no for an answer. It wanted Rod & Reel and its successful retail outlets. And so Double-X made a *tender* offer to each Rod & Reel stockholder. They agreed to buy the stockholders' shares on a set date at a set price almost 10% above its prevailing market price, provided enough other stockholders surrendered their shares so that Double-X could obtain control of Rod & Reel. If Rod & Reel stockholders signed the form agreeing to sell, they would have to tender their stock to Double-X on demand at the set price and on the given date.

Rod & Reel fought the tender offer and urged its stockholders not to sign up. In the end Rod & Reel won out. So few stockholders were willing to sell, even at the higher price, that

Double-X realized it could not gain control of Rod & Reel. So it was forced to withdraw its tender offer.

During the late seventies and early eighties, as ballooning start-up costs and rising interest rates made it more economical to buy existing businesses than to begin one from scratch, large cash-rich corporations waged increasingly heated bidding wars among themselves to acquire smaller established companies. Frequently these bidding wars drove the price of the merger target's stock up two- or threefold in a matter of weeks. Soon, ferreting out which smaller companies were the most likely candidates for a lucrative tender offer — by virtue of their assets, growth potential, and the undervaluation of their stock — had become one of Wall Street's more popular guessing games. Rod & Reel was one of the very few of these heavily romanced takeover candidates to escape assimilation by an acquisitive suitor during the heyday of merger fever.

This is the story of Rod & Reel, Incorporated, formerly Pocket Pole Company, Incorporated. It is a success story, as it was meant to be, to show the various kinds of stock operation that may mark a company's growth. But for that matter, it is no more a success story than the real-life stories of General Motors or International Business Machines, Xerox or Polaroid, or any of hundreds of other companies in which the original investors (or speculators) have seen the value of their stockholdings multiplied 10, 20, even 100 times over.

CHAPTER 5

What You Should Know
about Bonds and Investment Banking

DO you have a lot of money to invest — say, $20,000, $50,000, or more? Or is there some reason why you should be particularly conservative in your investments?

If either is so, then you ought to know about *corporate bonds*, the kind of bond issued by companies like Rod & Reel, Incorporated, and bought principally by *institutional investors:* banks, insurance companies, pension funds, colleges and universities, and charitable foundations.

If you don't have substantial sums to invest or some good reason for being especially conservative, chances are that there are better investments for you than corporate bonds.

But who can tell when you might get a lot of money? And anyway, every intelligent investor should know something about bonds just so he'll have a grasp of the whole securities business.

The easiest way to understand bonds is to consider the plight of Rod & Reel's treasurer at a time when the company needed $1 million of new capital — a much greater sum than it had ever had to raise before.

It needed that money because over the years it had grown rather haphazardly, acquiring a manufacturing plant here and another one there, a warehouse here and some retail stores there.

Now the whole operation had to be pulled together, made to function efficiently. An independent firm of engineers had figured out just what economies Rod & Reel could effect by centralizing most of its manufacturing operations in one big new plant and by modernizing its equipment. In the long run, the $1 million would unquestionably prove to be money well spent.

But how to get the money?

As company treasurer, you might first discuss the matter with the officers of your regular bank. They are perfectly willing to supply you from month to month with the credit you need for raw materials. But a million-dollar loan to construct a new plant — well, that is too much of an undertaking for them. What you need in the present situation, they suggest, is help from a very special kind of banker, an *investment banker*.

Investment bankers specialize in raising the kind of money that business needs for long-term use, usually in amounts considerably greater than the million Rod & Reel wanted.

Most times when a company wants money, it would like to get it without obligating itself to pay any set return on the money. In short, it wants *equity capital,* the kind of money it can get only by selling common stock.

If the company's condition is sound, if its prospects are good, and if the stock market is then very active and healthy, an investment banker may agree to *underwrite* such an issue of common stock. That means he will buy all the new stock himself from the company, then resell it at a set price per share to individual buyers. As a general rule, this is the only time in the entire life of a stock issue that its price will be fixed — at the time when it is originally issued, either to start a new company or to raise new capital. Once the stock is in public hands, its price will be determined solely by how much buyers will pay and how much the sellers want for the stock they own — the law of supply and demand.

For the risk that the investment banker assumes in underwriting an issue of common stock, the risk that he may not be able to resell the entire issue that he has bought, he expects to make a profit on each share of the issue.

On small issues, involving only $1 million or $2 million, he may be able and willing to carry the whole risk himself. But on most issues he shares the risk with other investment bankers, who join with him in forming an *underwriting group* or *syndicate* under his management.

When it comes time to sell the issue to the public, the underwriters usually invite other security dealers to join with them in a *selling group*.

The costs of underwriting and selling an issue of stock depend primarily on how salable the underwriting group thinks the issue will be when it is put on the market. Those costs might run anywhere from 3% to 10% of the final selling price, and they are wholly paid by the seller. The buyers get such stock at the announced price, free of all commission cost or other charges. On some issues, such as cheap mining or oil stocks offered at a dollar or two a share, charges might even run as high as 20%. That's because these *penny stocks* can usually be sold only by a costly merchandising effort. A third to a half of the total commission on any new issue might go to those who underwrite it, with the *manager* of the group getting an extra fee for his services, and the balance going to those who sell it. But if the issue looks as though it might be hard to sell, the selling commission is likely to be increased and the underwriting commission reduced correspondingly.

When a company wants to raise capital by selling a new securities issue, it usually shops around to see which investment banker will offer the best terms and handle the new issue at the lowest total cost. Once an underwriter is selected, the relationship between the company and the underwriter is apt to develop naturally into a close one. If the company needs to raise additional capital at some future time, it will usually expect to get help again from the same underwriter. When an underwriting is arranged in this fashion, it is described as a *negotiated* deal, as distinct from a deal that is arrived at through *competitive bidding* by various investment bankers interested in obtaining the business.

While most companies might prefer to raise new capital by selling stock, this is not the kind of securities issue that an investment banker is likely to sanction, especially in the case of a comparatively small company like Rod & Reel. He is far more apt to suggest an issue of bonds rather than an issue of stock. In normal years, the aggregate value of new bond issues may be five or ten times greater than the value of new stock issues. As a matter of fact, in the modern era, American business has raised little more than 5% of the money it has needed through the sale of stock. It has raised most of the balance by selling bonds. That is why the bond market is many times bigger than the stock market.

Bonds always represent borrowed money, which the company that issues them is obligated to repay. That's why they are called *obligations*. They are a kind of promissory note. When a company sells bonds, it borrows the money from the investors who buy the bonds, and the bonds stand as a formal evidence of that debt. Each bond is an agreement on the part of the company to repay the face value of the bond — usually $1,000 — at a specified time and in most cases to pay a set annual rate of *interest* from the day the bond is issued to the day it is redeemed.

The person who buys stock in a company actually buys a part of that company. The person who buys a company's bonds simply lends money to the company.

The stockholder expects to collect dividends on that stock and thus share in the company's profits. The bondholder expects only to earn a fixed return on that investment in the form of interest payments.

There's one other important difference between stocks and bonds. If a company is successful, the stockholder can hope to make a substantial profit because the price of the stock should go up. The bondholder enjoys no such extravagant hope. Market-price appreciation for a company's bonds is usually limited, regardless of how successful the company may be, although price changes sparked by interest rate fluctuations have often been quite dramatic, and in the late seventies and early eighties have frequently equaled, and sometimes even surpassed, similar price changes for common stocks.

On the other hand, if the bondholder can't expect to gain as much on invested capital, neither does he run the risk of losing as much. The investment is much better protected, thanks to the fact that bonds do represent debt. If the company is dissolved, the debt it owes its bondholders, like any other debt it owes for labor and materials, must be paid before the stockholders, either common or preferred, can get a nickel out of what's left of the company. The claims of bondholders come first, then the pre-ferred-stock holders — and last, the common-stock holders.

It is because the element of risk in bonds has historically been so comparatively slight that they have usually been such a popular form of investment with institutional investors. This is the market the investment banker has his eye on when he under-writes a bond issue. Very often, an issuer may succeed in selling an entire bond issue to just one or two large institutional cus-tomers — a bank, an insurance company, or a pension fund. This is known as a *private placement*.

Because the institutional market for bonds has over time been such a good market, underwriting and selling commissions are usually much lower on an issue of bonds than on an issue of stock. Otherwise, the two kinds of securities are issued and sold in much the same way.

From the point of view of any company treasurer, a stock issue has obvious advantages over a bond issue. The interest that must be paid on bonds represents a fixed charge that has to be met in bad times as well as good times. And bonds must be paid off when they come due. The stockholder has to be paid dividends only if the company makes money — and even that is not a bind-ing obligation.

If the company is successful, it can afford to pay interest on money borrowed from bondholders, provided it can make a substantially greater profit on the extra capital that it raises by the bond issue. Again, bond interest payments are an expense item deducted from a company's earnings before it pays its federal income *tax* on those earnings. In contrast, dividends are paid out of what is left after a company has paid the tax on its earnings. Thus, it actually costs a company less to pay a given amount of money to bondholders than it does to pay the same amount of money to stockholders.

For the company issuing the bonds the situation is not much different from what it would be if you as an individual sought to get a loan from a bank. If the banker knew you and knew that you would be able to repay the money, he might lend it to you without asking you to put up any collateral, such as your life insurance policies or other property, to guarantee the loan. But if he didn't know you or if it was a sizable loan, he might insist that you give him some collateral, such as a mortgage on your home.

It's much the same way with companies when they issue bonds. They would prefer to get the money without posting their property as a guarantee that the contract set in the bond will be fulfilled. That, as a matter of fact, is precisely the way the Rod & Reel treasurer felt when the investment banker told him the company would have to *float* a bond issue, not a stock issue.

As long as it had to be bonds, the treasurer proposed that the company issue $1 million of debentures.

A *debenture* is a bond that is backed only by the general credit of the corporation. No specific real estate or property stands as security behind it. It is, in effect, a giant-sized I.O.U. Debentures are the most common type of bond issued by big, well-established industrial companies today. But in the case of Rod & Reel, the investment banker was not disposed to feel that such an issue would be in order, because the company, though successful, was still relatively small and not too well known. He was afraid the debentures wouldn't sell.

The treasurer then asked if a debenture might not be made more attractive by including a convertible provision on it. There are many *convertible bonds* on the market, and their terms vary widely. But like convertible preferred stocks, all convertible bonds offer the owners the privilege of converting their bonds into a specified number of shares of common stock.

Such a provision may add a certain speculative appeal to the bond — the chance to make an extra profit if the common stock rises. But the typical bond buyer may look askance at such a "sweetener." He knows better than most security buyers that you don't get something for nothing in a security, any more than you do in any other kind of merchandise. A convertible bond may offer the possibility of price appreciation, but its guarantee of safety is not as substantial. Such issues are considered to be subordinate to other bonds.

In Rod & Reel's case, the investment banker did not feel that a convertible was feasible. In light of this attitude, the treasurer did not even raise the question of whether the company could issue some kind of *income* or *adjustment bond*.

These bonds are a kind of hybrid security, something like a noncumulative preferred stock, since they provide that the interest is to be paid on the bond only as it is earned. If earnings are sufficient to pay only a part of the interest on such bonds, the company must make whatever payment it can to the nearest $\frac{1}{2}$ of 1%. Thus on a 5% bond a company might pay only $2\frac{1}{2}$% or 3% or $3\frac{1}{2}$%, depending on its earnings. Hence, most income bonds have a very low quality rating.

There is still another kind of bond, the *collateral-trust* bond, which, like the income bond, used to be more popular than it is today. But Rod & Reel's circumstances were such that this type of security was obviously not suited to them. When a company issues a collateral-trust bond, it deposits securities with a trustee as a guarantee that the bonds will be redeemed and interest paid on them. Usually the securities on deposit are worth at least 25% more than the total value of the bond issue. And they are frequently the securities of subsidiary companies.

As the discussions progressed, it became apparent that the investment banker felt there was only one kind of industrial bond that Rod & Reel could offer. That was a *first-mortgage bond* — the kind of bond that is secured by a mortgage on all of a company's property: not only on its existing property but sometimes even on all property that it might later acquire.

Industrial bonds of this type are considered to be among the highest-grade security investments. They offer the investor an undisputed first claim on company earnings and the greatest possible safety. The claims of the holder of such a first mortgage take absolute precedence over the claims of all other owners of the company's securities, including the holders of debentures, adjustment bonds, or secondary-mortgage bonds that may be issued after a first mortgage has been made.

Having resigned himself to the fact that Rod & Reel would have to mortgage its property, including the new plant that it expected to build, in order to float a $1 million bond issue, the company treasurer next took up with the banker the question of what rate of interest the company might have to pay. Here the banker was in no position to supply an answer, because the rate a company has to pay always depends primarily on its credit standing and its earning capacity. And these were the crucial factors on which the banker could not commit himself without a thorough, painstaking investigation of all aspects of the company — the same kind of survey that every investment banker must make, with the help of outside accountants, engineers, and/or other needed specialists, before underwriting any new issue of securities for a company.

Bond interest rates vary not only with the health of the company but also with the bond's quality and with general business conditions. Whenever a new bond issue is floated, Moody's Investors Service and Standard & Poor's Corporation, America's two outstanding organizations in the field of securities research and statistics, assign it a quality rating. Most times the two companies agree on the ratings. But they don't quite agree on the form of the designation. Thus, Moody's grades bonds (downward in quality) as Aaa, Aa, A, Baa, Ba, et cetera, while Standard & Poor's prefers capital letters, using AAA, AA, et cetera, and also assigns plus and minus ratings to most major quality groups.

In 1920, Aaa or AAA bonds paid over 6%, while in 1945 they were paying only 2½%. In the early sixties, Aaa bonds were paying 4½% to 5% — a range that bond dealers consider fairly typical over a long period of years. By the end of the sixties, however, the return on such bonds had increased to 8%, then to 10% in 1974, and finally, by 1981, to as much as 14% as inflation soared to double-digit figures.

When money is "tight," as it was during the late seventies and early eighties, banks increase the rates they charge on mortgages and loans, and they pay higher interest rates on deposits. At such a time bond interest rates usually go up, too. If this happens at a time when stock dividends, expressed as a percentage of the price, have been going down, a situation develops where the investor can get a better return from bonds than he can from stocks. Thus, he is frequently tempted to shift to the "safer" investment.

This is why it is a mistake to think that bond prices never fluctuate. When new bonds are issued with interest rates of 13% or 14%, the prices of outstanding bonds, offered originally at 4% or 5%, are bound to decline. No one is going to pay face value for an old bond with an interest rate of 4% if he can buy a new bond of equal quality with an interest rate of 14%. The only way the old 4% bond could compete with the new 14% bond on even terms would be for the 4% bond to sell in the market at much less than one third of its original price. So, when interest rates rise, older bonds with low interest rates have a tendency to fall proportionately in price.

During the late seventies and early eighties, as the prime interest rate, the rate banks charge their most creditworthy customers, rose above the unprecedented 20% level, the prices of old bonds issued at substantially lower rates of interest fell precipitously. Thus, the once staid bond market, long treasured by conservative individual and institutional investors for the stability of its prices and the predictability of its return on capital, became the scene of frequent price swings as wide as any witnessed during the most dramatic of stock market fluctuations.

The interest rate of a bond is frequently referred to as the *coupon* rate, because traditionally bonds have appended to them a number of detachable coupons, one for each six months of the bond's life. The owner clips each coupon as it comes due and presents it to the company's paying agent for payment. Coupons were used at first because bonds were not registered on the company's books in the owner's name, as stock certificates are. Instead, they were the property of the bearer — whoever had them at a given time — and hence were called *bearer bonds*.

Today, there has been a departure from this practice. Nearly all companies now issue bonds that are registered in each owner's name, just like stocks. On some *registered bonds,* coupons are still used for the payment of interest. But on others the bondholder gets a check automatically from the company. This practice has become increasingly popular. In time, the phrase "coupon-clipper" to denote a wealthy individual who lives off the proceeds of bond interest may vanish from the language entirely.

Just as crucial as the interest rate of any company issuing bonds is the question of *maturity* — how long a life the bonds will have, how soon the company will have to redeem them, or pay them off. In general, the stronger the company, the longer the maturities. For a company like Rod & Reel, ten years might be considered the maximum time limit. Furthermore, the company would probably be required to establish a *sinking fund* and put enough into it every year to provide for an annual repayment of a portion of the issue, just as one pays off part of the principal on a mortgage each year. In view of its building and reorganizations plans, Rod & Reel would probably be allowed a breathing spell of two or three years before it had to start putting money into the sinking fund.

Like preferreds, most bonds have call provisions, which permit a company to redeem them before maturity if it has the money.

There is a wide variation in how long bond issues run, but a period of 20 or 30 years is about as common as any. Curiously, the railroads have issued bonds with the longest life on record, and they also have some with about as short a life as any. Many old rail bonds run for 100 years, and some have no maturity date. They were issued in perpetuity — a frank recognition of the fact that no one expects the railroads ever to pay all their debts.

At the other end of the time scale are *equipment trust* obligations, which mature in only one to fifteen years. These serial maturity bonds enable a railroad to buy freight cars, passenger cars, locomotives, and other such equipment virtually on the installment plan. Some have carried interest rates under $1\frac{1}{2}\%$. On this kind of bond, the equipment itself stands as the guarantee of repayment.

The maturity of a bond can affect the return you realize on it. You can buy a bond with a 6% coupon rate, but it may *yield* you something less — or something more — than 6%, depending on how much you pay for the bond and what its maturity is. If you pay exactly $1,000 for a bond and get $60 interest on it every year, you do realize a 6% yield. But if you pay $1,050 for the bond, the $60 annual interest payment obviously represents less than a 6% return on the money you've invested. Furthermore, if you hold the bond until it matures, you will get only $1,000 for it on redemption, a loss of $50. If the bond has a twenty-year maturity, that $50 loss would represent, in effect, a reduction of $2.50 a year in your interest payment. Furthermore, over the full twenty years you would have lost the amount of interest that you might have earned on that $50.

The net of it all is that if you pay $1,050 for a 6% 20-year bond, you will realize a *yield to maturity* of just 5.58%, but only if all coupons when paid are reinvested (interest on interest) at the yield they would provide if held to maturity. Of course, if you buy the bond at a discount instead of a premium — for $950 instead of $1,050, for example — you will earn more than 6% on it.

It was the yield to maturity that made many old bonds issued at 4% or 5% in earlier years especially attractive in 1981–1982. In early 1982, for instance, it was possible to buy a top-quality bond, such as American Telephone & Telegraph's 3⅞ bonds, due in 1990, at around 53. As the price of the old bond was forced down, its yield was increased so that it was able to compete in the marketplace with new bonds issued at 9% or 10%. The A.T.&T. bond — scheduled to be paid off in eight years at a full par — would have to gain 47 points before 1990, when it would be redeemable at full value. That built-in gain gave the bond a yield to maturity of over 19%. The capital gain portion of this 19% yield would be taxable like all capital gains, thus affording the investor a distinct tax advantage.

When a company like Rod & Reel floats a stock or bond issue to raise new capital, such an issue represents new *financing*. But very often preferred stocks or bonds are issued as part of a *refinancing* operation. Thus, when a company refinances, it may seek to substitute some new bond issue for an outstanding one that it issued many years ago — a process known as *refunding*.

Why should such a substitution be made? Because as business and investment conditions change, it is frequently worthwhile for a company to call an outstanding issue of bonds or preferred stock on which it may be paying a high rate of interest. Such an issue can then be paid off out of funds raised by the sale of a new issue carrying a lower rate.

When a company has a substantial amount of bonds or preferred stock outstanding in relation to the amount of its common stock, the common stock is said to have high *leverage*. This phrase is used because the price of such a stock is likely to be disproportionately influenced by any increase or decrease in the company's earnings. Here's why: suppose a company is obligated to pay $500,000 in bond interest and preferred dividends every year. If the company has earnings of $1 million before paying such fixed charges, it has only $500,000 left for the common-stock holders. But if the company has earnings of $3 million, it will have $2,500,000 available for the benefit of the common-stock holders, in the form either of dividends or of reinvested capital. This would serve to increase the value of the company and its stock. In this situation, a threefold increase in the company's earnings would have meant a fivefold increase in the amount of earnings available to the common-stock holders. This is because the holders of the bonds and preferred stock would still have received only the prescribed $500,000.

Of course, if the company's earnings decreased from $1 million to $500,000, there would be no earnings at all available to the common-stock holders. Because fluctuations in earnings can have such magnified effects on earnings available to the common-stock holders, high-leveraged stocks are likely to fluctuate more drastically in price than the stocks of companies that have relatively small amounts of outstanding bonds or preferred stocks.

CHAPTER 6

How New Issues Are Regulated

WHENEVER a company like Rod & Reel wants to raise capital by floating a new issue of stocks or bonds, it must comply with the federal law that governs the sale of any such issue offered to the public.

In the boom days of the twenties, many a new stock was sold with few facts and lots of glittering promises. In 1933, Congress changed all that. It enacted a new law, widely known as the *Truth in Securities Act*. Then in 1934, it passed the *Securities Exchange Act*, and, the same year, set up the *Securities and Exchange Commission* to administer both laws.

The S.E.C. requires *full disclosure* of all the pertinent facts about any company before it makes a *public offering* of new stocks or bonds. The company must file a lengthy *registration statement* with the S.E.C. in which it sets forth all the pertinent data concerning its financial condition: its assets and its liabilities, what it owns and what it owes. It must also furnish its profit and loss record for the past several years. It must describe all outstanding issues of its securities and their terms, list all its officers, and directors, together with the salaries of the top five who make over $50,000 and the cumulative salaries of all, and reveal the identity of anyone who holds more than 5% of any of its securities issues. Finally, it must provide a description of its operations.

If the data appear to be complete and honest, the S.E.C. gives a green light to the new issue. But this does not mean that it passes any judgment whatsoever on the quality of the securities, how good or bad they may be for any investor.

The Securities and Exchange Commission also sees that the information that is filed with it is made available to any possible buyer of the new issue. A company is required to put all the essential facts into a printed *prospectus*. Every securities dealer who offers the new stock or bond for sale must give a copy of that prospectus to everyone who buys the new issue and also to anyone who might request a copy. These prospectus regulations are generally binding on all publicly owned companies for 40 days after the new issue is offered for sale. If a company is offering its securities to the public for the first time, these prospectus regulations are binding for 90 days.

Before the price is set on a new issue, a preliminary draft of the prospectus is usually printed up. Such drafts, not yet reviewed by the S.E.C., are known as *red herrings*, because in the early days of its regulatory work, the S.E.C. often found them to be little more than outright sales promotion, designed not so much to divulge information as to distract the reader from facts about the new issue that the S.E.C. might regard critically. A red herring is usually distributed only to members of the underwriting and selling groups, but because some copies may reach the public, a red herring must carry on its face a warning printed in red ink to the effect that the prospectus has not yet been reviewed by the S.E.C.

The prospectus is usually about 20 to 30 pages long, sometimes even longer. But some well-established companies, notably utilities, that can meet certain high standards of financial responsibility have for years been permitted by the Securities and Exchange Commission to use a *short-form prospectus* on bond issues. In 1970 the S.E.C. relaxed its rules and extended the short-form privilege to stock issues of companies that had a strong financial position and a record of consistent earnings over a period of years.

During the period when a new issue is under prospectus regulation, no broker or dealer can provide the public with any additional information or opinion about that new issue or any outstanding issue related to it. If he wants he can publish the prospectus or a detailed summary of it as an advertisement. But apart from that the only other kind of advertising he can use for the issue is the so-called *tombstone* announcement. This is an advertisement in which no information is provided beyond the name of the issue, its price, its size, and the names of the underwriters and dealers who have it for sale. And above even this austere announcement the underwriters usually insert a precautionary note to the effect that the advertisement is not to be interpreted as an offer to buy or sell the security, since the offer is made only through the prospectus.

Sometimes you may see in the *Wall Street Journal* or one of the large metropolitan newspapers a tombstone ad announcing a new issue and stating that the issue has already been completely sold. You may well wonder why such an ad appears. The answer is simple. Underwriting houses are proud of their financing activities, and when they have arranged to sell all of a given issue — usually to big investors — even before it is scheduled for public offering, they go ahead and publish the new-issue advertisement as a matter of prestige. It is also a good piece of public relations for both the underwriter and the company whose offering has been sold.

Even if a company satisfies all the requirements of the Securities and Exchange Commission on a new issue, its troubles may not necessarily end there. Most of the individual states also have laws governing the registration and sale of new securities. While the requirements of these so-called *blue sky laws* are much like those of the S.E.C., they are sufficiently varied to cause a company a lot of trouble and a good deal of extra legal and administrative expense in filing the necessary forms to comply with the various state laws.

All told, preparing a new issue for sale can be a very expensive undertaking. The bill for preparing the necessary forms and printing a prospectus can run into the hundreds of thousands of dollars. This is the case when a large company brings out a new stock issue and has to offer rights to all its stockholders. Each of them must be supplied with a prospectus. Fees for lawyers and accountants can add a lot more to this bill.

However, the federal law, as well as most state laws, provides an "out" for little companies like Rod & Reel. For instance, if the new issue has a value of not more than $1,500,000, the company need file only a short registration form with the S.E.C. This is known as a *Regulation A* filing. Companies using it can satisfy the requirements of the law by distributing an *offering circular*, as it is called. On issues of less than $100,000, it isn't even necessary to prepare a circular. Again, if the new issue can be classified as a private placement — usually one that will be purchased by no more than 35 persons — rather than as a public offering, it doesn't even have to be registered with the S.E.C.

In the case of a small company like Rod & Reel, the investment banker would try to qualify any new issue as a private placement by lining up one or two institutional buyers, perhaps an insurance company or a charitable foundation, before the deal was finally set. If he succeeds in doing so, he would insist that the issue be of topflight quality, for such customers are only interested in high-grade securities. In Rod & Reel's case this would mean a first-mortgage bond.

While the Securities and Exchange Commission's "full disclosure" rules have undoubtedly done much to protect the investor, it is frequently argued that they are more exacting than they have to be, and that this may deter some companies from trying to raise new money for expansion. Again, the prohibition on disseminating *any* information about a company while its new issue is under prospectus regulation can deprive investors who own existing securities issued by that company of essential information about the company during the period of the prospectus blackout. The intent of the rule — to prohibit promotion of the new issue

— is good. But the application sometimes works hardships on investors.

Furthermore, it has been argued that the individual investor doesn't really benefit as he should from the protection that the prospectus regulations provide. Individuals who buy a new issue — and their number is few compared with those who buy securities already on the market — rarely examine the prospectus, or don't understand it if they do. As a matter of fact, if the buyer knows that the Securities and Exchange Commission cleared the issue, he is apt to believe that the commission has endorsed it — and anything that is good enough for the S.E.C. is good enough for him.

Nothing, of course, could be further from the truth. Full disclosure can protect against fraud. It can't quarantee a profit or protect against loss. *Caveat emptor* ("Let the buyer beware") is still the rule of the market. And it applies with particular force to new, unseasoned issues. This is especially true, for example, with respect to the low-priced oil and uranium shares that were unloaded on the public a few years ago. Many of these stocks were not worth the paper they were printed on. But the S.E.C. often lacked the necessary power to deal with the promoters behind them. Needless to say, many new issues of these worthless penny stocks avail themselves of the "small-issue" or Regulation A exemption so that they won't have to "tell all" in a full prospectus.

In times of general business uncertainty the number of companies with securities issues already outstanding that attempt to offer new stocks or bonds to the public diminishes markedly. Understandably, the number of new issues lessens proportionately. But in times of general business prosperity the number of little companies with big plans and lots of stock to sell increases with the optimism of the moment. And if the times are good enough, and the little companies' big plans are appealing enough, then demand for their offerings can be so great that it drives up the stock's first official traded price significantly from its initial offering price. Thus in the past fifteen years, during the increasingly frequent outbreaks of "new issue fever" that have periodically afflicted the market, it has not been at all unusual for the initial stock offering of a small computer company sold at $10 a share through the underwriting group to be resold on the first day of trading in the open market at $25 or $30 a share. Demand for such "hot" new issues can be so great, in fact, that broker participants in the offering may be forced to parcel out their allocations of stock in ten- or fifteen-share allotments. Some prospective buyers may not be able to obtain any stock at the offering price at all, and must buy it in the aftermarket at the substantially higher prices resulting from the heavy buying pressure on the stock when it enters the open market.

During periods of intense speculation in new issues it has become common for companies with no earnings, or even no product, to "go public" with an initial stock offering. Many of these companies never make a profit and are eventually forced into bankruptcy. During the late sixties, for example, scores of nursing home operators and fast-food franchisers sold their first batch of stock to a gullible public and were never heard from again. During the late seventies and early eighties the process repeated itself with the initial stock offerings of marginal energy exploration and biotechnological companies. At the same time, scores of other companies in these and similarly promising areas were going public for the first time and rewarding their charter investors with significant profits on their purchase of stock at the offering price.

There are both greater risks and rewards in buying new issues than in any other area of stock investing. The risk is great because the companies going public for the first time generally have limited track records. The rewards are potentially great because this factor is reflected in the comparatively low offering price of the stock.

What follows is a record of price fluctuations for a cross-section of new issues that went public from 1978 through 1981.

New Issue	Issue Date	Offering Price ($)	Bid Price 1/82 ($)	Percentage Change (%)
Advanced Semiconductor	5/12/81	15	8.50	−42
Avantek	11/16/78	1.87	16.50	+789
Biomedical Ref Labs	5/4/79	6	20	+238
Brae	5/4/79	19	7.75	−59
Brock Hotel	6/18/80	4.08	13.87	+240
Cetus	3/6/81	23	13	−43
Chem-Tronics	1/29/81	14.50	6.50	−53
Dimis	3/13/80	6.75	2.75	−57
Dreco Energy	12/3/80	17.50	8.75	−50
Evans & Sutherland	9/7/78	3.33	25.25	+666
Fafco	6/23/81	9	3.75	−57
Infotron	3/26/81	25.50	13.25	−47
I.S.C. Systems	9/16/80	4.87	14.75	+208
K-Tron Intl.	12/3/80	16	7.37	−54
Magnuson Computer	6/25/80	20	4.25	−78
Monolithic Memories	8/6/80	21	11.75	−43
N.B.I.	12/12/79	6.67	29	+337
Network Systems	11/3/80	9	18	+100
Odetics	7/14/81	18	9.50	−46
Petroleum Equipment	12/13/78	8	23.75	+200
Sanders Technology	7/17/79	9	2	−75
Sci Tex	5/21/80	5.50	15	+177
Siltec	3/11/80	20	8	−59
Spectradyne	9/17/79	4.89	12.37	+158
Stryker	5/2/79	9.33	20.50	+122
Tech America	8/6/81	13	6.12	−53
Unit Drilling	4/6/79	7	16	+129
Verbatim	2/15/79	17	37.50	+121
Walbar	8/7/79	15	33.50	+123
Xidex	10/26/78	10	27.50	+178

CHAPTER 7

What You Should Know about
Government and Municipal Bonds

THE *government bond* poses an interesting paradox. Here is the security about which more people know *something* than about any other. Yet here too is the security that is *fully* understood by fewer people than is any other.

An estimated 85,000,000 Americans learned what it meant to lend their money on a bond, with the promise of repayment and the assurance of interest, during World War II when they bought the famous Series E government bonds. Millions of other Americans have initiated their investment education by buying these savings bonds since the war.

But only the big institutional buyers of government bonds, plus a comparative handful of dealers who regularly buy and sell hundreds of millions of these securities for a profit measured in fractions of 1%, really understand the government bond market and know how it can be affected by subtle shifts in the credit and money policies of our own government or other governments half the world away.

There are scores of different government issues, carrying different coupon rates, different maturities, different call provisions. Some are issued for very short periods of time. These are *Treasury bills* with maturities as short as 91 days, and *notes* that may run up to ten years. On the short-term issues, interest rates have ranged from 2% to 3%, a level that was once considered fairly standard, to the high of 16.75% on May 22, 1982 for the 91-day Treasury bill. During World War II, the government pegged interest rates on bills at an all-time low of ⅜ of 1%. This practice was terminated in March 1951 by an agreement between the Treasury and the Federal Reserve Board.

Long-term issues of *Treasury bonds*, usually called *Treasuries,* have maturities ranging from ten to thirty years.

In periods of tight money, Treasuries usually sell in the open market at a discount, and the investor who buys a bond at less than par may well realize a yield in excess of its coupon rate if he holds to maturity.

Thus, when interest rates are high, a bond yielding only 4¼% would be so unattractive to investors that its price might drop 60%, and a $1,000 bond would be worth only $400. If you bought the bond at that price, you would still be collecting $42.50 a year in interest. That return on a $400 investment would mean that you would be earning an effective rate of 10.62%.

No matter how cheaply you buy a government bond, you can count on getting the full face value of the bond, the full $1,000, if you hold it till its maturity date. And all that time you would be collecting a higher effective rate of interest, based on the low purchase price.

While Treasuries may sell at a discount in the open market when competitive interest rates are high, it is equally true that they are apt to sell at a premium — a price above par — and return a lower current yield than the coupon rate when interest rates are generally low.

Treasury bonds, representing the great bulk of the federal debt, are always freely traded in the market at prices that change only slightly from day to day.

Regularly traded by the same dealers and on much the same basis as government bonds are those bonds issued by various government agencies, such as the Federal Home Loan Banks and the Federal Land Banks.

And there are other government bonds that are not traded in

any market, bonds that can be bought only from the government and sold back to the government at set prices, bonds that never suffer any fluctuations in market price. These are the *savings bonds* — *Series EE* and *Series HH* (formerly Series E and Series H). They can be bought at virtually any bank. No commission is charged. They are handled free as a patriotic service.

When savings bonds were first introduced during World War II, the maximum yield you could get on them was 2.9%. You paid $75 for an E bond; ten years later you could cash it in for $100, thus realizing an average annual return of 2.9%. If you cashed it in earlier, you got less on your investment.

As interest rates increased in later years, the government was forced to liberalize the return on its savings bonds. It accomplished this objective by shortening the maturity. Step by step, the length of time you had to hold an E bond before cashing it in at face value was cut from ten years down to five years and ten months in 1969. With this shortened maturity, the yield was boosted from 2.9% to 5%. A year later the Treasury added a bonus of ½ of 1% to encourage sales. By 1981, through the combination of shortened maturities and increased interest, an EE bond was yielding 9% for a five-year maturity. Additionally the Treasury now has the authority to adjust yields upward or downward 1% every six months.

All along the line, the Treasury also made similar changes in its Series HH bonds. Unlike EE bonds, which are sold at a discount ($75 for a $100 bond, for instance), HH bonds are sold at their full face value. The government sends the buyer an interest payment every half-year, smaller payments in the early years, larger payments as the bonds approach maturity. In early 1982 HH bonds were yielding 8.5% over their full term. Whereas EE bonds come in denominations as small as $50, the smallest HH bond is $500.

Despite all the differences among various issues, government bonds have one common characteristic: they are regarded as the safest investments in the world.

What security lies behind them? The pledged word of the government of the United States. Just that. Nothing else. As long as that word is believed and accepted — as it must be by all Americans, since we *are* the government, in the last analysis — government bonds, if held to maturity, offer the best protection you can find against the risk of losing any of your capital.

But because their prices do not rise with inflation, government bonds offer poor protection against the risk that your dollars will lose something of their purchasing power if prices generally go up. Thus, if you had paid $75 for an E bond in June 1964 and held it, that bond would have been worth $123 to you in June 1975. But the goods that you could buy with that amount of money would have cost you only $72.78 in June 1964. You would actually have lost $2.22 in buying power on the deal, thanks to the tremendous increase in the cost of living.

With the persistent double-digit inflation of the late seventies and early eighties, the buying power of savings bond yields has deteriorated even further, making these safest of all investments the least rewarding for the average investor.

Like the federal government, states, cities, and other units of local government, such as school districts and housing authorities, need capital — to build schools, roads, hospitals, and sewers and to carry on the many other public projects that are their responsibility. So they too issue bonds. These are called *municipal bonds*.

Unlike the federal government, which underwrites its own bonds, these local units of government go to the investment bankers for their money, just as a corporation does. Bankers underwrite municipal bond issues in very much the way that they underwrite corporate bonds.

The growth of municipal bond issues since the end of World War II has been little short of fantastic. In the early 1940s, when new municipal bonds were being issued at the rate of only about $1 billion a year, the total value of all outstanding issues was just short of $20 billion. By the end of 1981, thanks to our expanding economy and public demand for all kinds of new municipal facilities, that figure had grown to nearly $360 billion.

With approximately one million municipal bond issues on the market, the investor is confronted with a wide range of maturities, quality ratings, and yields. For many years, interest rates on municipal bonds ranged in the neighborhood of 3% to 4%, occasionally as high as 5%. But when interest rates surged to all-time highs in 1980–1981, municipals sold at prices that yielded returns of 12%, 13%, even 14%.

And what made those rates especially attractive was that the interest collected on a municipal bond is totally exempt from federal income tax. Thus an investor in the 50% tax bracket who got a return of 10% in dividends on common stock or in interest on corporate bonds would be able to retain only half the income. But if he got 10% on a municipal bond he would be able to keep all of it, free of federal income tax.

Not only that, but in many states if he bought a municipal bond issued by a city or town or other taxing authority within the state, the interest collected on that bond would also be exempt from state taxes. That might mean another 5% or 6% of tax-free income. In short, individuals with incomes in the $100,000 range might realize more "take home" income from municipal bonds than they would get from an investment that yielded a taxable return of 25%.

Is it any wonder then that municipal bonds have proved increasingly attractive to investors in the upper income brackets? So much so, in fact, that Congress has been repeatedly tempted to revoke their exemption from federal income taxes. On such occasions, however, cities, towns, and other local taxing authorities have complained so loudly that Congress has always backed down.

No one but an expert can hope to know all about the different characteristics, the different qualities, of municipal bonds. But in the main they offer the investor a good degree of safety, plus the assurance that he can always sell his bond in the open market if he doesn't want to hold it to maturity. Consequently, municipal bond prices are usually more stable than those of stocks, although in the 1980–1981 slump prices did fall precipitously, and it was this drop that resulted in the spectacular increase in yields, up to levels approaching 14%.

As far as the ultimate payoff on maturity is concerned, municipal bonds can be considered "safe" because the word of any unit of government, like the word of the federal government, can generally be believed and accepted.

There are six generally recognized types of municipal bond. *General obligation bonds,* which constitute by far the largest category of municipals, are generally considered the blue chips of the business. With rare exceptions they are backed by the full faith, credit, and taxing power of the state or municipality that issues them. Both the principal and interest on such bonds are virtually guaranteed by the ability of the state or city to tap tax revenues as necessary to pay off its obligations. In contrast, *special tax bonds* are payable only from the proceeds of a particular tax or some other particular source of revenue and do not carry a "full faith and credit" guarantee.

Revenue bonds are issued to finance specific projects — toll roads, bridges, power projects, hospitals, various utilities, and the like. The principal and interest on such bonds are payable solely from the revenues collected on such projects. In some cases a state will back a toll road project with its own credit. But this is not usual. Turnpike bonds are also known as *dollar bonds* because they are quoted on a price basis rather than in terms of their yields, as most municipals are quoted. Again, unlike most municipals, dollar bonds usually mature on a single date rather than over a period of time.

Housing Authority bonds are issued to finance low-rent housing projects. They are backed by the Federal Housing Assistance Agency. This guarantee gives them a top-quality rating, since the full faith and credit of the United States stands behind them.

Industrial revenue bonds are issued to finance the building of industrial plants, which will attract industry to a community and expand the local tax base. These bonds are secured by the lease payments that the issuing authority collects from the corporate tenants. Their popularity was such that $1.6 billion of these bonds were issued in 1968. But toward the end of the year Congress raised the question of whether such developments were entitled to tax exemptions and imposed legislative restrictions of such stringency that new issues were sharply curtailed.

There are no restrictions, however, on certain types of industrial revenue bonds, such as those issued to build airports, pollution control facilities, or hospitals. Hospital bonds have been especially popular in the past few years, because of a growing reliance on Blue Cross, Blue Shield, and other programs, which pay about 90% of all hospital bills. *Refunding bonds* are issued to replace an outstanding issue that is being recalled, usually because interest rates have become more favorable.

Most municipal bonds are bearer bonds. They mature serially — that is, a certain number of bonds in each issue mature in each year over a period ranging up to 50 years. Quality ratings are provided on municipal bonds (Aaa, Aa, A, Baa, et cetera) just as they are on corporate bonds.

Municipal bonds are bought principally by banks, fire and casualty insurance companies, and estates. But the wealthy individual constitutes a steadily growing market because of that all-important tax exemption feature.

The table on page 58 shows just what return an individual at various income levels would have to earn on stocks or other taxable investments in order to retain the same amount after federal income taxes that he could realize from tax-exempt municipal bonds with coupons ranging from 8% to 14%. These figures are based on tax rates as they existed in 1982.

The Advantage of Owning Tax-free Municipal Bonds

Comparative after-tax yields from taxable and tax-exempt securities based on federal tax rates as of January 1982. At the various income levels shown in the column at the left, you can realize as great a return from municipal bonds with yields shown on the top line as you can from taxable dividends or interest shown in the corresponding line below.

| 1982 Taxable Income | | Tax | | | | | | |
Joint Return	Single Return	Bracket	7%	8.4%	9.8%	11.2%	12.6%	14%
24,601–29,900		29%	9.86	11.83	13.80	15.77	17.75	19.72
	18,201–23,500	31%	10.14	12.17	14.20	16.23	18.26	20.29
29,901–35,200		33%	10.45	12.54	14.63	16.72	18.81	20.90
	23,501–28,800	35%	10.77	12.92	15.08	17.23	19.38	21.54
35,201–45,800		39%	11.48	13.77	16.07	18.36	20.66	22.95
	28,801–34,100	40%	11.67	14.00	16.33	18.67	21.00	23.33
45,801–60,000/34,101–41,500		44%	12.50	15.00	17.50	20.00	22.50	25.00
60,001–85,600		49%	13.73	16.47	19.22	21.96	24.71	27.45
Over 85,600/Over 41,500		50%	14.00	16.80	19.60	22.40	25.20	28.00

CHAPTER 8

How Stocks Are Bought and Sold

THE stocks of the biggest and best-known corporations in America are bought and sold on the New York Stock Exchange. In World War II days, the average daily trading volume was less than a million shares. But with increased interest in share ownership, trading volume has expanded almost steadily so that even in a market slump like that of 1973–1974, the daily volume averaged 15 million shares, and when the bull market really took hold at the beginning of 1976, the turnover rose to 30 million shares or more a day. During the early eighties, trading had risen to a daily average of 46 million shares a day. The all-time trading record was broken on January 7, 1981, with 92.88 million shares. Prospects were that even that record wouldn't last long.

A 40 million-share day is likely to represent about $3 billion worth of stock. That much money has a lot of glamour about it. It builds its own folklore. As a consequence, the New York Stock Exchange has become one of the most publicized institutions in the world, the very symbol of American capitalism.

But somehow that publicity has got in the way of public understanding, so much so that the stock exchange could almost be described as the business nobody knows — but everybody talks about.

A lot of people think the stock exchange sells stock. It doesn't. It doesn't own any, doesn't sell any, doesn't buy any. If stocks sold on the exchange lose or gain $100 million in the aggregate on a given day, the exchange itself neither loses nor gains a nickel. It is simply a marketplace where thousands of people buy and sell stocks every day through their agents, the brokers.

Nor does the stock exchange have anything to do with fixing the price at which any of those stocks is bought and sold. The prices are arrived at in a two-way auction system. The buyer competes with other buyers for the lowest price, and the seller competes with other sellers for the highest price. Hence, the stock exchange can boast that it's the freest free market in the world, the one in which there is the least impediment to the free interplay of supply and demand.

When the buyer with the highest bid and the seller with the lowest offering price conclude a transaction, each can know that he got the best price he could at that moment. As buyer or seller, you may not be wholly satisfied. But you can't blame the stock exchange any more than you can blame the weatherman if it's too hot or too cold for you.

Stock prices can and do fluctuate sharply — they dropped 36% in 1969–1970 and 45% in 1973–1974. But these price movements simply reflect the optimism or pessimism of shareowners about business prospects at that time.

Perhaps you've heard that the stock market is "rigged," that big operators drive prices up or hammer them down to suit themselves and make a profit at the little fellow's expense. Yes, that did happen — as recently as the 1920s. Big market operators resorted to all kinds of questionable devices then to *manipulate* stock prices to their own advantage.

But today there are laws, stringent laws, to prevent price manipulation. And they are vigorously enforced by the Securities and Exchange Commission. The abuses of the twenties, which were blamed in part for the great market crash of 1929–1932, when prices fell 89%, brought the Securities and Exchange Commission into being in 1934. Thirty years later, after an exhaustive study of the securities business, the commission got from Congress a substantial grant of additional power to help it in its work of policing the markets. This was the Securities Acts Amendment of 1964.

The Securities Reform Act of 1975 not only augmented that power by revising certain old regulations and introducing new ones, but it also gave the S.E.C. additional funds to increase its staff. This enabled the S.E.C. to supervise the markets more closely and to enforce its rules and regulations more rigorously.

Actually, the commission leaves much of the regulatory work in the hands of the exchange, which, in turn, clamps down on its members' firms. The N.Y.S.E. rules are generally designed to prevent unfair trading practices and protect the individual investor. They were tightened when the exchange was reorganized in the thirties. And they were tightened again in many areas as a result of the enactment of the 1964 amendment. But these reforms were as nothing compared to that imposed on Wall Street by the Reform Act of 1975. Repercussions to that reform will be felt right down the line for a long time to come — from top management right down to the *"runners,"* or messengers, who make daily deliveries and pickups all over the financial district.

Today, there is probably no business in the world that operates under more stringent regulation or with a stricter self-imposed code of ethics than the New York Stock Exchange.

For instance, the exchange has a computerized *stock-watching* service that keeps under constant surveillance the price and volume movements of all stocks traded on the exchange. The computer is programmed to flag automatically any unusual movements in a stock. These indications are followed up by investigators. Sometimes a rumor can make a stock "act up." Is there anything to it? If not, the exchange takes immediate steps to scotch the rumor. Sometimes it asks the company itself to clarify the facts in the situation and announce them to the public. And if the computer ever turns up evidence of illegal manipulation, the exchange turns those facts over to the S.E.C. for action.

When the original securities law was first enacted in 1934, Congress even undertook to protect the buyer of securities (and the seller too) against himself — against his own greed and rashness. Before 1934, you could buy securities with only a small down payment, or *margin*. Typically it was 20%. Often it was less. And an occasional customer even "bought" securities 100% on credit — without putting up a dime. That's how a few people made a fortune on a shoestring. But it's also how more of them brought disaster on themselves and thousands of others in the 1929 crash.

When stocks bought on zero to 20% margin began declining in the fall of 1929, brokerage houses began sending out calls for more cash from the stocks owners in order to protect their own precarious position as lenders on an asset whose value was rapidly deteriorating. If, for an example, a stock cost $20 a share, and the broker had lent his customer $16 of that cost in order to generate a commission and make a profit on interest charges, and that stock had declined to $14, not only had the customer's entire $4 equity in the stock been wiped out, but the broker now had a $2 loss on his loan. He needed more cash to keep operating. But frequently the customers either did not have the cash necessary to prop up the sagging stock, or did not want to throw good money after bad in the interest of protecting their position in a declining investment. So the brokers were forced to sell the customer out, to dump the stock into a declining market in order to raise cash. This wholesale dumping drove stock prices down still further, which led to more margin calls, which led to more selling, and so on and on in a snowballing decline, which quickly turned into the greatest investment market debacle of all time.

Nowadays, the *Federal Reserve Board* decides what the minimum down payment shall be, and its decision is binding on everybody. The board changes the figure from time to time, depending on how much restraint it thinks it should apply to the market. Since 1934, it has ranged from as low as 40% of the purchase price up to 100%. When the 100% rule prevailed, that meant there was no credit at all; the buyer had to pay in full for his stocks.

This power alone — the power of the Reserve Board to say what the minimum margin shall be — guarantees that there will never be another market crash quite like the one in 1929. Stock prices are bound to go down from time to time, and down sharply. Indeed, in 1937–1938, despite the regulatory powers of the federal government, they dropped about 50% in just twelve months. There have been many other drops of 25% or more since then. But it can still be said that the market can never crash as spectacularly as it did in 1929.

That can't happen again because under the Reserve Board's margin regulation prices can never be as overinflated as they were when people bought hundreds of millions of dollars' worth of stocks by putting up only a small fraction of that amount in cash.

One noteworthy result of all the regulations that have been imposed on the market has been a change in the character of the market itself. It has become more of an investor's market, less of a speculator's market. Of course, speculators still buy and sell stocks in the hope of making a profit. This function is not only legitimate but useful and desirable in the main, because it helps provide a continuous and liquid market. It also helps stabilize prices, thus permitting the investor to buy and sell more readily and at fairer prices.

Nevertheless, more of the people who buy stocks today are doing so for the sake of earning a good return on their money over the long pull. They are not "in-and-outers," people trading for a small profit on every market move. Generally, they hold their stocks for years and years. They're investors — people who want to be part owners of those biggest and best-known corporations.

All told, on the New York Stock Exchange, the stocks of over 1,500 of these companies were *listed* as of January 31, 1982. Collectively, these listed companies employ about 20% of all American workers. But they account for almost 40% of sales and over 70% of all corporate profits made in the United States every year.

To qualify for listing on the exchange a company has to pay an initial listing fee of $29,350, plus a small per share charge. It also must pay an annual fee for as long as its stock is listed. This fee ranges from $11,750 to $58,700, depending upon the number of listed shares. More important, it must meet certain requirements, which have become more exacting over the years. In 1982, these were the principal qualifications a company had to meet if it wished to have its securities traded on the New York Stock Exchange:

(1) A minimum of 2,000 holders of 100 shares or more.
(2) A minimum of 1,000,000 common shares outstanding, which must be owned by the public, not by the company itself.
(3) A market value for its publicly owned shares of at least $16 million.
(4) Annual earnings of at least $2.5 million before taxes in the most recent year and at least $2 million in each of the two preceding years.
(5) Net tangible assets of at least $16 million.

Most of the listed companies exceed these regulations by a wide margin. The most widely held of the companies, American Telephone & Telegraph, had 3,026,000 shareholders at the beginning of 1981. General Motors ranked second with 1,191,000. American Telephone also held top ranking in the number of shares listed, with 740.6 million, and in the market value of listed shares, with nearly $43 billion.

Not all companies prosper, of course. That's why the exchange has a set of minimum standards that a company must meet in order to keep its stock listed there. It might be *delisted* unless it has at least 1,200 shareholders, each of whom must own a minimum of 100 shares; unless publicly owned shares total at least 600,000 with a market value of $5 million; or unless the aggregate market value of all its common stock is at least $8 million and net earnings of the past three years have averaged $600,000 minimum. About 54 common stocks have been delisted every year over the past fifteen years for various reasons, although many of these delistings resulted from mergers with other listed companies.

But these mathematical standards are not the only basis for delisting. In recent years, companies have been delisted because management refused to give voting rights to holders of its common stock, or because of consistent failure to produce timely and meaningful financial reports. Indeed, the exchange may suspend or delist at any time a security whose continued trading it no longer considers advisable, even though that security still meets listing standards.

All listed companies must agree to publish *quarterly reports* on their financial condition, as certified by independent accountants. In the old days, only annual reports were required. And some companies were admitted on these terms. Nevertheless, almost all listed companies now report quarterly.

A company must agree not to issue any additional shares without exchange approval. And it must have a *registrar* in New York City to see that no more shares of stock are issued than a company has authority to sell. It must also have a *transfer agent* who keeps an exact record of all stockholders, their names. addresses, and number of shares owned.

The companies whose stocks and bonds are traded on the exchange have nothing to say about the exchange's operation. The brokers run their own show, although the paid chairman of the exchange must be a man who has no connection with the securities business. The 21-man board of directors, which includes the chairman, must contain ten public members who also have no identification with the securities business. The chairman is chosen annually by the board of directors.

Although the exchange was incorporated in 1971, primarily to relieve its officers and directors of individual liability in the event of lawsuits against the exchange, it remains essentially what it has always been: a purely voluntary association of individual members, whose number totals 1,366. It is this "private club" image of the exchange that has always disturbed the S.E.C. Although in recent years, as the exchange has become increasingly aware of its social responsibilities, it has begun to operate more like a publicly owned business and less like a club.

The business of trading in stocks in New York goes back to the early eighteenth century, when merchants and auctioneers used to congregate at the foot of Wall Street to buy and sell not only stocks but wheat, tobacco, and other commodities, including slaves.

In 1792, two dozen merchants who met daily under a buttonwood tree on Wall Street to trade various stocks agreed from then on to deal only with each other and to charge their customers a fixed commission. Thus began the New York Stock Exchange.

How do you become a member of this association today? If you are approved by the exchange's board of directors, you buy a *seat*. Since nobody but a mailman is on his feet more continuously than a broker, this term is one of the classic misnomers of our language. It had its origin in the leisurely days of 1793 when the new association took up quarters in the Tontine Coffee House and the members could be seated while they transacted business.

What does a seat cost? That depends on how good business is on the exchange at the time of the sale. In 1929, seats were sold for $625,000 each. Later the number of seats was increased 25%, so that none was worth quite as much. But it is hard to believe they could ever fall again to the low they hit in 1942, when one was sold for $17,000, which is less than the amount given today as a gift to the family of a deceased member out of the exchange's *gratuity fund*. In 1968, a seat was sold for $515,000, and, considering the 25% increase in the number of seats, this figure represented an even higher price than in 1929. So discouraging were the succeeding market slumps of 1969 and 1973–1974, however, that in 1975 a stock exchange seat brought only $55,000. By 1982, however, the price of a seat had rebounded to $250,000.

A number of the seats are owned by men who aren't really brokers at all. They are *registered floor traders,* men who buy and sell stocks wholly for themselves. Because they pay no commissions, by virtue of their membership in the exchange, they are able to make money by moving in and out of the market, trying to make a quarter of a point here, an eighth of a point there — usually in the most active stocks.

In its extensive study of the market, which supplied the groundwork for the 1964 act, the Securities and Exchange Commission took the position that floor traders performed no useful economic function and that they should be phased out of existence. The exchange has strongly resisted doing this. Nevertheless, it did come up with a set of new rules to govern traders' activities. These rules provide that 75% of a trader's transactions must be of a "stabilizing" nature. To qualify as "stabilizing," a purchase can be made only when the price on the preceding sale was down, and a sale can be made only when the price on the preceding sale was up. Other rules are designed to make sure that the traders, who now account for less than 1% of total volume, enjoy no advantage over the public.

Many brokers on the floor earn their living by executing buy or sell orders for the public, especially for large institutions, either directly or indirectly. In 1982, there were 603 *member firms* represented on the exchange, of which half were partnerships and half were corporations. In 1981, these brokerage firms operated 4,174 offices throughout the United States and 247 offices abroad. In still other cities they are represented by thousands of *correspondents.* Usually these correspondents are local security dealers or banks that have wire connections to some member firm.

More than a million miles of private telephone and teletype wires keep all the offices of these brokerage firms, the so-called *wire houses,* in almost instantaneous touch with the exchange. As a result, the person who has an office next door to the exchange has no advantage in contacting his broker over someone who lives 3,000 miles away.

CHAPTER 9

What It Costs to Buy Stocks

FROM the time the New York Stock Exchange was founded in 1792 until May 1, 1975, any broker in the business could have told you to the penny just how much commission you would have to pay on the purchase or sale of 100 shares or 1,000 shares of any listed stock. It was all very simple because those two dozen founding fathers of the New York Stock Exchange had agreed from the outset to charge the same commission on any security transaction. They had further agreed to deal only with each other — no outsiders admitted. For more than 192 years, the succeeding members of the New York Stock Exchange maintained that same tight little monopoly.

Then came May 1, 1975, the day the Securities and Exchange Commission put an end to all fixed commissions on the stock exchange. In one fell swoop the S.E.C., on "Mayday," blasted away the very cornerstone of the exchange.

So how much will it cost you to buy stocks today in this new era of competitive commissions?

There are several different answers to that.

The first is — a lot less than you probably think, especially if you are thinking in terms of the 6% to 10% commission you might pay on a real estate transaction, or the even higher commissions paid to automobile or life insurance salesmen. The fact is that no goods or services of comparable value change hands at as low a commission cost as do stocks. And that has always been true, whether commissions were fixed or unfixed.

The second and more realistic answer is to tell you that the amount of commission you pay is going to vary with the total dollar value of your transaction. If your transaction is a modest one — say, an investment of $2,000 or $3,000 — the commission is apt to be somewhere near 3% from a full service broker. But if your investment involves $10,000 or $20,000, the commission may be only around 2% from the same firm. And if you're a really big operator, with a transaction involving $100,000 or more, you might well bargain yourself into a commission cost that is only a fraction of 1%.

Despite the outlawing of fixed commissions, don't be surprised if you find three or four full service firms all quoting you pretty much the same commission on a modest transaction involving only a few thousand dollars. That won't be the case, however, if you are talking big money — anything above $10,000 or $15,000. Then it's going to pay you to shop around for the best commission deal if you agree to pay for stock in advance. And if you are willing to give the broker an extra day to execute your order.

Besides charging you a commission, the broker might also exact a service charge for executing your order. Service charges come in a variety of different packages. Some brokers may charge you for keeping your stocks for you, thus saving you the cost of renting a safe deposit box. They might even add a further charge for collecting dividends on your stocks and crediting them to your account.

Of course, if you are a good customer, if you buy and sell stocks frequently, your broker might be willing to waive such service charges on your account just to keep you happy. But remember, no firm wants to hold 100 shares of stock for you year after year, credit dividends to your account, and send you regular statements unless the firm gets some financial reward out of it.

Such service costs the broker money, and he likes to see a little action in your account to generate commissions that will offset the firm's out-of-pocket costs.

Service charges may also be exacted to cover the cost of statistical reports that he furnishes you on individual companies — reports that the broker may buy from one of the large securities research firms or that his own research department may produce.

And if you hold stocks in a number of different companies and want advice from his research department on what to hold, what to sell, and what to buy as replacements — with reasons why — you may well be charged for that kind of service, too.

So when you go shopping for a broker, don't just ask about his commission rates. Ask about his service charges too.

There are some brokers who make no service charge of any kind. They figure they ought to be able to give the average customer whatever he wants just for the sake of the commissions they earn on his business.

The Securities and Exchange Commission, however, looks with some disfavor on this one-charge-for-everything concept. It is a strong advocate of what it calls *unbundling* — hanging specific price tags on all the services that a broker may render, over and above the commission that he earns just for executing orders. The S.E.C. argues that if a broker provides various services for customers, the customer has to pay for those services, and the cost of each should be clearly marked. They shouldn't just be wrapped up together in the total commission cost. Brokers who follow a "no-service-charge" policy reply that the S.E.C. has no right to tell them how to run their business. They contend that it's their business if they want to absorb the cost of supplying special services to their customers, all for a single commission. If they can cover those costs and still keep their rates competitive with other brokers, they figure they will be able to attract more customers.

One thing you should always remember is that some brokers will have an interest in your business if you want to buy only 10 or 20 shares, and some brokers won't. And their commission schedules are geared that way. Some brokers may be willing, even anxious, to execute a small order for you, even if they lose money on it from a cost accounting point of view. They are willing to gamble that somewhere down the line you will become a more substantial customer, maybe even a big trader. But many brokers, probably most of them, aren't willing to take that gamble. They are interested in the big-ticket customer — and you can be sure their commission schedules will be skewed to discourage you from bringing them your ten-share order.

One final word about brokerage service: you can get as much or as little as you want and are willing to pay for, so it pays to find your kind of broker. If you are an investor who makes up his own mind about what he wants to buy or sell — a person who doesn't want any advice or help from his broker — you might as well take your order to one of the scores of new discount, or "no service," brokers who have sprung up all over the country in the wake of the commission deregulation of 1975. These brokers will buy or sell stock for you at savings of 60% to 75% over the full service brokers' charges. But that is all they will do for you. They will not provide you with research reports on potential investments. They will not advise you on which stocks to buy and sell. They will not sit down with you for a long, friendly chat on your investment objectives. They will simply execute the buy or sell directives you give them and then deliver the stock you've bought or send you the proceeds from the stock you've sold. They are "no frills" order executors. And their low commission schedules reflect the narrowness of their services.

On the other hand, you may want or need a good deal of help — maybe even a little psychological support. If you're that kind of person, then the old-line full service brokers will happily give you everything you want — at a price.

So while you're shopping around for a broker and collecting commission rate schedules, consider the different kind of service provided by various brokers to their customers. And find out what that service is going to cost you. However, one thing you needn't bother looking for is a cut price below that paid by other customers on transactions of the same size. When a broker sets a commission schedule, he expects all his salesmen to stick by it. And if you think a special exception should be made in your case, you're probably going to have to argue your case with somebody pretty far up the line. And you're not likely to win this argument easily.

While you are looking for a broker, you may find yourself wondering what brought this revolution to Wall Street. For almost 200 years you had to pay the same commission charge no matter what member firm you dealt with. And now brokers are really competing with each other. What accounts for the change?

The explanation is really very simple. Even the monolithic, monopolistic New York Stock Exchange could not withstand the pressures of the marketplace — the inexorable effects of supply and demand. This is what actually brought the stock exchange's fixed fee schedule to its knees. The S.E.C. simply administered the coup de grace.

It all began in the fifties, when big-money institutions — banks, insurance companies, foundations, trusts — began to realize that common stocks were pretty good investments in inflationary times. When such a big institution goes into the market, it's apt to make quite a splash, because it buys and sells stocks in big blocks — 10,000, 25,000, maybe even 50,000 shares at a time. But back in the fifties and sixties the lowest commission rate charged by the New York Stock Exchange was the commission on 100 shares, a round lot. If somebody wanted to buy 5,000 shares of stock, he simply had to pay 50 times the fixed round-lot commission. If he wanted 10,000 shares, he had to pay 100 times the round-lot commission.

That didn't make much sense to the institutions. They felt they deserved a commission break on their big-volume business — a better deal than the fixed round-lot commission rate gave them. True, the New York Stock Exchange did provide various means by which big buyers and sellers could circumvent the exchange's ironclad commission rules. But these devices were at best cumbersome and cost the institutions more than they thought they should have to pay.

So the big institutions began looking for a better way, a way to trade blocks of stock more easily and at a lower cost to themselves. And they found it — outside the New York Stock Exchange. They found that there were big securities dealers — firms like Weeden & Co., that were not members of the exchange, hence not bound by its commission rules — who were quite willing to trade big blocks of stock for reduced rates. They were able to buy, or *position,* a block of stocks, thousands of shares at a crack, and then assume the risk of reselling it, hopefully at a profit, over an extended period of time.

Such nonmember firms didn't even bother with commissions. They simply bought the stock at a *net price,* a price a little lower than the price prevailing on the exchange but high enough to guarantee the seller a better net return than if the seller had sold the stock on the exchange and paid the commission cost.

Thus the *third market* was born — "third" because the two big exchanges, the New York Stock Exchange and the *American Stock Exchange,* had long ago usurped the right to be known as the first and second markets for securities in the United States.

Alarmed by the sensational growth of the third market — and the loss of institutional business — member firms in 1966 went to the S.E.C. and asked for the right to relax the regulatory shackles that the exchange had forged for itself.

First, they asked for an amendment to *Rule 394,* the rule that compelled members to execute all orders for listed stocks on the floor of the exchange and effectively prevented any trading with nonmembers or splitting commissions with them. This rule, of course, was the twentieth-century successor to the agreement that the founding fathers had reached under the buttonwood tree in 1792 that they would buy and sell securities only with each other. Obligingly, the S.E.C. permitted a modification of Rule 394 to permit a member to buy or sell off the floor of the exchange — in short, to participate in the third market — if he could demonstrate that such a deal would result in a more advantageous trade to his customer.

That amendment helped. But still the shackles of the fixed commission system chafed. In 1969, rates were reduced on orders of 1,000 shares or more. But that still wasn't enough to satisfy the institutions. Soon member firms began agitating for total abandonment of fixed commissions on all big-ticket orders. The S.E.C. tentatively suggested that commissions on all orders exceeding $100,000 be made subject to negotiation between the member firm and the buyer or seller.

That suggestion shocked many of the more staid members of the exchange who were used to doing business with a select clientele that definitely did not include hard-bargaining institutions. But then came the real bombshell. Robert W. Haack, then president of the New York Stock Exchange, advanced the revolutionary idea that no commissions should be fixed on orders of any size executed on the exchange. He suggested that the law of supply and demand, the rule of free competition, should supplant the monopolistic schedule of fixed commissions.

This was heresy, indeed — and from a paid hand at that! And when Merrill Lynch, Pierce, Fenner & Smith, Inc., the world's largest brokerage firm, and Salomon Brothers, a member firm that played a dominant role in handling institutional business, endorsed the no-fixed-commission proposal, the fears of many smaller firms were scarcely allayed.

Caught between the big firms that wanted a larger slice of the institutional business, and the smaller firms that feared they might go under without the protection of a fixed-commission system, the S.E.C. finally stuck a timid toe in the water. In April 1971, the commission ruled there should be no more fixed rates on orders involving $500,000 or more. From that time forward, commissions on all such orders should be subject to negotiation or bargaining between customer and broker. Soon member firms began to get more and more of the big-ticket business. Institutional transactions, which had accounted for only about 20% of exchange volume in the early sixties, soon doubled. Such trades were destined to account for 60% of exchange transactions in a decade — some days even as much as 75%. However, as long as the third market also continued to prosper, the big-ticket brokers weren't happy. So within a year, they were back knocking on the S.E.C.'s door asking for the right to negotiate commissions on all transactions of more than $300,000.

It was then, just when the S.E.C. was putting its case together to ask Congress for many basic reforms in the law governing the securities business, that the decision was made to go all out and order the abandonment of fixed commissions on all exchanges, effective May 1, 1975. This position was strongly supported by the Antitrust Division of the Department of Justice.

Ten years earlier, a Chicago investor had brought suit against the New York Stock Exchange, contending that its fixed commission system violated the *antitrust laws*. But the United States Supreme Court held finally that the exchange was exempt from the antitrust laws because the S.E.C. had the power to regulate its commission rates. Despite this defeat in the *Kaplan* case, the Antitrust Division, which bluntly told the S.E.C. that it considered all "private rate fixing illegal," persisted in its campaign against the exchange. Ironically, the United States Supreme Court, still turning a deaf ear to the Antitrust Division, ruled in June 1975 (*Gordon* vs. *New York Stock Exchange*), as it had before, that the exchange was immune to the antitrust laws because of the S.E.C.'s authority to fix commission rates. But by that time, the whole question was purely academic. Mayday had come and gone and the fixed commission schedule had become a dead letter — by order of the S.E.C. and with the obvious blessing of Congress.

In the end, the New York Stock Exchange, responding as it did to the pressure of outside competition for institutional business, had no one but itself to blame — or credit — for the result.

With the fixed-commission cornerstone blasted away, the question arose whether the New York Stock Exchange could continue to stand. Or maybe the question was how long it could stand. As long as Rule 394 remained on the books, exchange members were obligated to try to execute an order there before concluding a deal with a nonmember in the third market. But the S.E.C. had the power of life and death over Rule 394. How would it use that power?

There was no clear or immediate answer. On the one hand, it was obvious that the commission was dedicated to the concept of a *central securities market* in which exchange members and other *market-makers* would compete with one another in offering the best prices for securities. On the other hand, it was equally obvious that the S.E.C. could not sign the death warrant of an institution so vital to the stability of stock trading as the New York Stock Exchange.

The S.E.C. adopted the first alternative when in May 1976 it introduced a second set of rules that increased the competition among brokers on the trading floor. By forcing them to bargain among themselves over the commissions they charged each other, the S.E.C. hoped to reduce eventually the cost of handling all transactions, regardless of the market where they took place.

In the long run it could be that the answer to the question of the exchange's future might not be supplied by the Securities and Exchange Commission — or even the Congress of the United States — but again by the inexorable laws of the marketplace, the interplay of free competition.

Only a few days after Mayday, Weeden & Co., probably the biggest factor in the development of the third market, announced that it had formed a subsidiary, Dexter Securities Corporation, which would buy a seat on the New York Stock Exchange. This would enable Weeden & Co. to work both sides of the street, dealing alike with members and nonmembers.

Actually, that idea was not a new one. Five months before Mayday, Dreyfus Corporation, an institution that buys and sells many millions of N.Y.S.E. stocks, had applied for membership on the exchange. Although the application was turned down because exchange rules forbade any such institution to own a seat on the exchange, the message was writ on the wall for all to see.

Day by day, year by year, pressure was mounting. The exchange could not fend off forever the big institutions that sought the right to buy and sell securities without paying tribute to an intermediary — in short, without paying a commission. Within days after May 1, 1975, some member firms of the exchange — and many nonmembers — were cutting their rates on big volume orders right down to the no-profit bone. They were seeking to appease the institutional customer and trying to postpone the day when they would demand seats on the exchange for themselves.

And in this brave new world of free competition, what was the future of the brokerage business? Probably not much different from that of the broker's customers. The big and efficient firms seemed likely to grow bigger and more prosperous, whether they did business on the New York Stock Exchange or in the new national marketplace. As for the smaller firms, the future was not rosy. Without the protection of the fixed-rate schedule, such firms seemed likely either to be swallowed up by their big competitors or to fall by the wayside. By 1982 scores of firms had closed their doors and many others had been swallowed up by bigger, stronger firms. And there were those in Wall Street who freely predicted that only a comparative handful of brokerage firms would be doing business a decade hence.

Meanwhile, among the big brokerage firms with their worldwide networks of offices, few were content to sit back and simply count the commission dollars rolling in. They too had reason to worry. Nobody was guaranteeing them the fruits of a future monopoly in the stock-trading business. Not as long as those big institutions were intent on getting rid of all middlemen and handling their own securities transactions. To protect themselves, many firms were diversifying their business as rapidly as possible, moving into new fields.

Even before Mayday, Merrill Lynch & Co. had ventured into the insurance field, real estate, merchant banking abroad, and investment counseling. Other big competitors were following Merrill's lead.

Clearly, the order of the day in Wall Street was to diversify. As rapidly as they could, brokers were putting out anchors to windward. They knew that the storms which had ravaged the Street for a decade had not really abated.

But despite Wall Street's revolution, despite the ever-growing dominance of the big institutional customers in the stock market, the average individual investor could still count on doing business with his friendly broker in almost any bigger-than-average town in the United States. And there was even the chance that that broker would get friendlier and friendlier as the new competition between member firms of the New York Stock Exchange grew keener in the years ahead.

CHAPTER 10

How the Stock Exchange Works

WHAT actually happens on the New York Stock Exchange when a broker gets an order to buy or sell stocks? How is the transaction completed with another broker so that both buyer and seller are assured of the best price possible on the exchange at that moment?

Consider first the physical layout of the stock exchange. It is a big building at the corner of Wall and Broad streets in New York City. The trading room looks somewhat like an armory, with a high ceiling and a *trading floor* about three-fifths the size of a football field.

All around the edge of the trading floor are *telephone booths,* as they are traditionally called, although today they might more appropriately be called teletype booths. These booths bear no resemblance to any other phone booths you have ever seen. Most of them are open at both ends. Along the two sides there are spaces at which a dozen or more clerks, representing various brokers, can work. At each clerk's space, there is a narrow shelf at which he stands and does his paperwork. (Once a bastion of male chauvinism, the stock market community has, since the first edition of this book was published, become considerably more enlightened in offering career opportunities to women. Despite the fact that there are more and more women turning up in positions of responsibility on Wall Street every day, however, we shall

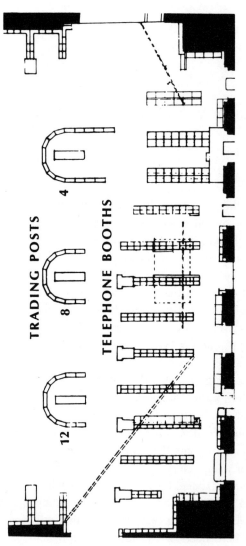

TRADING POSTS

12   8   4

TELEPHONE BOOTHS

At trading posts on the main trading floor of the New York Stock Exchange such well-known stocks as General Motors and R.C.A. (post 10), Greyhound and Boeing (post 11), and Ford (post 6) are traded. If you place an order to buy General Motors, the floor broker representing your firm will pick up the order from the clerk at his telephone booth and walk to a precise spot on the outside perimeter of post 10. Here he knows he will find the specialist in General Motors stock, as well as all other brokers who have orders to buy or sell that stock at that time. Here he will execute the trade for you. As he walks between his booth and the trading post he is likely to keep one eye on the ticker tape projected on fluorescent screens (dotted lines) in each corner of the trading floor. That way he knows how the market as a whole is moving. Prices are flashed on the screens from elevated projection booths (dotted rectangle, bottom center) around the floor.

retain the use of the masculine pronoun when referring to such employees for the purpose of simplicity.) Above the shelf there is a bank of telephones connecting him with his home office. These phones were once the nerve ends of the entire stock exchange business. It was through them that all public orders to buy or sell stocks came to the floor of the exchange. The phones are still used, but as part of its modernization program, the exchange permitted most large brokerage firms to install teletype equipment in or near the telephone booths so that they could receive orders directly from their branch offices. This eliminated the necessity for relaying orders by phone from the home office to the floor clerk. Since teletype orders are printed, the possibility of error was also reduced.

Spaced at regular intervals on the trading floor are 22 *trading posts,* twelve on the main trading floor, six in the "garage" or annex, and an additional four in the new trading room, called the blue room, opened in July 1969. Each trading post, or station, used to be a horseshoe-shaped counter, occupying about 100 square feet of floor space. Behind the counter, inside the post or station, there was room for a dozen clerks and for several paid employees of the exchange. Looking to the future, the exchange, in 1979, launched a major facilities upgrade program to help assure its ability to handle anticipated trading volumes of up to 150,000,000 shares a day. At the hub of this program were sleek new trading posts fitted with a dazzling array of electronic equipment. By 1981 all of the old horseshoe posts had been replaced and donated by the exchange to various museums across the country.

All buying and selling is done around the outside of the trading post. About 90 different stocks are assigned to each post in different sections around the perimeter, ten or so to each section.

Indicators above the counter show just which stocks are sold in each section. Below each is a price indicator showing the last price at which a transaction in that stock took place and whether this price represented an increase or decrease from the last different price — a plus sign or *up tick* represents an increase, a minus sign or *down tick* a decrease.

When a customer decides to buy or sell a stock he simply calls his local broker with the order. The broker then calls his firm's headquarters office in New York City, which in turn phones the order to a clerk in that firm's telephone booth on the exchange floor (unless, of course, the order comes directly to the floor by teletype). Some firms have booth space for only one or two clerks, while one big wire house has about 40 spaces in nine booths. When the clerk gets the order over the phone, he writes it out in a kind of shorthand and hands it to his *floor broker* to execute. This is because only members can trade on the floor. If the broker is not at the booth, the clerk can summon him by means of a pocket-sized radio receiver, or by pushing a button located in the firm's booth. Every broker has a number. When the clerk pushes the button, the broker's number is flashed on large *annunciator boards* in each of the trading rooms.

If the clerk knows his broker is busy with other orders, he employs the services of a so-called *two-dollar broker,* an independent member of the stock exchange who is not connected with a member firm. These brokers own their own seats on the exchange and make their living by executing orders for other brokers or for wire houses that are sometimes too busy to transact all of their own business. The two-dollar brokers got their name in the days when they received that fee for every order they executed. Nowadays their commission, called *floor brokerage,* is negotiated.

Let's assume that with the passage of years Rod & Reel, Inc., has grown to the point where its stock is listed on the New York Stock Exchange. Let's further assume that the order that the clerk gives his broker is a *market order* to buy 100 shares of Rod & Reel. A market order is one that a broker must execute as soon as he can at the best price he can get. As soon as the broker has the actual order in his hands he walks — no running is permitted on the floor — over to the trading post where Rod & Reel is traded.

Here he knows he will find all other brokers with orders to buy or sell Rod & Reel.

As he approaches the post, the broker looks at the price indicator and notes that the last sale of Rod & Reel took place at 18¾, which means $18.75 a share. However, some broker may now be willing to sell it for less than that price. So as he enters the "crowd" of other brokers — two, three, or more of them at the trading position — he simply asks, "How's Reel?" He doesn't disclose whether he wants to buy or sell; he just asks the question. Another broker may answer, "Eighteen and three-eighths to eighteen and three-quarters," or simply, "Three-eighths, three-quarters." This means that 18⅜ is the best bid, the most any broker is then willing to pay, and 18¾ is the best offer, the lowest anyone will sell for.

Our broker will try to get the stock cheaper if he can. So he waits a few seconds for other offers. Finally he decides to tip his hand and make a bid. He says, "One-half for a hundred," by which he means that he will pay $18.50 a share for 100 shares.

If he gets no response, he may raise his bid by ⅛ of a point. This is the minimum fluctuation in the price of most stocks. So he announces, "Five-eighths for one hundred." At this point, perhaps, the first broker, who was offering the stock at 18¾, may have decided that he can't get that price. Or another broker, who may have entered the crowd later, will decide to accept this bid of 18⅝. If either one of them decides to "*hit*," or accept, the bid he says, "Sold," and the transaction is concluded, simply on the basis of that spoken word. Conversely, if a broker decides to accept an offering price announced in the course of an auction, he simply says, "Take it." No written memoranda are exchanged by the brokers. Each broker simply makes his own note of the other broker to whom he sold or from whom he bought and the price that was agreed on.

The rules of the New York Stock Exchange provide that all bids to buy and all offers to sell must be made by open outcry. No secret transactions are permitted on the floor of the exchange.

Furthermore, a broker cannot conclude transactions between his own public customers without presenting on the floor their orders to buy or sell. For instance, the broker may have a market order to buy 100 shares of Rod & Reel and another market order to sell 100. He can't just "*cross*" these orders privately and effect a transfer of the stock between his two customers. He must send both orders to the floor, where the appropriate bids and offers must be made. Only in very rare cases, usually involving thousands of shares, are off-the-market crosses permitted. Even in these cases, both buyer and seller must know that the cross is being made, and the stock exchange must grant permission.

No broker is permitted to execute any orders on the floor except during the official trading hours of the exchange. These are from 10 A.M. to 4 P.M., New York time, Monday through Friday, excepting holidays. (From mid-1968 to mid-1970, when brokers were struggling with an unprecedented volume of orders that they were not equipped to handle, the exchange operated on a reduced schedule of trading hours so as to catch up with the paperwork generated. But by 1976, efficiency had so improved that the exchange did not have to resort to early closings despite the record-breaking volume.)

As soon as a transaction such as the Rod & Reel purchase at 18⅝ is completed, the broker who bought the stock and the broker who sold it have their clerks report back to their respective home offices. This is done so the buyer and seller may each be advised that the transaction has been concluded and be told what the price was. Brokerage firms with teletype order service direct to the floor simply send the information from the floor back to the originating office.

After the market closes, the two brokerage firms involved in the Rod & Reel transaction must arrange for the real transfer of the stock and the payment of the amount due. Actually these two firms might have concluded many transactions with each other in the course of the day, and, in turn, each of them might have dealt with dozens of other brokers.

Thus, on a given day one firm might have sold 1,100 shares of Rod & Reel for its customers and bought only 1,000 shares for other customers. The transfer of 1,000 shares from its customers who sold the stock to the customers that bought the same number of shares is purely an internal bookkeeping problem for the firm to settle. But it would still owe some other broker 100 shares.

Time was when the broker who owed shares at the end of the day would deliver the actual certificates to the *Stock Clearing Corporation,* where other brokers to whom shares were due would pick them up. Later, all member firms simply kept a supply of all stocks at the clearing corporation. The transfer of shares between brokers would be accomplished simply by debiting or crediting each broker's account. Dollar balances — the net amounts due them — were settled in the same fashion.

Now, the *Depository Trust Company* (a subsidiary of the New York Stock Exchange, formerly known as Central Certificate Service) has eliminated nearly all that shuffling of certificates by handling more than 75% of all clearing operations. It conducts a central certificate operation, which relieves its participants — broker-dealers, banks, clearing corporations, insurance and investment companies, among others — of the burden of handling hundreds of pieces of paper each day in both the receiving and delivery functions.

In the vaults of major banks and in the Depository Trust's own vault are stored about 4 billion shares of stocks, including those sold on the exchange and those traded elsewhere. Corporate securities held here are worth more than $530 billion. Including registered corporate bonds, more than 16,000 issues are represented.

When certificates are deposited, they are held in nonnegotiable form until it is necessary to transfer them out in the name of a customer or a firm. The participants in a stock trade do not have to handle or even see the certificates until they are delivered upon request.

Computers make daily bookkeeping entries to reflect changes in the participants' position after the securities have been traded. All of this has obviously reduced the number of securities under a participating broker's care, thus freeing valuable space and personnel. At the end of the business day, only one check need be delivered or received from each active participant.

Ultimately, the problems involved in handling stock certificates may be further simplified by the introduction of a certificate like an IBM card on which all the essential data can be "read" by a computer. Another proposal would involve adding a half-inch to the width of the present 8" x 12" certificate and incorporating into that half-inch all the essential data in characters that could be read electronically by an *optical scanner*. But either change would be only a stopgap measure, for in 1975 Congress directed the S.E.C. to take steps to eliminate altogether stock certificates as a means of settling securities transactions. A system of computerized bookkeeping entry would probably be substituted. Thus, one of Wall Street's most cherished and colorful traditions will have vanished from the scene.

To return to our Rod & Reel order, after the sale took place at 18⅝, one of the *floor reporters*, paid employees of the exchange who stand outside each trading post, would see that the price indicator on the post was changed from 18¾ to 18⅝. And since this sale was below the preceding sale, he would be sure that a minus sign showed beside the price figure.

For unnumbered years, the reporter then used to write a report of the sale — the name of the stock, the number of shares involved, and the price — and hand it to a pageboy, who would take it to the pneumatic tubes that led directly from each post to the ticker room. There a notation of the sale was typed onto the *ticker tape,* and it was carried by wire to the *tickers* in every broker's office throughout the country.

Here again, modern technology has come to the rescue of the beleaguered exchange and vastly speeded up operations. Now when a transaction is completed all the reporter has to do is draw pencil lines through the appropriate coded boxes — stock symbol, number of shares, price — and insert the card into the electronic scanner. The machine automatically "reads" the essential data from the card and transfers the information to the computer. The computer is used to drive the ticker and produce the printouts, showing each transaction on the tape, or electronic screen. Thus, in a matter of seconds, the public knows all the essential information about every transaction.

With automation of floor operations increasing, some brokers are wondering seriously if the day is coming when computers will take over the entire trading function and render both them and the exchange obsolete. After all, they have seen what a revolution computers have wrought in just a few short years in the accounting, bookkeeping, traffic, and even research departments of their home offices.

On the tape the name of every stock appears only as initials or a combination of letters, such as C for Chrysler Corporation, CP for Canadian Pacific, and CRR for Carrier Corporation. The single-letter symbols are, of course, the most highly prized and best known. Thus F stands for Ford, T for American Telephone & Telegraph, and, probably the best known of all, X for U.S. Steel.

Rod & Reel might have the symbol RAR, in which case the sale of 100 shares at $18\frac{5}{8}$ would appear on the tape simply as:

RAR

$18\frac{5}{8}$

If 200 shares, instead of 100, had changed hands, the transaction would be noted this way:

RAR

2S $18\frac{5}{8}$

If 1,000 shares was involved, it would appear on the tape this way:

RAR

10S $18\frac{5}{8}$

When sales volume is so heavy that the ticker, which can print 900 characters a minute, falls as much as one minute behind in reporting transactions, the price information is abbreviated to the last digit plus a fraction, except when that digit is a zero. If the ticker was one minute late, our sale at 18⅝ would appear as:

RAR

8⅝

It is assumed that people who are following the stock closely on the ticker will be able to supply the missing first digit. If the stock were to go up to 20 or above, hence involving a new first digit, this price would be noted in full, such as 20⅛. on the first such sale.

When the ticker falls two minutes behind in reporting, the volume of sales is deleted. Thus, even if 1,000 shares of Rod & Reel were sold at 18⅝, the transaction would still appear:

RAR

8⅝

The ticker rarely falls three minutes or more behind and then only on big volume days. But when it does, *repeat prices* are omitted. In other words, succeeding transactions in the same stock at an identical price are not printed. As soon as the tape recovers lost time, it returns to normal routines.

If the tape can't keep up with the pace of trading, you may wonder why the exchange doesn't simply introduce a faster ticker. The answer is that anything above 900 characters a minute would be "blurred," almost impossible to read. Although a high-speed data processing ticker is planned for the future, it will be available only to financial vendors and to press associations.

When most people think of buying or selling stock, they think of doing so on the basis of a market order. This is an order to be executed as soon as possible after it reaches the floor, at the best price then prevailing. Actually, an individual very often wants to buy or sell a stock only if it can be done at a certain price or better. Thus, you might want to buy 100 shares of Rod & Reel if you don't have to pay more than 18½. You could place an order to this effect with your broker. It's called a *limit order,* and you can tell him whether it's good for a day, a week, a month, or "good till canceled." All limit orders are treated as day orders, unless they are clearly marked for a longer period of time. If they are not so marked they are canceled if they are not executed by the end of that day's trading.

The stock purchased for you on this hypothetical Rod & Reel limit order will be bought for you only if it can be bought at 18½ or less. Perhaps when the order is actually executed, your broker will be able to get the stock at 18¼. On the other hand, it can happen that the stock may actually drop to 18½, and your order still won't be filled. That's because other orders to buy at 18½ were placed ahead of yours, and the supply of the stock offered at that price was exhausted before your order was reached. In that kind of situation, if you ask your broker why your order wasn't executed, he will tell you that there was *"stock ahead."*

Limit orders can also be used in selling stock. Thus, if you owned Rod & Reel stock, you might be willing to sell it, but only if you could get $19 for it — or more. You could place a *sell-limit order* to that effect with your broker. Sometimes, you might like to place a day limit order to buy or sell at a specified price. But you would still like to have your order executed that day even if the stock didn't quite reach the price level you set. You could accomplish that by having the order marked for *execution at the close* regardless of the market level at 4 P.M.

There's still another kind of suspended order: the *stop order.*

Suppose you bought Rod & Reel at 12 or 13, and the stock rose to a level where you had a nice profit — perhaps to 19 or 20. You might want to protect that profit in case the market dropped sharply. You could do so by instructing your broker to sell the stock if it declined to 18. This would be a *stop order to sell.* Your broker would see that it was executed if Rod & Reel ever fell as low as 18. Whenever it hit that mark, your stop order would become a market order to be executed at the best price then possible. Again, because other people might have placed orders ahead of yours to sell at the 18 figure, the price might slip to 17¾ or even 17½ before your order could be executed.

Conversely, you might not want to buy Rod & Reel when it was selling at 18 because you felt it might fall further. But on the other hand if there were a sharp rally, you wouldn't want to miss your opportunity to pick up the stock before its price went up too high. In that case you might place a *stop order to buy* by instructing your broker to buy Rod & Reel for you at, let's say, 19.

Occasionally, the exchange will exercise its authority to prohibit stop orders in individual stocks. Such action is taken only when the stock in question has followed a very volatile pattern of price movements and when the exchange fears that the execution of stop orders to sell it would trigger a sharp sell-off.

In theory these fixed-price orders, both limit orders and stop orders, look pretty attractive as a means of controlling your profit or losses. In common practice, however, they don't work as well for the average investor as you might think. To have any real utility, a limit order has to be pegged fairly close to the prevailing market price. For instance, if Rod & Reel is selling at 18½, there might not be much point in placing an order to buy it at 16 or even 17. And if you place a limit order at 18, you might just as well buy it outright at 18½. The same logic applies in reverse when it comes to selling stock.

In short, decisions to buy or sell that turn on getting an extra point or fraction of a point above or below the market price prevailing are usually not apt to be sound decisions for the average investor.

CHAPTER 11

How a Market Is Made

WHENEVER you place an order to buy or sell stocks, your brokerage firm is responsible for executing it at the best price possible, the highest price if you are selling, the lowest if you are buying. Often this responsibility requires the firm's floor broker to spend far more time on your order than he can afford to spare if he is going to attend to all his other duties. Thus, for instance, if you were to place an order to buy Rod & Reel at the specified price of 18 and the stock was then selling at 19, you could hardly expect your broker to spend all his time keeping an eye on Rod & Reel, waiting to see if it dropped to 18.

In a case like that, he would turn your order over to another broker, who, as his agent, would watch the stock for you and execute the order if he could. This agent is usually the *specialist* in Rod & Reel stock.

A specialist is a broker who has elected to confine his buying and selling activities to a particular stock or stocks that are traded at one spot around the perimeter of a trading post. He never moves away from that spot. He is always there to accept orders from other brokers and, for a negotiated commission known as floor brokerage, to assume responsibility for their execution. The individual investor does not pay anything extra for the specialist's services.

A specialist must not only function as an agent for other brokers, executing orders that they leave with him; he must also be willing to buy and sell for his own account those stocks in which he specializes. In fact, this is his primary responsibility, fulfilling the obligation imposed upon him by the exchange to maintain a "fair and orderly market" in these stocks.

All told, there are about 407 members of the exchange who operate as specialists. They work for 64 separate specialist organizations — mostly partnerships or two or three firms working together — that handle the stocks of all the companies listed on the exchange. Some big specialists units handle as many as 150 stocks; some only a few.

No member can operate as a specialist except with the approval of the stock exchange. The specialist must also be a member of substantial means. Every specialist unit is required to have enough capital to buy as many as 5,000 shares of the common stocks and 1,000 shares of the convertible preferred stocks in which their members are authorized to deal. In the case of a common stock priced at $50 a share, a specialist unit would thus need a quarter-million dollars just to handle that one stock.

Moreover, each specialist firm must have at least $100,000 readily available for its use, or 25% of the cost of 5,000 shares of all the common stocks and 1,000 shares of all the convertible preferreds it's authorized to deal in, whichever amount is the greater.

This means that the big specialist firms that handle dozens of stocks must have access to many millions of dollars. Some specialists rely principally on their own resources. But most supplement their own capital through private financing arrangements. Some specialist firms are so well-heeled that they can buy as many as twenty or thirty thousand shares of one or more of the stocks they handle.

When a specialist executes orders for other brokers, he is himself operating as a broker, for technically, that is what the word broker means, a man who acts as agent for others. But when a specialist buys or sells for his own account, he is acting as a *dealer*. That is the distinction between a broker and a securities dealer. A broker simply bargains *for* you. A dealer bargains *with* you, and acts as a principal in the transaction. He sells you securities that he owns himself, or buys such securities from you at an agreed price.

When a member firm broker comes to the trading post with an order to sell a stock and there are no other brokers with buy orders for that stock at the post, the specialist will make a bid for the stock himself. Similarly, when a broker wants to buy a stock and there are no other sellers, the specialist will offer it for sale himself.

Normally, about 30% to 40% of stock exchange volume results from this kind of buying and selling by specialists for their own accounts. And normally, the specialists count on making about half their income from these transactions. The other half comes from executing orders for other brokers.

On each of the stocks in which he specializes, the specialist keeps a book. In this *specialist's book* are entered all the limit or stop orders that other brokers have given him for execution which could not be executed because they were "away from the market" — either too high or too low in relation to the price at which the stock was then being traded. If a specialist gets two or more orders to buy a stock at the same price — or to sell it at the same price — he enters them in his book in the order in which he receives them. Those that are received first are executed first, whenever the price auction permits, regardless of all other conditions or circumstances.

Thus, if your order for Rod & Reel at 18 was the first one in the specialist's book, and if the stock was offered at that price, your order would be filled first. Even if he wanted to, the specialist couldn't buy the stock for his own account at 18 until your order, and all others in his book at that price, had been executed.

If the last sale of Rod & Reel was made at 18½, the specialist's book might typically show one or two limit orders to buy at 18⅜. That's because most customers place limit orders in round figures rather than fractions. On the sell side, his book might show a couple of orders to sell at 18⅝, a few at 18¾, and several at 19 or higher. These might be either limit orders or stop orders, and would be so marked in the specialist's book.

In that situation, if a broker came to the trading post with a market order to buy Rod & Reel and there were no other brokers there with stock to sell, his query "How's Reel?" would be answered by the specialist. The specialist would reply, "Three-eighths, five-eighths," meaning 18⅜ bid and 18⅝ offered, since 18⅜ was the highest buy order and 18⅝ the lowest sell order that he then had in his book. This would be the *bid-and-asked* quotation as of then.

Since a specialist's primary responsibility is to see that there is no violent fluctuation in the price of any stock he handles, he usually undertakes to see that the difference between the bid and the asked price is only ½ of a point or so, although it might be more on high-priced issues.

Because specialists are generally faithful to their obligations to maintain orderly markets, well over 90% of all transactions on the exchange take place at prices that show a fluctuation of ¼ of a point or less from the previous transaction. Whenever there is a larger than normal gap between bid-and-asked quotations, the specialist, under the rules of the exchange, is expected to do something to narrow the gap. Specifically, he is expected to make appropriate bids or offers of his own — to buy or sell the stock as necessary, for his own account.

Furthermore, if one of his stocks is moving rapidly up or rapidly down, he is expected to *stabilize* the market in that stock. If there is a heavy pressure of sell orders that pushes the price down, he is expected to buy the stock for his own account. If buy orders are pushing the price up too rapidly, he is expected to sell the stock from his own inventory. He may even be forced to sell stock he doesn't have, hoping that somewhere along the line he will be able to buy an offsetting amount of the stock at a lower price to make good the stock he has sold to other brokers.

The obligation to maintain a fair and orderly market can impose fearsome and expensive responsibilities on a specialist. Important news developments can drastically affect a company's prospects and result in a sudden torrent of buy or sell orders. Sometimes such a development will delay the opening of a stock for hours. Sometimes it will force suspension of trading for a much longer period of time. In such situations, the specialist will consult with floor officials and one or two directors of the exchange. Together they will decide what constitutes a fair price quotation. When trading in the stock begins again, that's the price at which the specialist is obligated to buy or sell.

A classic illustration of the kind of dilemma that frequently confronts specialists is that which occurred in early 1964 when Lockheed announced that it had developed the A-11, a jet plane whose performance, in the words of President Johnson, far exceeded that "of any other aircraft in the world today." The President made that announcement on a Friday. Lockheed had closed that day at 38. At what price would it open on Monday? On Monday morning the Lockheed specialist was confronted with market orders to buy 30,000 shares. In his book, he had offsetting sell orders that totaled only 17,000 shares — 13,000 less than were needed. Floor traders were willing to sell 3,200 shares, and the specialist had 5,600 in his inventory. As for the remaining 4,200 shares, the specialist had no choice but to sell shares he didn't have, hoping to cover his shortage by buying 4,200 shares later at a reasonable price.

After conferring with floor officials, the specialist set an opening price of 40¾ — $2.75 above Friday's close. Trading opened on a block of 30,000 shares at that price. Lockheed closed that day at 40⅜, after 299 individual transactions valued at some $5,500,000 had taken place, but the most significant thing about the day's trading was that the specialist ran such an orderly market that not one of those transactions was carried through at a price that varied more than ¼ point from the preceding transaction.

Occasionally, there may be such an overnight accumulation of buy or sell orders for a stock that the specialist is unable to arrange an opening price, even with the help of floor traders or floor officials. On Monday, January 11, 1982, for instance, after the government announced it was dropping its lengthy antitrust suit against IBM, the giant computer corporation, its stock wasn't traded at all on the New York Stock Exchange until just before the close. When it finally did open on a block of 714,500 shares, it was up $1\frac{3}{4}$ points to $58\frac{5}{8}$.

In addition to stabilizing the market and being willing to buy or sell when there are no brokers with offsetting orders, the specialist performs another important service, which is called *stopping a stock.*

Suppose your broker came to the trading post with your market order for Rod & Reel when the best offering price in the specialist's book was $18\frac{5}{8}$ and when there were no other brokers present with better offers. Anxious to get a lower price for you, yet not wanting to miss the market if it went up, your broker would ask the specialist to "stop" 100 shares for him at $18\frac{5}{8}$. If another broker came up then and offered Rod & Reel at $18\frac{1}{2}$, the specialist would buy it for your broker and earn a floor brokerage commission. On the other hand, if the stock was not offered at a lower price, but sold again the next time at $18\frac{5}{8}$, the specialist would execute your buy order at that figure. He could not execute your order at more than $18\frac{5}{8}$, for when he was asked to stop the stock, he agreed that $18\frac{5}{8}$ would be the maximum price your broker would have to pay. He'd try to buy it cheaper if he could, but $18\frac{5}{8}$ would be the top price.

After every sale a whole new auction starts. Thus, if a transaction in Rod & Reel had just been concluded at $18\frac{5}{8}$, other brokers in the crowd who might be trying to buy 100 shares apiece would immediately restate their bids, maybe the same bid — $18\frac{1}{2}$. These simultaneous bids would have parity. If a broker then came up and offered 100 shares of stock at $18\frac{1}{2}$, the brokers who wanted to buy at that price would settle the matter of who got the stock by tossing a coin.

The brokers who lost out might then report to their customers that they had *matched and lost*. Customers who get such a report often wonder why they never match and win. The answer is that the broker never reports when he matches and wins. The customer simply gets the stock.

In the case of simultaneous bids, if one broker has an order for 200 shares, while the others are trying to buy only 100 shares apiece, the larger order takes precedence if the seller offers a block that is as big or bigger. If the seller offers 200 shares, the broker who wants 200 will get them all. If the seller has 300 shares, the broker who wants 200 will get his first, and the others will have to match for the remaining 100.

Very often, before placing a market order a customer wants to have an idea of what he'll have to pay. To accommodate such a customer, the floor broker will try to *"get the market and the size."* This means that he will ask the specialist for the current bid-and-asked prices and for the size of the orders at these prices. The specialist will reveal only the highest bid and the lowest offer, such as on Rod & Reel. "Three-eighths, five-eighths," or $18\frac{3}{8}$ bid, offered at $18\frac{5}{8}$. He is not permitted to reveal any of the lower bids or higher offering prices shown on his book. As far as the size of the orders is concerned, he might say, "One hundred either way." By this he would mean that he has 100 shares to buy at $18\frac{3}{8}$ and 100 to sell at $18\frac{5}{8}$. If he had 100 to buy and 500 to sell, he would say. "Three-eighths, five-eighths, one and five."

The specialist is not required to divulge the size of the orders on his book at either the bid or asked price if he feels that it would not be in the best interests of the buyers or sellers.

Because the specialist's book gives him a "feel" for the market that no other broker or investor can possibly have, and because he not only can, but *must*, buy and sell for his own account to maintain an orderly market, he is obviously in a position to affect the trend of prices in a very important way.

To be sure that the specialist does not abuse his privileged position or manipulate prices in any way to his personal advantage, the exchange has circumscribed his operations with a set of highly technical rules, which have become steadily more stringent over the years.

Despite the fact that various surveys, including the S.E.C.'s own, have not turned up any evidence of wrongdoing by specialists on the New York Stock Exchange, and have even demonstrated what a useful service they render, the S.E.C. continues to regard their operations with grave suspicion. There is no doubt that those operations will continue to be kept under very close surveillance by both the exchange and the S.E.C.

Specialists are now required to submit to the exchange — about eight times a year — details of their dealings for various one-week periods, selected at random by the exchange and not revealed in advance. These reports make it possible for the exchange to study the orderliness of the market in an individual stock, the continuity of price, the spread in quotations, and to render a judgment about how well the specialist is fulfilling his obligations.

Specialists must also report weekly to the stock exchange every trade they make for their own account — stating the time, the "tick" (whether up or down in price), and the number of shares involved. They are then graded on their stabilizing record — whether they bought on down ticks and sold on up ticks, as they are expected to.

In addition, the exchange maintains an on-line price surveillance program based on trading data obtained from the computers that run the stock ticker. This program monitors all trades reported on the ticker throughout the market session. When the price movement of a stock exceeds preset standards, the computer calls attention to that fact. The transaction — stock symbol, time, and price — is reported on a teletypewriter machine in the exchange's surveillance section. The surveillance section then retrieves from the computer's memory bank the chronological sequence of sales, before and after the suspicious transaction, and analyzes the record. If there is no apparent cause for the fluctuation, the surveillance section alerts a trading floor official in the area where the stock is traded. The official will then speak to the specialist to find out just what happened — and why.

Whenever the cry is raised that specialists should not be allowed to trade for their own accounts, that their functions should be restricted to running the book and executing orders for other brokers, specialists ask what would have happened to the stock market if they had not been able and willing to step into the breach at the time of President Eisenhower's heart attack in 1955, or on the day President Kennedy was assassinated in 1963.

On Monday, September 16, 1955, after the news of Eisenhower's heart attack had broken over the weekend, the market opened with sell orders far outnumbering buy orders. It was virtually impossible to open trading in any stock. The sell orders would have depressed prices beyond all reasonable levels before buying sentiment could be generated. The specialists met the challenge. They bought steadily for their own accounts at prices only moderately below the levels that had prevailed at Friday's close. All told, one-quarter of the stock purchases that day were made for the specialists' own accounts — 1,759,360 shares with an estimated market value of $80 million. Eisenhower's recovery enabled the specialists as a group to work off the stock they bought without loss — indeed, with profit. But when they took the risk, they did not know whether or not they would be wiped out.

"How," ask the specialists, "could you get a computer to do that kind of job?"

On November 22, 1963, the performance of the specialists was equally noteworthy. The story can be summarized in terms of what happened to 25 key stocks between 1:40 P.M., when news of President Kennedy's assassination hit the exchange floor, and 2:07 P.M., when the exchange was closed down by the governors. At

1:40 P.M. specialists in these 25 issues held 126,000 shares, worth over $7 million, in their own inventories. When panic selling engulfed the floor, the specialists stepped in to buy, risking their own personal solvency. In the following 27 minutes, 570,000 shares of these 25 stocks were traded on the floor. Of this total, specialists bought more than 144,000, increasing their inventories to almost 230,000 shares, worth $12,348,000. Floor traders also helped stabilize the market in these stocks, buying 31,000 shares on balance. True, the specialists sustained no loss, thanks to a rapid market recovery. But that's something they couldn't count on when they took their big gamble.

The S.E.C. contends that specialists have not always behaved in such exemplary fashion. But, then, perhaps no one can be a hero all the time.

CHAPTER 12

How Large Blocks of
Stock Are Handled

SUPPOSE you owned a sizable block of stock in a company. Maybe you acquired the shares as part of your retirement benefits from that company. Maybe you inherited the stock. Or maybe you simply bought the block bit by bit over a long period of time. Now, you have decided you want to sell 5,000 shares, or 10,000 shares, or more. How would you go about selling that much stock?

Obviously, if you just dumped it on the market all at once, it would depress the price and you wouldn't get as much for the stock as you should. Moreover, it might be a period of days or even weeks before you could dispose of all that stock in ordinary trades of one or two hundred shares at a time.

In a situation of this kind you would be well advised to let your broker solve your problem for you. The first thing he would do is try to "find the other side of the market," to uncover a buying interest in the stock that would match your own desire to sell. To do this the department of his firm that specializes in block business would contact various sources to find a buyer for your block. These sources would include other member firms, but also nonmember firms known to have an interest in the stock. If the stock was not popularly traded in the market, your broker might see if the company itself was interested in buying back its own stock, as many large companies often are.

Your broker might also turn to the specialist who handles that stock who, in his role as market-maker, often helps brokers dispose of sizable blocks.

Time was when a broker could turn a block order over to the specialist to execute on a *not-held* basis. On this basis the specialist would be free to exercise his own best judgment about when and how to feed the stock into the market. He might, for instance, hold the stock back in expectation that prices would rise. If they dropped before he finished executing the complete order — if other orders were filled at prices higher than what he finally realized on his not-held order — he was at least assured that the broker for whom he was acting would "not hold him to the tape," that is, hold him responsible for failing to sell at those better intervening prices.

For some years, however, the S.E.C. has insisted that specialists not accept not-held orders. This restriction makes the handling of such orders difficult for the broker. About all he can do is try to get the customer to change his order to a limit order. If he succeeds, the broker can then turn the order over to the specialist to execute as best he can at prices above the minimum set in the limit order.

In the last analysis, the specialist is as interested as your broker is in disposing of your block with the least possible impact on his market. The specialist might, for instance, know some floor traders who would be interested in buying all or part of the block. Or the specialist might be willing to buy it outright for his own account, thus assuming the entire risk that he could sell the block at a profit.

If he took on a block on this basis, it would be known as a *specialist block purchase*. However, under stock exchange rules, such a transaction may take place only when the stock cannot be sold in ordinary exchange transactions without disturbing the market. (A *specialist block sale* — just the reverse of a block purchase — is, of course, subject to the same restriction.)

Occasionally, a broker with a big order will be able to find buyers or sellers for the whole block among his own customers and handle both sides of the transaction. This is called a cross — because the broker actually crosses the buy and sell orders on the floor in a regular trade. The biggest block handled in this fashion in N.Y.S.E. history involved the sale of 5,240,000 shares of American Motors on March 14, 1972. The biggest trade in terms of dollar value was a $103,086,500 transaction in Cutler-Hammer on June 12, 1978.

In this kind of "in house" transaction, if a broker can't find enough buy orders among his customers to equal the sell order, he will often buy the balance of the shares for his own account and assume the risk of selling them later.

If a member firm takes on a big block — too big for it to handle alone — the technique it is most likely to use to sell the block is the *secondary distribution* (secondary, as distinguished from an original underwriting, or primary distribution). A secondary distribution, like a new issue, can be handled either by a member firm of the New York Stock Exchange or by a securities dealer who is not a member. It will usually involve the participation of member firms as well as nonmembers.

If the block offered in a secondary is a listed stock, an announcement of the impending offering is made on the exchange ticker on the day of the sale. The actual offering to the public generally takes place after the close of the market. This advance publicity that a sizable block of stock is hanging over the market can, of course, have a negative effect on the price of the stock during the day's trading. Actually, if the exchange community is in any way concerned about the overhanging block, the price may already have drifted downward for a day or two. News of an impending secondary gets around as soon as the broker or dealer who is handling the sale sets about organizing his underwriting group.

The underwriters participating in the secondary buy the block outright from the seller and assume the risk of reselling it to the public, often inviting other brokers and nonmember dealers to join them in the selling group. The underwriters charge the seller a *gross spread*, which typically will amount to three or four times the going commission rate, although it can range from as little as twice to as much as six times the going rate. This spread covers the manager's fee, the underwriting commission, and the *selling concession*, which normally runs from a third to a half of the gross spread. Since negotiated commissions became effective, the spread or cost to the seller has generally been reduced in order to meet competition.

The price at which the block is offered in a secondary distribution involving a listed stock is usually the price at which that stock is sold in the last transaction on the floor that day, although it might be either lower or higher depending on the attractiveness of the offering.

If you had no particular desire to buy a given stock at the close of the market, you may wonder how you could be interested in buying that same stock at the same price just a little later the same day. The answer is simple. To induce you to buy, the underwriters offer the stock on a commission-free basis, no matter how many shares you buy. The seller pays all the costs, and that's why the gross spread is so big.

On a secondary distribution the underwriting group usually undertakes to stabilize the market with S.E.C. sanction, just as they do on an original underwriting. Obviously, it would not be possible for them to sell their stock at the price fixed in their agreement with the seller if the same stock was being offered in the open market at substantially lower prices — prices that more than offset the commission saving to the buyer. In such cases, the underwriters would have to buy up the stock offered at the lower price and add it to their own block. If large quantities of the stock appear at considerably lower prices, they may have to give up their price *stabilization efforts*, withdraw the block, and wait for a better market, a happier day.

The largest secondary offering of common stock ever made was the Ford Foundation's first public offering of stock in the Ford

Motor Company in 1956. This was handled by seven securities firms operating as *joint managers*. It had a gross value of $657,-900,000. The next-largest secondary — and the largest ever handled by a single firm — was the sale by Merrill Lynch, Pierce, Fenner & Smith in 1966 of Howard Hughes's holdings in TWA — a block of 6,584,937 shares worth $566,304,582.

A second technique for distributing a large block of stock is the *special offering*. A special is handled the same way as a secondary, except that participation is limited to members of the New York Stock Exchange. Specials take place on the floor of the exchange during regular trading hours.

A third technique — the *exchange distribution* — is also available, although it has declined substantially in popularity. Such a distribution is usually handled by a single brokerage firm. The block is disposed of wholly by that firm's own sales organization to its own customers. It is, in effect, a giant cross. The seller gives the broker what amounts to a market order. The broker's sales force then seeks to develop buying interest among its customers on the assumption that the stock will be available at or near the price then prevailing on the exchange. When the sales organization has developed buy orders that match the size of the block, the broker checks the seller a last time to be sure he is satisfied with the price then prevailing. If he is, the floor broker will offer the block on the exchange and simultaneously bid for it, usually at the last sale price or at a price somewhere between the bid-and-asked quotations.

There are two big advantages to an exchange distribution from the seller's point of view. Since there is no public announcement of the offering, and since the entire transaction is usually handled within a single broker's organization, there is little likelihood that news of the impending block sale will depress the price of the stock before the offering is made, as often happens with secondaries or specials. Again, since there is no need to organize an underwriting syndicate or a selling group, the cost to the seller is lower — generally about half of what he would have to pay on either a secondary or a special. The buyers, of course, get their stock without paying any commissions, since all costs are borne by the seller.

Banks, insurance companies, and other institutions are more apt to encounter a serious problem in selling a large block of securities than they are in buying one, although institutional business has grown so rapidly recently that it is sometimes also difficult for these big purchasers to acquire the stock they want at a fair price without disturbing the market. To meet this problem, the stock exchange in 1956 established a mechanism known as the *exchange acquisition*. This works exactly like the exchange distribution, except in reverse. The broker who handles such a transaction solicits sell orders from his customers at a net price, free of all commission, until he accumulates a number of shares equal to the buyer's order. The buyer usually pays at least a double commission.

The exchange acquisition has never been popular. And it isn't hard to see why. It's one thing for a broker to ask a customer if he wants to buy a stock commission-free. It's another — and more awkward — thing to ask him if he wants to sell a stock commission-free. The customer is immediately suspicious. Why, he asks himself, should his broker want him to sell that stock, particularly if it is one the broker recommended that he buy in the first place?

While the New York Stock Exchange has developed all these techniques for handling the purchase or sale of blocks of all sizes — and almost automatically grants the required approval for any secondary, special, or exchange distribution — many an institution in recent years has found it easier to take the block to the third market and sell it in toto to a securities dealer who is willing to position the stock and assume the entire risk of selling it. Obviously, for assuming such a risk, the dealer expects to buy the stock at a substantial discount from the prevailing market price. If he is selling a block instead of buying it, he expects to get a price concession on that side.

The marked success that nonmember dealers have enjoyed in developing block business for the third market has induced more and more member firms to employ the same tactics. Instead of resorting to the machinery of the stock exchange to move a block of stock, they buy the block outright from the seller, position the stock, then devise ways and means of selling it, just as a nonmember would in the third market. With one small difference: if a member firm wants to dispose of all or part of the block to a nonmember, he is required to see that all limit orders for the stock on the specialist's books at the same or a higher buying price are satisfied first.

Institutions also have available to them a fourth market — the Institutional Network, or Instinet, as it is called — to help them trade big blocks of stocks.

Instinet is a privately owned computerized network. Subscribers can notify Instinet of their interest in block purchases or sales via a cathode ray tube. If a seller announces that he wants to sell a particular block, and if another subscriber indicates an interest in buying that stock, the two of them can negotiate prices and terms with each other through a computer terminal. Instinet claims that some of its subscribers have been able to save up to 70% of the commission they would have had to pay under the exchange's old fixed-rate system. Instinet makes its money not by collecting commissions but by charging each subscriber a flat annual fee.

Once a subscribing institution has indicated its interest in selling a block of some stock, that indication of interest is placed in the Instinet file. Perhaps a little later another subscribing member decides on the basis of its own information that it would like to buy that stock. When it reports that interest to Instinet, the file is checked and the would-be buyer is put into computer contact with the organization that has decided to sell it. Since the whole transaction is handled privately, there is no chance that a rumor about such-and-such an insurance company wanting to sell a block can depress the price of the stock for the seller. Conversely, the potential buyer doesn't show his hand publicly and run the risk of bidding up the price.

While institutions are the principal sellers of large blocks, sizable offerings are sometimes made by the directors, officers, or prinicipal stockholders of a company. Such blocks often pose a difficult problem for the broker. S.E.C. rules provide that no one in a *control* position can sell stock unless it has been registered with the commission. The whole question of just who is and who isn't a control person is not easily defined. So most brokers play it safe and insist on S.E.C. approval before undertaking to sell a block of stock for any company executive.

CHAPTER 13

How Small Orders Are Handled

ALL stocks bought and sold on the stock exchange are traded by brokers on the exchange in round lots, units of 100 shares, with the exception of a few relatively inactive stocks that are sold in ten-share units.

But what if you want to buy or sell just twenty shares of our hypothetical Rod & Reel Company on the exchange? The answer is that you can buy or sell an *odd lot* — anything from one to 99 shares — of any stock listed on the New York Stock Exchange. But chances are that your cost of buying or selling it, figured as a percentage of the total value of your order, will be slightly higher than it would be on a round-lot trade.

One reason for that is that brokers generally charge higher commission rates on smaller orders. How much higher depends on your broker. Generally speaking, you will find that brokers who do a broad public business charge less to handle an odd-lot order than do houses that cater to an exclusive clientele or specialize in institutional business.

But there's a second reason why it will probably cost you proportionately more to buy and sell odd lots. That is that historically the odd-lot customer has been obliged to pay a kind of service fee, over and above the commission. The charge used to be mandatory under the rules of the New York Stock Exchange. But on January 23, 1976, competition entered the picture and the mandatory service charge rule was broken. Thus, another time-honored monopoly was shattered.

To understand the significance of that development, it is necessary to understand just how the odd-lot system formerly operated.

For many years there were two *odd-lot brokers* — Carlisle & Jacquelin and DeCoppet & Doremus. They handled 99% of all the odd-lot orders that reached the floor of the exchange. In 1969 they merged to form the firm of Carlisle, DeCoppet & Company. This odd-lot brokerage firm wasn't really a broker at all. It was a securities dealer. If you bought twenty shares of Rod & Reel, Carlisle, DeCoppet would supply your broker with the twenty shares from its own inventory. If you sold twenty shares, Carlisle, DeCoppet would buy the odd lot from your broker and put it in its inventory. If you ordered twenty shares of Rod & Reel, and Carlisle, DeCoppet didn't have it in its inventory, it would buy a round lot of the stock, sell you your twenty shares, and put the other 80 shares in its inventory — an inventory that might run to many millions of dollars.

Under the rules of the exchange, as they existed just before fixed commissions were abolished, the odd-lot broker had to fill your market order for any stock at whatever price prevailed on the next round-lot transaction after your order reached the trading post. For this service the odd-lot broker charged a fee, known as the *odd-lot differential*, which was ⅛ of a point, or 12½¢ a share, on every share of stock bought or sold.

If you bought an odd lot, you paid ⅛ point above the price at which the next round lot was sold after your order got to the trading post. If you sold, you got ⅛ point less. At an earlier time, the odd-lot differential had been ¼ point on stocks selling at $40 or above. Later that ¼ point was changed to apply only to stocks selling at $55 or more. The odd-lot house never dealt directly with the customer, only the customer's broker. In that sense, the odd-lot house was really a broker's broker. Although in the sense that he was always trading on his own account, positioning stocks, and buying for, or selling from, his own inventory, he was a securities dealer.

In January 1976, this time-honored system of charging an odd-lot differential was challenged. Over the objections of the stock exchange — but with the obvious blessing of the S.E.C. — Merrill Lynch, Pierce, Fenner & Smith announced that it would begin buying and selling odd lots out of its own inventory and, in certain circumstances, would not charge the odd-lot differential on market orders.

That was a serious blow to Carlisle & DeCoppet. Merrill Lynch, which accounted for about a quarter of all odd-lot business on the exchange, was by all odds the biggest customer of the odd-lot broker.

Here is what the Merrill Lynch plan offered the odd-lot customer.

(1) If you place an odd-lot order on a given day and don't mind waiting until your stock opens on the exchange the following day, Merrill Lynch will fill your odd-lot order at the price that prevails on the first round-lot transaction. It will charge you only its regular commission, no odd-lot differential.

(2) If you place an odd-lot market order for immediate execution during a trading day, Merrill Lynch will execute it for you at the bid or asked price then being quoted by the specialist in your stock. If you are buying, you will get the asked price — the lowest at which any round-lot owner is then willing to sell. If you are selling, you will get the bid price — the highest any round-lot buyer is then willing to pay. Either way, you pay only Merrill Lynch's regular commission, no odd-lot differential.

If you pick the first option, you realize a clear and obvious saving of 12½¢ a share. But you do have to wait for the next day's opening to have your order executed. This could work either in your favor or against you, depending on which way the market moved after you placed your order. Almost a quarter of

Merrill Lynch's odd-lot customers appeared willing to take this gamble in the first few months of the plan's operation.

As for the second option, if the spread between the bid and asked prices is only ⅛ of a point, as it often is on heavily traded stocks, you have a 50-50 chance of saving that 12½¢, depending on whether the next sale takes place at the bid or the asked price. Suppose Rod & Reel is quoted at 30½ bid, 30⅝ asked when you give Merrill Lynch your order to buy 20 shares. Your order will be filled at 30⅝. If the next round-lot sale takes place at that price, you will indeed have saved yourself ⅛ of a point, the odd-lot differential you would have had to pay under the old system. But if the next round lot is sold at 30½, you come out even, for you paid just what you would have under the old system: 30½ plus ⅛ differential, or 30⅝. So if the spread is only ⅛ of a point, and you trade at the bid or asked price, you may or may not save money. But at least you know you can't pay more than you would have paid under the old system.

If the spread is more than ⅛ point, the odds on saving the odd-lot differential aren't quite so good. Suppose Rod & Reel were quoted at 30½ to 30¾. Your odd-lot order to buy would be executed at 30¾. The next round-lot transaction would generally take place at any one of three prices — 30½, 30⅝, or 30¾. At 30½, you would lose ⅛, compared to what you would have paid under the old system. At 30⅝, you would break even. At 30¾, you would be ⅛ point ahead of the game.

As the spread between bid and asked prices widens, your chance of saving that odd-lot differential by trading on the bid-and-asked prices diminishes. Thus, if the spread were ⅜ point, you would have one chance of saving the odd-lot differential, one chance of breaking even, and two chances of paying more than you would have under the old system.

If the customer doesn't want to place an order to buy or sell at the bid-or-asked price, he doesn't have to. He can insist that his odd-lot order be executed in the traditional manner — at whatever price prevails on the next round-lot sale. But if he does, he will pay the standard $\frac{1}{8}$ point differential.

As a matter of fact, this conventional method is the way Merrill Lynch announced it would handle all odd-lot limit orders — through Carlisle, DeCoppet. The execution of an odd-lot limit order differs from the execution of an odd-lot market order in one particular. A buy order for 10 shares of Rod & Reel at a limit price of $18\frac{1}{2}$ is filled on the next round-lot transaction at $18\frac{3}{8}$, so that when the differential is added the buyer gets his stock at the $18\frac{1}{2}$ limit and the odd-lot broker is assured his $\frac{1}{8}$. Conversely, an odd-lot sell order is executed when a transaction takes place $\frac{1}{8}$ above the limit price.

The first reaction of the exchange, when it was faced with this competitive threat from its single biggest member firm, was to announce that it would buy out Carlisle, DeCoppet and use its computer facilities to go into the odd-lot business itself, relying on floor specialists to supply the required odd lots from their round-lot inventories.

Then second thoughts set in. Maybe the Merrill Lynch odd-lot system didn't pose as big a threat as it seemed to at first. Maybe competition would be a good thing for the odd-lot business. Maybe the old and new methods of odd-lot trading could coexist. Or, if worse came to worst, the exchange itself could adopt the Merrill Lynch system — something the exchange obviously had in mind. It had ordered Carlisle, DeCoppet, even before it had actually acquired the firm, to execute odd-lot orders at the market opening without charging a differential.

With Merrill Lynch competing for odd-lot business and with the New York Stock Exchange handling odd-lot orders itself, it appeared that even the small investor might get something of a break in the new era of competition.

How important is the odd-lotter in the overall brokerage picture? One answer to that question is that he is both more important and less important than he used to be. With the great growth in the number of shareholders since 1950 he has become numerically much more important. Yet collectively he has accounted for a steadily decreasing percentage of the volume of total shares traded.

In the era that culminated in the bull market of 1929, the little man represented almost 20% of stock exchange volume. Twenty years later, odd-lot trading was still accounting for about 15% or 16%. But from then on it headed pretty steadily downward to a level of less than 10% in 1968 and below 5% in 1974. By 1981 it had fallen to only 1.6%.

CHAPTER 14

Monthly and Other Accumulation Plans

UNTIL January 1954, the smallest amount of stock anyone could buy was one share. In that month, however, member firms on the New York Stock Exchange initiated the Monthly Investment Plan — commonly known as M.I.P. — under which it became possible to buy a fractional share of stock, a fraction figured out to the fourth decimal point. The plan wasn't formulated, of course, just to permit an investor to buy part of a share. It was designed to permit people to invest a set sum of money every month — or every quarter if they preferred — and to acquire for that money full or fractional shares of any stock listed on the New York Stock Exchange, except those few sold in ten-share units.

By the method of systematic saving and systematic investing inherent in the M.I.P., a person is able to acquire a worthwhile interest in the stock of some company on a regular budget basis. He does not have to wait to become an investor until he has acquired enough money to buy five or ten shares of the stock.

The Monthly Investment Plan, in short, is geared to the tempo of life today, since most American families are used to settling their bills and making their installment payments on a monthly budget basis.

M.I.P. is a method of buying stock by the dollar's worth, regardless of how the price may change from month to month, just as you buy $10 or $20 worth of gasoline, regardless of what the per-gallon price is.

In March 1976 the exchange announced that it was abandoning its sponsorship of the Monthly Investment Plan. But many individual member firms continue to offer small investors the opportunity to buy stocks on an M.I.P. basis, or through various accumulation plans of their own devising. Merrill Lynch, for example, offers its customers a "Sharebuilders" plan, which is based closely on M.I.P. principles. In early 1982 Sharebuilders had over 400,000 accounts buying stocks on a regular basis. The exchange withdrew its sponsorship because it did not want to handle the business itself, as it would have had to do after its acquisition of Carlisle, DeCoppet & Co. That odd-lot house had handled 17,000 M.I.P. plans for a number of small brokerage firms. Although Carlisle, DeCoppet's M.I.P. business was only 5% of all M.I.P. business, it was more than the exchange wanted to deal with, so it disowned its own brainchild.

Under M.I.P. types of plans, the buyer signs a "contract" — it is actually nothing more than a declaration of intent — with a member firm of the exchange. Under this contract the buyer agrees to accumulate shares of a particular stock listed on the exchange and to invest a regular sum of money every month, or every quarter, toward the purchase of that stock.

Since M.I.P. contracts can be canceled by the buyer at any time, and are so drawn that the buyer can skip payments without penalty, they are in no sense binding or obligatory.

Here's how the plan works: suppose you want to buy shares in Rod & Reel at the rate of $50 a month. Out of each payment, the broker gets a commission, and with the balance the operator of the M.I.P. plan buys whatever number of full and fractional shares he can for you, at whatever price prevails at the opening of the market the day after each payment is received.

When the buyer closes out his M.I.P. contract, he gets a stock certificate for whatever full shares he has purchased. Any fractional share that may remain is sold at the prevailing price and the proceeds remitted to the buyer. The broker may levy a minimal extra charge for stock certificates representing anything less than 100 shares.

Dividends become due and payable on all shares, including fractional shares, from the moment any shares are bought. These dividends, as they are received by the broker, are credited to the customer's account and can be automatically applied to the purchase of additional shares. This is one of M.I.P.'s unique features. The investor can automatically reinvest the dividends he collects in any one of the common stocks available through M.I.P.

The small investor always pays the highest commission rates percentagewise — and no investor can be smaller than an M.I.P. customer. Still many brokers, since the arrival of negotiated commissions, have shaved their charges on M.I.P. business, partly to encourage new, small investors, and partly because computerized operations have made it possible to cut handling costs. Thus, Merrill Lynch, Pierce, Fenner & Smith cut its commission about 25%. Nevertheless, because they may get a better commission break on purchases involving larger dollar amounts, some M.I.P. customers let their funds accumulate for three months, in order to buy bigger dollar amounts on a quarterly basis.

No matter how high commission costs may be, M.I.P. types of accounts have the advantage of helping investors establish regular habits of thrift. Then, too, consistent buying of the same stock provides protection for the small buyer in the event of a decline in price. If he continues buying in the same dollar amount while the price declines, the average cost of all the shares he owns will be reduced. Then, if the market rises again, he stands to make a tidy profit. Of course, if he stops buying in a downtrend and sells out when the value of his accumulated shares is less than their purchase cost, he will incur a loss.

In general, however, the "dollar cost averaging" technique of buying stocks — buying a set amount of a certain stock or stocks at regular intervals regardless of the current price of the stock or general market conditions — has proven to be one of the most successful methods of buying stocks over the years, whether it is done within an M.I.P. format or by an individual investor on his own. Because it eliminates the luck involved in guessing periodic market swings, and concentrates instead on the gradual accumulation of participatory positions in top-drawer companies at averaged prices over a long period of time, it eventually rewards the patient investor in quality stocks to a much greater extent than more random trading patterns can.

The big reason M.I.P. caught on so well initially was that in 1965 several brokers began pushing M.I.P. as a means by which listed companies could initiate *employee stock purchase plans* on a voluntary, payroll-deduction basis. Hundreds of companies joined forces with brokers to promote such plans. Tens of thousands of their employees thus became stockholders in their companies for the first time.

There is nothing new, of course, about company-sponsored stock purchase plans. Many N.Y.S.E.-listed companies have them in some form. But the M.I.P. angle has been particularly attractive to many managements because the broker carries the onus of selling the plan. Therefore the management feels less responsible for the price action of its stock. The plan is attractive to the employees because they acquire their stock commission-free, since the company usually picks up the commission tab. Also, the employee escapes payment of virtually all fees charged for purchasing in small lots, since the company purchases the stock for all the employee accounts monthly in a single block.

In addition to sponsoring automatic stock purchase plans for their employees, many publicly traded companies have also begun offering their own Dividend Reinvestment Plans (D.R.P.). In these plans dividends paid by the company's stock are automatically used to buy additional shares of that stock for the shareholder instead of being remitted directly to that shareholder in cash. Some companies even offer discounts up to 5% on the price of the stock being bought through D.R.P.'s.

Utilities have been the most frequent sponsors of Dividend

Reinvestment Plans. And the Economic Recovery Tax Act of 1981 made their plans even more attractive to investors when it stipulated that an individual (but not a trust or an estate) could exclude from taxable income up to $750 ($1,500 for a joint return) of dividends paid by a public utility if the dividends were reinvested in the utility's stock through a D.R.P. The shares, however, would have to be held more than a year to get the exclusion. When sold after a year, the capital gains rate would apply.

Certain banks too have initiated accumulation plans or variations of M.I.P. for the benefit of their customers. The Chase Manhattan Bank, for instance, offers an *Automatic Stock Investment Plan* through which depositors can agree to have funds withdrawn automatically from their checking account each month and applied toward the purchase of any or all of a selected list of stocks. The bank then combines the funds that are allocated to particular stocks, makes bulk purchases, and divides the shares up in proportion to individual payments. The stock accumulation plans of other banks operate in essentially the same way.

Since the *Pension Reform Act* of 1974 and the *Economic Recovery Tax Act* of 1981 were signed into law *Keogh Tax-Shelter Retirement Plans* and *Individual Retirement Accounts* have become increasingly popular. The Keogh Plan permits self-employed individuals to postpone payment of taxes on 15% of their earned income up to a maximum of $15,000 annually. The I.R.A. Plan allows persons earning wage and salary income to postpone payment of taxes on $2,000 of that income, even though they may already be participating, through their employer, in another retirement program. The income tax on such funds put into a Keogh or I.R.A. plan — as well as taxes on capital gains and dividend or interest income to be earned in the future — is deferred until the person retires. Since his tax bracket then is likely to be a lot lower than it was during his high-earning years, he will pay a lower tax on all the money he set aside than he would if he paid it when he earned it. Meanwhile, he has had the use of all that money for years. The basic concept of the Keogh and I.R.A. plans is to defer taxes as long as possible; to build a nest egg for the future.

The growth of tailor-made accumulation programs and other regular investment plans demonstrates the willingness of investors to pay premium prices for new and special brokerage services offered in package form. The appeal of these programs lies in their streamlined, automatic operation, and in their minimum transaction costs.

Many M.I.P. investors have become regular brokerage customers, having learned to accumulate money until they could afford to buy an odd lot in a regular brokerage account. But others, many others, have fallen by the wayside. They found it easy to drop out of M.I.P. because there was no compulsion, actual or implied, to keep up their payments.

If M.I.P.'s performance has been somewhat disappointing, reasons are not hard to find. Since M.I.P. began, the market has been extraordinarily active. And brokers' sales representatives are generally too busy attending to their regular customers to undertake much missionary work on behalf of M.I.P. It is no overstatement to say that M.I.P. is seldom sold by the brokers, but rather it is bought by the customers.

There is a second explanation for the disinclination of brokers to push M.I.P. Many of them feel that it is not right to impose relatively higher commission rates on the investor who characteristically is least able to pay them. On the other hand, it can be argued that the high commission cost is justified because America has to pay a price to learn thrift. Consider the current high interest rates charged for mortgage money, as high as 20% in 1981–1982; indeed, the high rates for any type of loan. Consider the high carrying charges on all installment purchases. The pay-as-you-go person is used to paying both going and coming.

CHAPTER *15*

Other Exchanges — Here and in Canada

ALTHOUGH they differ somewhat in rules, regulations, and operating mechanics, the other registered exchanges in the United States function fundamentally the same way as the New York Stock Exchange does.

In dollar volume, about 80% of the business is still done on the New York Stock Exchange — the *Big Board*, as it is called — with 2,220 common and preferred stocks listed on January 1, 1982. However, in recent years other exchanges have been steadily increasing their volume — twenty-six years ago the New York Stock Exchange had 85% of total exchange volume.

The American Stock Exchange has been this country's second biggest stock exchange for generations. With 918 companies represented, the Amex normally handles about an eighth as large a volume as the New York Stock Exchange. But, because the average price of its shares is much lower, it accounts for only about one-tenth of the total dollar volume in trading.

Rightly or wrongly, the American Stock Exchange has long been regarded as a kind of prep school for the New York Stock Exchange. Many important companies like General Motors and the various Standard Oil companies got their start on the Amex. But there are many other well-known companies such as Hormel, Horn & Hardart, and Prentice-Hall, which remain faithful to the American Stock Exchange.

Until 1953, the Amex was known as the New York Curb Exchange. It got this name from the fact that it actually began as a curbstone market, first on Wall and Hanover streets in New York City, and later on Broad Street. It remained an outdoor market until 1921, when it finally moved indoors, thus depriving the city of one of its most colorful spectacles. Before it moved inside most of its trading was done by hand signals. Orders were relayed to the brokers in the street by shouts and whistles from the clerks perched on the windowsills of their offices in adjoining buildings. Even in its spacious headquarters today, far more modern than those of the New York Stock Exchange, phone clerks relay their orders to floor brokers by hand signals.

Included among the 661 members of the American Stock Exchange are all of the nation's major brokerage firms. With increased trading activity during the sixties, seat prices rose steadily — to an all-time high of $350,000 in 1969. But the market decline of 1973 hit the American Stock Exchange hard, just as it did the Big Board, and seat prices tumbled to $27,000 — the lowest since 1958. By 1982, however, the price of an Amex seat had rebounded to $250,000.

The two New York exchanges operate in rather similar fashion. On the American Stock Exchange odd lots were always handled by specialists, just as they are now on the New York Stock Exchange, instead of by an odd-lot broker. An odd-lot differential was charged by the Amex until January 1976 when Merrill Lynch, Pierce, Fenner & Smith went into the odd-lot business and established a new schedule of fees. The American Stock Exchange decided to meet that competition at once and initiated the same rates as those quoted by Merrill Lynch. If you want to place an order through your broker for an odd lot on the Amex to be filled at the opening on the following day, it will be filled at the price of the first round-lot transaction in your stock, and you will not be charged any odd-lot differential. If you place a market order during the trading day, it will be filled at the bid price in the specialist's book if you are selling, or the asked price if you are buying. By paying the ⅛ point odd-lot differential, you can have your order executed at whatever price prevails on the next round-lot sale. You also pay the ⅛ differential if you place a limit order to be executed at a set price. Because the average price per share is much lower on the American Stock Exchange, a greater proportion of its traders buy and sell in round lots rather than odd lots.

Although it was a price-manipulation scandal involving two specialists on the American Stock Exchange that touched off the whole S.E.C. investigation of the market and led to the 1964 securities legislation, it must be said that this exchange moved more rapidly than the Big Board to put its house in order and conform to S.E.C. standards of self-regulation. The reforms were pushed through by the American Exchange in 1963 as part of its complete reorganization program.

The American Stock Exchange also moved more rapidly than the New York Stock Exchange to automate its procedures and to maximize computer application in the conduct of business — including a stock-watch technique to spot unusual trading patterns. The American Exchange also installed electronic equipment to speed reports of transactions from the floor to the ticker before the Big Board did. Moreover, it introduced its own market averages one month sooner, in 1966.

In 1975, the Amex scored another "first" when it introduced trading in odd-lot quantities of certain United States government securities on the floor of the exchange. It later augmented this innovation with trading in government agency issues. The Amex also provides a marketplace for all outstanding issues of U.S. Treasury bonds and notes.

In a spirit of cooperation rather than competition, the two big exchanges in 1969 announced that they would undertake to combine many of their key services and computer operations. Not only did they consolidate their stock-clearing systems, but on the trading floors of both exchanges they developed joint automation programs that can save member firms an estimated $5 million annually in duplicate costs.

Such cooperative efforts naturally gave rise to a proposal that the New York and American exchanges be merged into one market. A study of the feasibility of such a merger was given top priority by both exchanges in 1970. Although neither exchange expressed any great enthusiasm for the idea of a complete merger, they did form the jointly owned *Securities Industry Automation Corporation* in 1972 to consolidate all their technical facilities and agreed to pursue still further the idea of combining the two exchanges into one. However, in July 1975, the death knell was sounded for the merger concept when the Amex board of directors voted unanimously against it. Still, no one would be surprised if the proposal was resurrected someday.

The third biggest United States exchange, the *Midwest Stock Exchange*, came into being in 1949, when the Chicago Stock Exchange undertook to effect a consolidation of its activities with those of other exchanges in Cleveland, St. Louis, and Minneapolis–St. Paul.

Other *regional exchanges* include the Pacific Stock Exchange, located in both Los Angeles and San Francisco; the Philadelphia Stock Exchange, which opened a Southeastern Stock Exchange division in Miami in 1974; and the stock exchanges in Boston, Cincinnati, Salt Lake City (Intermountain Stock Exchange), and Spokane.

All of these exchanges are registered with the Securities and Exchange Commission, which means that the S.E.C. has approved their rules and regulations and adjudged them adequate for the discipline of any member who violates his public trust.

The regional exchanges were originally organized to provide a marketplace for the stocks of local companies. But as these companies grew and acquired national reputations, many of them wanted their securities listed on an exchange in New York City, the nation's biggest money market. And as the Big Board succeeded in luring many issues to New York, the regional exchanges languished.

But in recent years the regional exchanges have managed to turn the tables on the Big Board. They trade many of the same securities that are listed on the New York Stock Exchange, and in recent years the amount of business they did in these stocks accounted for 75% to 85% of their total volume. It was a business that kept growing every day, and local or regional issues account for less of their volume all the time.

To attract this business in Big Board stocks, the regional exchanges either induced some N.Y.S.E. companies to list their securities on one or more of the local exchanges as well as on the New York Stock Exchange, or, if a company didn't want to go to the expense of *dual listing*, made arrangements to trade in those securities without formal listing. Such arrangments have to be approved by the Securities and Exchange Commission. But in view of the S.E.C.'s determination to break up the Big Board's monopoly, such approval has never been hard to get.

More than half of all Big Board stocks are now also traded on one or more regional exchanges. In the main, these are the most popular stocks, those that account for over 80% of Big Board volume. (The American Stock Exchange has not been able to share in this dual trading bonanza because, under S.E.C. rules, a stock cannot be traded on two exchanges in the same city.)

The reason for the great growth of trading in Big Board stocks on the regional exchanges traces back to old Rule 394 of the New York Stock Exchange. This is the rule that for years forbade a member firm to split commissions with a nonmember.

Formerly, when a securities dealer who did not belong to the Big Board had a sizable block of some Big Board stock to buy or sell, he often arranged to have the order executed on a regional exchange by a firm that had memberships both on the Big Board and on the regional exchange and that undertook to develop the other side of the order — finding a purchaser to match the dealer's sell order or a seller to match his buy order. The nonmember dealer and the member firm split the commission, and everybody was happy. Everybody except the New York Stock Exchange.

A 1965 amendment to Rule 394, permitting Big Board member firms to deal with nonmembers, made it seem likely that some of the regional exchange business in Big Board stocks would dry up. But such was not the case. Under the 1975 securities law, the Big Board and all other exchanges were required to scrap any rules that restricted off-board trading by member firms.

Though the Big Board offered to ease Rule 394 in an attempt to offset more radical moves by the S.E.C., the commission turned a deaf ear and set a deadline of April 1, 1976, for lifting all restraints on the freedom of a member firm to execute a customer's order for a Big Board stock wherever he pleased — in the over-the-counter market, on a regional exchange, or on the New York Stock Exchange.

Additionally, much of the competition that faces the New York Stock Exchange comes not only from the regional exchanges in the United States but from the exchanges north of the border, where the big boom after World War II stimulated worldwide interest in the ownership of Canadian stocks.

Of the five Canadian exchanges, by far the largest is the Toronto Stock Exchange. From the standpoint of dollar volume, Toronto does more than twice the business of all the other Canadian exchanges combined. Almost 30% of its business is in securities listed on the other Canadian exchanges as well. In 1981, the Toronto Stock Exchange ranked fourth among all North American exchanges in dollar volume.

The other Canadian exchanges are in Montreal, Calgary, Vancouver, and Winnipeg. Interest in oil and mining shares runs especially high in western Canada, while industrial shares are still the prime attraction on the more staid market in Montreal.

In the main, stocks are traded on the Canadian exchanges much as they are in the United States. But there are several significant differences.

For one thing, floor trading in Canada is not restricted exclu-

sively to member brokers. Thus, on the Toronto ⟩change, authorized nonmember brokers are entitled to split ⟩mmissions.
There are also significant differences in the units of ⟩ling. On
the Toronto Stock Exchange, stocks selling at less th⟩ 10¢ a
share and those selling at more than 10¢, but under $1, are⟩ ded
in units of 1,000 and 500 shares, respectively. If the price⟩ ⟩t
least $1 but under $100, the trading unit is 100 shares. Sto⟩
selling above $100 are traded in ten-share units. All of these
different units are known as *board lots*, rather than round lots.

Moreover, the minimum allowable price fluctuation is not ⅛
point (12½¢), as on the New York Stock Exchange. On stocks
selling below 50¢, the minimum spread is ½¢; at more than 50¢
but under $3, it is 1¢; at more than $3 but under $5, it is 5¢; at $5
and over, it is 12½¢.

Odd lots are also bought and sold in Toronto, but they are
called *broken lots*. Whether a particular order is classified as a
broken lot or a board lot depends on how many shares constitute
a board lot of that particular stock.

If a floor broker has a broken lot to sell, he cannot look to
either an odd-lot dealer or a specialist to help him, for there are
none on the Toronto exchange. He turns instead to a registered
trader, the nearest equivalent to a specialist. A registered trader
has the responsibility for maintaining a market in certain stocks,
and a broker with a broken-lot order on his hands can compel the
registered trader in that stock to take it off his hands. If it is a buy
order, the registered trader must supply the stock at the current
quotation, plus a premium. If it is a sell order, the trader must
buy the stock, but he is allowed a discount from the current
quote.

Canada does not have a national agency like our S.E.C. to
regulate its securities business. Instead, each province has its own
commission. The control these commissions have exerted over the
securities business has been something less than rigorous. As a
consequence, *boiler shop* operations, involving the sale of questionable oil and mining stocks, flourished in Canada for many

years. Typically, a promoter of such a stock would offer an unsuspecting prospect the "chance of a lifetime" to buy some new issue of stock at a price below that at which it was presumably scheduled to be offered to the public.

The promoter would try to high-pressure the prospect by long-distance telephone, assuring him that he had to "act now" if he wanted to get in on the ground floor. He would glibly cite "engineers' reports" that established the value of the mineral deposit or oil field that the new company intended to work. The prospect would rarely be able to lay his hands on a copy of any such report, much less a prospectus. As a matter of fact, whether or not the company actually proceeded with its venture often depended on how many suckers the promoter was able to sell his scheme to.

Many of these boiler shops used to operate in Ontario and prey on prospects in Boston, New York, and other big eastern cities. But they have generally been put out of business as a result of the Ontario Securities Acts — enacted in 1966 and 1970 as a result of widespread public complaints.

But there's always a chance that you'll be invited someday to buy a block of stock at a bargain price in the Pipe Dream Mining Company. If you are, check with some reputable broker first. Don't worry about missing out on your big chance by failing to say yes right away. If the stock is worth buying, it will be as good a buy tomorrow as it was today.

CHAPTER 16

How the Over-the-Counter
Market Works

IF you can buy the stocks and bonds of only a few thousand companies on the registered stock exchanges, where can you buy or sell the securities of the tens of thousands of other companies that exist in this country?

Where, for instance, would you have bought the stock of the Rod & Reel Company in the days when it was growing up, before it could ever hope to be listed on any exchange?

The answer is that you would have bought it in the *over-the-counter* market, the place where all unlisted securities are traded. Actually, this market isn't a place. It's a way of doing business, a way of buying or selling securities other than by trading them on a stock exchange. Buying interest is matched with selling interest, not on a trading floor, but through a massive network of wires linking thousands of securities firms.

The over-the-counter market is difficult to define or describe, because transactions that take place in this market have few common characteristics.

You might, for instance, conclude a purchase or sale with a securities dealer who operated a one-man shop in a small town. Or you might deal with a large securities firm in Wall Street that used the facilities of the over-the-counter market to trade large blocks of stock at lower cost.

You might buy an unlisted stock, or one that is regularly traded on the Big Board, the Amex, or a regional exchange.

You might buy a security that the dealer himself owned and sold to you from his inventory, or you might buy a security that he bought from another dealer just to fill your order.

You might pay a negotiated commission, or you might pay a flat price. You might buy a highly speculative $2 stock in some little-known company, or you might buy the stock of such well-known corporations as Chubb Corporation, Tampax, or U.S. Sugar. You might even buy stock in some well-known foreign company by purchasing an *American Depositary Receipt*. (An A.D.R. certificate is simply the evidence that the shares you bought in such a foreign company are deposited to your credit in a foreign office of an American bank or one of its correspondent banks abroad. Such certificates are traded in the over-the-counter market — only a few are listed on the exchanges.)

You might buy the initial stock offering of a new company like Rod & Reel, for this is where all companies first offer their securities to the public. Or you might buy stock in a bank that has paid dividends for over 190 years — fifty years longer than any New York Stock Exchange security. The stocks of all but a score of major banks are bought and sold exclusively in the over-the-counter market, as are virtually all insurance company stocks.

Finally, your over-the-counter transaction might not involve stocks at all. It might involve the purchase or sale of a bond. More than 99% of all United States government bonds, all municipal bonds, and the great bulk of corporate bonds are traded in the over-the-counter market, not on the exchanges.

The over-the-counter market is, indeed, all things to all men, whether they be conservative investors or wild-eyed speculators, and whether they have millions or simply hundreds of dollars to put in the market.

Despite the diversity of this market, all over-the-counter transactions have about them one common characteristic. The price arrived at in any transaction is not determined by a two-way auction system, such as prevails on a stock exchange. It is arrived at by negotiation — negotiation between the securities dealers on both sides of the transaction, and further negotiation between one of those dealers and you, his customer.

Probably the most common kind of over-the-counter transaction is one that takes place on a net price basis. A net trade is one in which no commission is charged. Instead of a commission, the securities dealer expects to make a profit by selling the stock to you at more than he paid for it, or by buying it from you at less than he expects to get by selling it to somebody else.

Suppose you got interested in Rod & Reel when it was a new company and decided you would like to buy 50 shares of it. You can buy any number you like in the over-the-counter market, because there are no round lots or odd lots — no standardized trading units.

Now, it might happen that the securities dealer to whom you gave your order was able to fill it from his own inventory, since he had bought some shares recently from another customer. Thus, he would be able to quote you a price and conclude the sale on the spot.

At the time you made that purchase the prevailing quote might have been 18 bid, offered at 18½. Your dealer might quote you that same offering price of $18.50 a share. Or he might offer it cheaper, say $18.25, if he were anxious to move it out of his inventory, especially if he had been able to purchase the stock at $17.00 or $17.50 originally.

Now, let's suppose he doesn't have 50 shares of Rod & Reel in his inventory. He would have to buy the stock from another dealer in order to fill your order. So he checks with other dealers and finds that the lowest price at which he can buy the stock is 18¼, or $18.25. That's the price to him, the price one dealer quotes another. Such a price is called the *wholesale price* or *dealer price* — sometimes the *inside price*. It is not the price at which he will sell the stock to you. That price, the *retail price*, might be $18.75 or $19.00 a share, perhaps even more. The difference between what he paid the other dealer for the stock and the price he charges you is his *markup*. Since this is a net trade, it is this markup that he takes, instead of a commission, as his profit on the transaction.

If you were selling the stock instead of buying it, the dealer would simply reverse the procedure. If he knew that $18\frac{1}{4}$ was the best inside price, the highest price at which another dealer would take the stock off his hands, he might offer to pay you $17\frac{3}{4}$ or $17\frac{1}{2}$ for your stock. The difference, or *markdown*, would represent his profit.

Of course, once he bought the stock from you, the dealer might decide not to sell it. Instead, he might decide to hold it in his inventory. In such a case, he would be said to be *taking a position* in the stock. If he then began to trade the stock actively, buying and selling it in substantial volume, he would be *making a market* in the stock.

Price differences or spreads between the wholesale and retail, such as those on your Rod & Reel transaction, are fairly typical of spreads on net trades of low-priced stocks that aren't too well known in the over-the-counter market. If you were buying or selling one of the actively traded stocks in the market, the spreads between the retail and wholesale prices might narrow to $\frac{1}{4}$ point on low-priced stocks. The difference between the bid and asked quotations might be only $\frac{1}{2}$ point.

On the other hand, if the over-the-counter stock you wanted to buy or sell was almost unknown, if it did not enjoy any public market to speak of, there might be a spread of a full point or more on the wholesale market and of several points between the retail bid and asked quotations.

Suppose, for instance, you were in New York and wanted to dispose of some stock you owned in a little lumber company out in Oregon, a company that was virtually unknown outside its hometown. Your dealer would try to find a bid for the stock by contacting other dealers, principally in New York, where most dealers are located. He might then try his luck in Chicago or San

Francisco or Portland by calling or teletyping dealers in those cities. Ultimately, to promote a bid, he might wire or phone local banks in the area to see if they knew of any possible buyers. He might even phone the company itself to see if it wanted to buy back any of its own stock. For such special service the dealer is obviously entitled to an extra profit.

In ordinary transactions, trades that involve no special effort on the part of the dealer and in which he assumes no risk, the *National Association of Securities Dealers* (N.A.S.D.) has long taken the stand that the dealer should restrict his markup to a maximum of 5%. Thus, if the inside market for Rod & Reel were 19 bid, offered at 20, when you placed an order to buy, your dealer would be entitled to mark the offering price up 5%, or 1 full point. His retail price to you could be $21 a share ($20 plus 5%). Another dealer might have quoted you a retail price of $20.50 or $20.75. But this is not something you are likely to know unless you shop around. The S.E.C. has long looked with disfavor at that 5% markup on a *riskless transaction* and feels that the customer should demand that his dealer reveal the amount of his markup. As a result, some securities firms now voluntarily disclose the amount of their markup on the trade confirmations that they send their customers.

Remember, when you buy a stock from a dealer on a net price basis, you are negotiating or bargaining with him. You are asking, "How much will I have to pay?" And the dealer, in effect, is asking, "How much will you pay?" He is not acting as your broker or agent, trying to buy or sell something for you at the best price possible, plus a commission. He is dealing with you as a *principal* in the trade. As a dealer, he doesn't collect a commission; he expects to make a profit on the price you are willing to pay.

While the great majority of over-the-counter transactions are handled on a net price basis, it is possible, especially if you are dealing with one of the big national brokerage firms, to buy or sell over-the-counter securities on an *agency basis*. Operating as an agent, your broker would seek the best possible inside price.

He would buy or sell the stock for you at that wholesale price and charge you a commission, just as he would if he were buying or selling a stock on an exchange for you. The commission he charges is usually the same as he would charge for buying or selling the same number of shares at the same price on an exchange.

In the big brokerage firms, over-the-counter business is handled by a separate *trading department* located in the headquarters office. But sales representatives in the firm's offices across the country still handle orders for both stock-exchange and over-the-counter securities. Most firms that operate both as dealers and as brokers usually make a market in a specified number of over-the-counter stocks. That number may run into the hundreds in the case of really big firms. If you buy or sell one of these stocks, the transaction will almost certainly be handled on a net price basis. On other over-the-counter stocks in which the dealer does not make a market, he is generally willing to act as your agent or broker in concluding a trade.

Whenever you buy an over-the-counter stock, you may wonder whether your dealer really did get the best possible inside price for you. Nowadays, you can get a clear-cut, instant answer to that question if you are buying or selling any one of the several hundred most popular and widely held over-the-counter stocks. You merely consult the automated quote system developed in the late sixties by the Bunker Ramo Corporation, a company specializing in quotation equipment for the securities business, and the National Association of Securities Dealers, the industry's self-regulatory agency. The N.A.S.D. represents over 4,000 dealers in the over-the-counter market and operates under the authority of the Securities and Exchange Commission.

Before the development of the National Association of Securities Dealers' *Automated Quotation System,* popularly known as *NASDAQ,* there was no way a dealer himself could be absolutely sure that he was getting the best possible price on a particular stock. There was no way he could know all the firms throughout the country that might be making a market in the stock or what their current price quotations were. He might be able to contact the principal *market-makers* in New York and Chicago, maybe even San Francisco. But at any given time some dealer in Cleveland or Atlanta or Denver might be making a better market in the stock.

For a long time, the *National Quotation Bureau* has provided at least a partial solution to that problem. Every day this privately owned price-reporting service publishes in its *pink sheets* the wholesale prices of more than 10,000 over-the-counter stocks and half as many bonds. These are the prices at which hundreds of different dealers are currently buying or selling various securities in trades between themselves.

Any dealer who wants to have his prices quoted in the pink sheets simply supplies them to the bureau every afternoon. The quotation sheets are printed overnight and distributed nation-wide prior to the opening of the N.Y.S.E. Since any dealer who has an important position in a stock wants to stimulate inquiries about it from other dealers, the pink sheets, subscribed to by almost every important dealer in the country, render a valuable service. In its study of the over-the-counter market however, which preceded the 1964 Securities Acts Amendment, the S.E.C. expressed its concern about how dealers used — or abused — the pink sheets.

The S.E.C. wants to be sure that every dealer stands behind the prices he announces in the sheets, that they are not used to create a false impression of value or market activity. If a dealer announces a price he is willing to pay for a given stock, he may get away with a refusal to buy the stock that is offered to him at his announced bid on any one particular day — he might defend himself by saying that the market had moved away from his bid — but if he publishes the same price the next day, he has to take any stock offered to him at that price or run the risk of having an official complaint lodged against him.

When the 1964 act was under consideration, the commission made it clear that it felt automation was in order for the over-the-counter market. It wanted a computerized electronic system, operating on a national scale, which would assure a more accurate and rapid exchange of price and market information. And that is how NASDAQ was born.

Beyond question, NASDAQ has revolutionized the over-the-counter business. By hooking dealers together in one wire system, capable of providing exact, instantaneous wholesale price quotations from all dealers who make markets in important over-the-counter stocks, NASDAQ has virtually eliminated the vast jumble of telephone wires on which the business previously depended. NASDAQ has become, in effect, a new kind of securities exchange in which the computer and assorted electronic gear constitute a 3,000-mile-long trading floor stretching from coast to coast, to which securities dealers in some 6,000 offices have immediate access.

NASDAQ began its operations by supplying bid-and-asked quotations on 2,500 over-the-counter stocks. It has been gradually increasing that number ever since. It will not put any stock into the NASDAQ System however unless there are at least 100,000 shares in the hands of 300 or more stockholders, and unless the company has total assets of at least $1 million and net assets of a half-million.

At any time during the trading day, a market-maker can feed into NASDAQ the price at which he is willing to buy a particular stock and the price at which he is willing to sell it, changing these quotations during the day as competition dictates. NASDAQ records all these thousands of different entries in its memory bank. Whenever a dealer wants to know at what price other dealers will buy or sell a stock, he simply turns to his NASDAQ machine.

NASDAQ provides different levels of service. Level 1 is a quote machine for the use of securities salesmen. Simply by pushing buttons for the alphabetical symbol of the stock on his desk-model machine, the saleman can get a *representative bid* price and a *representative ask* price on that stock. The data appears on a small fluorescent screen, which is part of the machine. The representative bid is the median wholesale bid of all the firms making a market in the stock. Thus, if five dealers quoted bids on a particular stock of 40, 40¼, 40½, 40¾, and 41, the representative bid would be 40½.

If a customer finds a representative quotation to his liking, he may decide to make a purchase or a sale. With the order in hand, the salesman now turns to the Level 2 machine in the trading department. Again, by punching out the stock symbol, he gets the actual quotes of five firms making a market in that stock. The names of those firms are shown beside their quotes on the screen. There may be fewer than five market-makers in the stock, but if there are more than five, the indication MOR appears on the screen. When the MOR button is pushed, the bid-and-asked quotes of the additional dealers, ranked in order of best price, appear. Once a trader knows what firm offers the best quotation, he contacts that market-maker by phone or wire and concludes the purchase or sale in the usual manner. All trades in over-the-counter securities are settled and cleared through the *National Clearing Corporation* (N.C.C.), a wholly owned subsidiary of the N.A.S.D. The N.C.C. has facilities in numerous major cities to serve hundreds of clearing members.

The N.A.S.D. does not attempt to dictate what the spread should be between bid and asked prices on any stock. It leaves that to be determined by the competition of the marketplace. But, the automatic quotation system is geared so that each time a market-maker enters a bid-and-asked quotation it is checked by computer against the *"representative spread"* — the average spread of other market-makers in that security. If this representative spread is half a point and the market-maker enters a spread that is a point or more, he is notified instantly that his spread is excessive. This report of excess spread is forwarded from the computer to the N.A.S.D., which may then take disciplinary action against the market-maker.

A company whose stock is included in the NASDAQ system

generally must register under the Securities Exchange Act of 1934 and meet the same disclosure requirements as a listed company. Furthermore, there must be at least two dealers who make a regular market in the stock, and each dealer must have a net capital of $25,000, or $2,500 for each security in which he is registered as a market-maker, whichever is more.

Once he registers with the N.A.S.D. as a market-maker in a stock, a dealer must be willing to buy it or sell it at any time and announce through NASDAQ the prices at which he will trade.

Perhaps the single most dramatic new development the S.E.C. initiated with the 1964 act was the newspaper publication of more accurate and dependable quotations on over-the-counter stocks, thanks again to NASDAQ.

Over-the-counter quotes were not — and are not today — actual prices. They have always been only indications of the price range within which the customer might then expect to trade. Prior to 1966, quotes on the bid, or buy, side furnished to newspapers by the National Association of Securities Dealers were always reasonably accurate. But the asked, or offering, prices were characteristically inflated by 4% or 5%, sometimes even more. Thus, a stock with a published quote of 21 on the asked side might actually have been available at 20 — and the customer who was asked to pay only 20½ would be delighted at the "bargain" he thought he got.

The S.E.C. took a dim view of this practice, and after a bitter fight with many small dealers in the industry, the commission forced the daily publication of more realistic quotes on the 2,500 stocks with national or regional markets. As a result, virtually all prices for over-the-counter stocks that are now published in newspapers are reliable quotes, not inflated on either side. Throughout the trading day, NASDAQ releases to the press lists of closing representative bid-and-asked quotations for all issues quoted in NASDAQ. These lists also indicate the trading volume and the price change, if any, in the bid from the previous day's close.

Quotations and trading volume figures for securities on the national NASDAQ list (approximately 1,400 issues) are published in more than 200 newspapers across the country. In addition, over 130 local N.A.S.D. quotations committees select securities with local investor interest, and newspapers are supplied with additional NASDAQ quotes on these. The NASDAQ system also computes a number of market indexes and trading statistics, which are furnished to newspapers and radio and television stations.

In addition to the publication of reliable wholesale quotes, many other reforms have flowed from the enactment of the 1964 and 1975 legislation. One of the most important is the requirement that companies whose stocks are sold over-the-counter (except insurance companies, which are regulated by state insurance commissions) must make annual reports to the Securities and Exchange Commission, and to their shareholders, if they have assets in excess of $1 million and more than 500 stockholders.

One of the chief benefits of the S.E.C.'s long-envisioned central securities market, which would link stock exchanges and the over-the-counter market, is a *composite quotation system* for securities transactions. At the S.E.C.'s request, the exchanges eliminated the rules and practices that formerly restricted the use of stock quote information. Thus, the consolidated quotation service was introduced in early 1977 and expanded in 1978.

Slowly but surely over the years, the Securities and Exchange Commission has forced on the over-the-counter market most of the regulations that have long been imposed on stock exchanges and their member firms. Thus, provision has been made for the regular inspection of all dealer organizations by the N.A.S.D., with authority to compel compliance with all rules and regulations. Salesmen of both member and nonmember firms must take tougher examinations, and controls have been established to assure the honesty of advertising and sales literature.

Since the 1964 act gave the S.E.C. the authority to suspend trading in any over-the-counter stock for ten days, it now has the necessary power to control the so-called *hot issues*. These are the over-the-counter stocks, often little-known, which in past bull markets have skyrocketed in price in a relatively short time, only to plummet back to their starting point, or lower, just as rapidly, without any provable price manipulation.

Intent on preventing such disorienting price swings, the Securities and Exchange Commission has been using a computer since 1966 to help it police its over-the-counter beat. The computer makes regular surveys of the market. It can scan 32,000 quotations in 90 minutes. Regularly, it turns up 300 or 400 suspicious price jiggles, sharp rises or drops that suggest the need for further investigation. In each such case, the computer supplies the name of the dealer involved. Unless investigation proves there was sufficient reason for the price movement, that dealer becomes a marked man. From then on, his name can be fed into the computer regularly and all his trades subjected to close scrutiny.

Despite this improved climate of regulation, the phrase "over-the-counter" will probably continue to suggest to some investors the kind of questionable dealing associated with the phrase "under-the-counter." The unfortunate term "over-the-counter" — which goes back to colonial times, when the few securities that existed were often traded by a merchant, just like his other merchandise, right over his store counter — will not die, despite concerted efforts to substitute other terms, such as unlisted, or *off-board*, or *off-exchange*.

However, as more people have become familiar with the over-the-counter market and come to have more confidence in it, thanks to S.E.C. reforms, its business continues to increase. Nowadays share volume in the over-the-counter market is apt to be a third of Big Board volume, although the dollar value of shares traded is apt to be somewhat less than on the Big Board because of the lower-priced stocks.

Because the over-the-counter market is essentially a negotiated market instead of an auction market like the New York Stock Exchange, day-to-day price fluctuations may not be as pronounced. But the long-term trend is usually pretty much the same in both markets.

CHAPTER 17

Investing — or What's a Broker For?

SUPPOSE you decide that the time has come for you to put some of your extra savings into securities. What do you do next? How do you go about buying stocks or bonds?

You might go to your local banker and ask him how to proceed. He'll know several investment firms in your general community and probably at least one broker in each of them. But don't forget that the banker is actually in competition with those security houses for your savings. He is quite apt to look with a jaundiced eye on *your* buying securities rather than adding to your savings account or employing your money in other ways through his bank — by its investing in a local business, real estate, or mortgages, for example.

Most bankers are extremely conservative. It's their business to be. When it comes to investing the bank's own money, they have been legally compelled to confine investments largely to government and other high-grade bonds. They may have little familiarity with stocks and understandable misgivings about them. They don't realize that an individual investor's investment problem probably differs considerably from a bank's.

This is apt to be true of lawyers too. They are likely to be almost as conservative, because they think of investments principally in their roles as trustees, individuals legally responsible for the administration of estates and the preservation of the capital in those estates.

So where else may you turn for help if you want to buy securities?

The ultimate answer to that question is to a broker, because a broker is obviously the one person best qualified to help you with your investment problem. That's his whole business. If you don't know the name of a broker, one of your friends or associates surely does. And if you don't want to ask, look in the financial section of your daily newspaper or the *Wall Street Journal* or the Sunday *New York Times*, where you'll find many brokers' advertisements. Study those advertisements for a while. Decide which firms have the kind of policy you like and the service you need. Then visit the firm. You don't need a letter of introduction.

But can you trust brokers' advertising? After all, advertising is always special pleading, notoriously given to overstatement, exaggeration, and excessive claims. While that may be generally true, you can place much greater confidence in brokers' advertising than you can in the advertising of virtually any other product or service. This is equally true of all their sales promotion literature. Almost all member firms submit their advertising and their sales literature to the scrutiny of their own legal counsel, as well as to the exchange, because any misstatement in such promotional material can subject a broker to expensive lawsuits.

In the early sixties when the S.E.C.'s study of the securities industry pointed up the need for many reforms, the exchange tightened up its regulation of advertising and all other forms of communication, spelling out its standards in meticulous detail. Specifically forbidden is language that is promissory or flamboyant or that contains unwarranted superlatives; opinions not clearly labeled as such; forecasts or predictions not stated as estimates or opinions; recommendations that cannot be substantiated as reasonable; testimonials; boasts about the success of past recommendations unless they meet a set of exacting requirements; and any evasion of a broker's responsibility to disclose special interests he might have in a security he recommends.

Shortly after the exchange adopted its standards, the National

Association of Securities Dealers adopted roughly similar regulations, which apply to all over-the-counter dealers in that association. Both the N.A.S.D. and the exchange are continually tightening those regulations — strictly enforcing them and adding new ones. The can't afford not to.

Still, lots of people shy away from brokers for a variety of reasons. Some of them feel embarrassed about the small amount of money they have to invest. Maybe they have only a few hundred dollars to put into stocks, perhaps only $40 or $50 a month. They figure a broker wouldn't be interested.

Maybe some brokers wouldn't be. But the big wire houses have been spending millions of dollars in advertising every year to tell the smaller investor that they definitely are interested in him and in helping him invest his money wisely.

Still people hesitate. Perhaps they think of the broker as a somewhat forbidding individual who gives his time only to Very Important People, people who are well heeled and travel in the right social circles. That's not true. There's nothing exclusive about the brokerage business today.

Another thing that stops a lot of people is the jargon that brokers talk. You know now that there's nothing mysterious about words like "debenture" or "cumulative preferred." True, they're specialized words, because they apply to very specialized things. But there's nothing difficult to understand about either the words or the things they stand for, if you take the trouble to learn them.

Finally, some people shun brokers because, frankly, they distrust them. They're afraid of being sold a bill of goods, a block of stock in some worthless company. That used to happen occasionally. Nobody can deny it. Maybe it happened to people you know — your father, your uncle, some other member of your family.

Can it happen today? Yes, it *can*. Because no law or regulation has ever been devised that can guarantee that some dishonesty will not exist in the marketplace. Occasionally — very, very occasionally — you may still encounter a con artist in the securities business intent on unloading some stock on you so he can run the price up and then sell out his own holdings at a fat profit, leaving you to hold the bag when the price subsequently plummets.

Occasionally — but again, very occasionally — you might be sold such a stock at a highly inflated price by a thoroughly honest but somewhat naive or irresponsible broker who himself has been taken in by the propaganda con artists always spread. The S.E.C. and the exchange are constantly on the alert to track down and scotch such false and misleading *tips* or rumors. Their circulation is a clear-cut form of illegal price manipulation or outright fraud. But, alas, brokers — like all human beings — can fall prey to propaganda that promises an easy dollar.

A broker may logically and legitimately try to sell you on the idea of buying a particular stock because he believes in it. But unless his firm is involved in underwriting or selling a large block of that stock, he hasn't any selfish reason to try to sell you that particular stock rather than another. His only reward is a percentage of the commission his firm charges. And there is usually not much difference in the commissions generated when you buy one stock rather than another. So it doesn't matter to your broker which stock you buy.

Of course, when you buy stocks on a net price basis — over-the-counter stocks — there is more chance that you can be sold something the dealer has an interest in unloading at a profit.

And there is always the outside chance that you will come across the occasional unscrupulous broker who is more interested in the level of activity in your account than in the quality of the transactions that activity represents. Such brokers do not care what you buy or what you sell as long as you buy or sell something, and do so often enough to keep the commission dollars rolling their way. Such *churning* is usually easy to spot, as when a broker frequently calls his customer to recommend the sale of a stock the purchase of which he had advocated only a short time ago. Churning occurs most frequently in *discretionary* accounts,

accounts in which individual investors have given complete trading authority over to the broker.

None of these abuses occurs often. Few businesses are as competitive as the American securities business. Every broker and dealer in the country is anxious to get customers and keep them for a good many years to come. In that kind of situation there's not much room for the second-story operator who plays fast and loose with the customer's best interests.

Credit the Securities and Exchange Commission, if you wish. Or credit the stock exchange's own housecleaning. Or credit the moral influence of healthy competition.

But credit also the fact that the people in the securities business are, in the vast majority, individuals of conscience and probity, responsible to a standard of ethics as high as prevails in any business you can name.

What it all comes down to is this: the safest way to begin investing in stocks is to choose some listed stock through a member firm of the New York Stock Exchange. Then study that stock, and the company behind it, before you buy.

If there's no member firm near you, you can write to one and buy by mail. You should request a copy of the broker's commission schedule and inquire about possible extra charges — what they are for, and what added cost they could mean to you.

You can also order stock through virtually any bank or securities dealer in the country. You will probably have to pay an additional handling charge if you make your stock purchases this way. Such a charge is wholly legitimate.

One last word of caution: if any broker or securities dealer tries to dissuade you from buying stock in some well-established company, if he tries to switch you into Wildcat common or Pipe Dream preferred or some other dubious stock, you had better check with another brokerage house.

To help protect investors against the high-pressure, "fast-buck" peddlers of dubious stocks, the S.E.C., with the cooperation of industry trade groups and the Better Business Bureau, has published an investor's guide, which make these ten recommendations to all investors:

(1) Think before buying.

(2) Deal only with a securities firm you know.

(3) Be skeptical of securities offered over the telephone by any firm or salesman you do not know.

(4) Guard against all high-pressure sales.

(5) Beware of promises of quick, spectacular price rises.

(6) Be sure you understand the risk of loss as well as the prospect of gain.

(7) Get the facts. Do not buy on tips or rumors.

(8) Request the person offering securities over the phone to mail you written information about the corporation, its operations, net profit, management, financial position, and future prospects.

(9) If you do not understand the written information, consult a person who does.

(10) Give at least as much thought when purchasing securities as you would when acquiring any valuable property.

CHAPTER 18

How You Do Business with a Broker

LET'S assume you finally make up your mind to buy some stock. You go to a broker, a member firm of the New York Stock Exchange, to place your order.

What's likely to happen? What's a broker's office like? What do you say and what do you do? How does a broker operate?

Lots of people go in and out of brokers' offices every day, people who want to know how the market is doing or people who just like to watch the passing show. So if nobody pays any attention to you when you first walk in, don't feel you're being neglected. Just walk up to the first person who looks as though he works there and tell him you would like to talk to somebody about buying some stock. That will get action fast.

Maybe that person will take you to the manager, who in turn will introduce you to a *registered representative* with whom you can discuss your interest in more detail. Maybe you'll skip the manager and be referred directly to a registered representative.

What's a registered representative? In the twenties he was called a *customer's man*. That's not a title in favor anymore, because the customer's man got a bad reputation as a fast-work artist with a glib line when it came to selling bonds to old college chums or clubhouse cronies. Today's registered representative bears little resemblance to that character.

The old customer's man used to "play the market" a good deal himself too. Most brokerage firms today are happy to see their employees invest in securities, but they frown on too much "in and out" trading by registered representatives for their personal accounts. In fact, New York Stock Exchange rules, with rare exceptions, prohibit any employee of a brokerage firm from buying or selling securities except through the firm for which he works.

Many customers refer to the registered representative as "my broker." Actually, of course, he isn't a broker at all. He is an employee of the brokerage firm, and as such simply represents the firm's floor broker to you. It is this floor broker who will actually execute your orders on the exchange. The "registered" part of the registered representative title means that he has been licensed by the S.E.C. and approved by the exchange as a person of good character who is thoroughly informed about the operations of the securities business. In fact, he has had to pass a searching examination, administered by the New York Stock Exchange, on the subject. The National Association of Securities Dealers gives the same kind of examination to representatives of nonmember dealers.

Registered representatives — also called *customer's brokers* or *account executives* by some firms — come in all kinds and qualities. Some are young. Some are old. Some are Democrats. Some are Republicans. Some are men. Some are women. Some have been in the business for years. Some are comparative newcomers.

These newcomers deserve a special word, because their entrance into the field is itself evidence of how the business has changed. From the time of the depression to the end of World War II, only a handful of college graduates went into Wall Street. They looked for greener pastures — the big corporations.

But nowadays, the securities business can count on getting its share of individuals from every graduating class. Many an old customer's man coasted for years on his reputation as an all-star halfback. His successor's career is apt to be based more on a record of scholastic achievement, plus extracurricular leadership.

Often, he will have earned a degree at some university's graduate school of business.

Again, the customer's man of yesteryear rarely bothered to acquire any formal training in the business. He just picked it up as he went along. The present-day registered representative usually has served a much more painstaking apprenticeship. More often than not, he has attended some firm's training school, plugging away eight hours a day for several months at basic lessons in accounting, economics, security analysis, and investment account management. It costs a sponsoring firm thousands of dollars to train each representative. He or she has really to make a serious commitment to succeed.

The registered representative is "your broker" in the sense that he's the person you deal with when you do business with a brokerage firm. He's usually assigned to you by the manager of the office. If at any time you find his service less than satisfactory, all you have to do is ask the manager to be assigned another.

And if you don't like the brokerage firm itself, try another. There are plenty of them, some big and some little, some offering a wide variety of special services and facilities, and some specializing in just one phase of the securities business, such as municipal bonds or institutional investment.

All of them can buy and sell securities for you. And all of them will execute your orders faithfully. They won't "bucket" them.

A *bucket-shop* operator is a man who accepts your order to buy a stock at the market. He takes your money. But he doesn't execute the order. Instead he pockets your money and gambles on his ability to buy the stock for you sometime later at a lower price and make a profit for himself on your order. He reverses the method on a sell order. Needless to say, all such operations are thoroughly illegal. Today they are virtually nonexistent, thanks to the vigilance of the Securities and Exchange Commission and the stock exchange.

You can talk to your registered representative with complete candor, because whatever you tell him about your affairs will be held in strict confidence. A broker never reveals who his customers are, much less anything about their circumstances.

The more you tell your registered representative about your finances — your income, your expenses, your savings, your insurance, and whatever other obligations, like mortgage or tuition payments, you may have — the better he will be able to help you map out an investment program suited to your particular needs.

It is a part of his job to see that you get information or counsel whenever you need it. Don't be embarrassed about asking him the simplest kind of question about investing — about a company, about some financial term, or about the way your orders are handled.

At the same time, you should remember that you have certain obligations to your broker, just as he has to you. You should pay promptly for any securities you buy. You should inform him of any change in your address and whether the securities you buy and pay for are to be transferred into your name and mailed to you, or held by the broker in your account. And you shouldn't keep him on the phone for long periods of time during trading hours passing the time of day. Registered representatives are essentially salesmen, and like all salesmen they make their living on the phone.

If you give your broker an order to buy or sell, be sure there is no misunderstanding about what you want him to do. He may seem overly meticulous and careful about your order. This is not only because he wants to give you prompt and efficient service, but also because the cost of correcting errors has gone up like everything else. Moreover, the firm he works for very likely penalizes him for any error, an error which might very well be attributable to you. Indeed, the phrase common to many boardrooms for decades, "Put it in the error account," is translated today to mean "Charge it to the registered representative."

The ticker tape itself is no longer what it was in the days when conquering channel swimmers, visiting statesmen, and astronauts rode up Broadway through paper snowstorms.

Paper ticker tape began to fade from the scene over a quarter-century ago when the eight-foot *Trans-Lux* screens became a standard fixture of brokerage offices. The tape itself, printed on cellophane, was magnified and projected on the Trans-Lux screen, and quotations marched across the screen from right to left, so that the brokers, customers, and boardroom loafers could all watch the market action on both the New York and American exchanges.

The Trans-Lux screens were replaced in the late sixties by electronic screens on which the stock symbols and prices marched across a black background, as in an animated electric sign. These electronic displays give brokers and their customers ready and convenient access to an almost bewildering array of last-second market information, all right at their fingertips.

Gone with the paper ticker tape is the old-fashioned quote *board* on which board markers chalked up quotations for various stocks as they came in on the ticker. It has given way to the highly sophisticated computer-operated *desk model quote machines.*

Simply by pushing a few keys, the registered representative can get an incredible array of statistical information on thousands of different stocks — all those listed on the New York and American exchanges, as well as many on leading regional and Canadian exchanges, plus many hundreds of leading over-the-counter stocks and mutual funds. On most stocks, he can instantly obtain the latest price, with an indicator to show whether it is an up tick or down tick, the bid-and-asked prices, the open, high, low, and previous close, the volume of trading, earnings, dividend and percentage yield per share, the price-earnings ratio, and the time of the last sale. Some machines will also provide essential news about the stock or a brief appraisal of it. Equally comprehensive information on the trend of the market as a whole can be obtained on the desk-model screen. On some models the current tape is also projected.

With the development of computers and various electronic

gear to provide instantaneous price and market information for thousands of stocks, listed and unlisted, it was only a matter of time before the securities industry developed a *consolidated ticker* system covering all major markets.

Under the sponsorship of the *Consolidated Tape Association,* composed of the principal exchanges and the National Association of Securities Dealers, a consolidated stock tape was introduced in June 1975. It consisted of two sections: *Network A* and *Network B,* Tape A reporting all transactions on Big Board stocks — both common and preferred — regardless of the exchange where the trade took place. Thus, when a transaction is effected in any Big Board stock on a participating exchange, in the over-the-counter or third market, or in any other market such as that operated by Instinet, the stock symbol printed on the New York Stock Exchange consolidated tape is followed by "&" and then a letter identifying the marketplace: M (Midwest), P (Pacific), X (Philadelphia), B (Boston), T (Third Market), O (Other Markets, including Instinet). Transactions in Big Board stocks that are executed on the New York Stock Exchange, of course, have no identifying letter since that is the primary market for those listed stocks.

For instance, a trade involving 1,600 shares of Ford Motor that took place in the third market at a price of 22 would be reported on the upper line of the consolidated ticker tape by the letters "F & T," followed on the lower line by "1600S22." In order to report trade executions of N.Y.S.E.-listed issues on the Pacific Stock Exchange, which remains open an hour and a half later than the Big Board, the tape runs until 5:30 P.M., E.S.T.

Here's a sample section of the consolidated tape, showing transactions made in Occidental Petroleum (N.Y.S.E.), Northern States Power (Third Market), Fluor Corp. (Philadelphia), duPont (Midwest), and Transamerica (Philadelphia).

QXY	NSP&T	FLR&X	DD&M	TA&X
3S7⅞ 4S7⅞	4⅞	39⅛	118⅜	4S8¾

Since all brokerage operations have become more streamlined

and efficient, it is easy to visualize the day when a central securities market and a national clearance and depository system will be introduced. The traditional broker's boardroom might disappear completely. There would no longer be a quote board, nor any reason for having one. There would no longer be quote machines, which in many brokerage offices can even now be operated by the customers themselves if they want the latest price information on a stock.

These and other innovations will inevitably change the character and atmosphere of the broker's office.

Far more important then the change in physical appearance, though, will be the improvement in the quality of service that the broker will be able to supply his customers — instant information on any stock or on any market as a whole — and instant information on the customer's transactions and on the exact position of his account, whether cash or margin.

CHAPTER 19

How You Open an Account

EVERY new customer of a brokerage firm must open an *account* with that firm before the customer can either buy or sell securities.

Opening a *cash account* with a brokerage firm is very much like opening a charge account at a department store. It simply involves establishing your credit so that the broker is sure you can pay for whatever securities you order. The New York Stock Exchange has a rule, widely known as the know your customer rule, which it requires all member firms to enforce strictly. If the broker doesn't know you, he might ask you to make a *good faith* deposit on opening an account. But most times he will be satisfied with a bank reference.

He has to be sure of your credit responsibility because when you place a market order for a stock, neither you nor the broker knows to the exact penny what you will have to pay for the transaction. You may know that the last sale took place at 18½ a share, but when your order is executed, even a few minutes later, the price may have gone up or down. When the purchase is made, the broker assumes the responsibility of paying for the stock and sends you a bill. This bill must be paid in five business days, not counting Saturdays, Sundays, or holidays, because your broker must settle his account within that time.

Because no one can know just when an *open order* — a limit order or a stop order — may be executed, and because the customer may be away from his home or office at the time of execution, brokers can in their own judgment extend the payment date to seven business days after the transaction. But if payment is not received by then, a further extension can be granted only by the exchange. This is because by your delay you will have violated the Federal Reserve Board's *Regulation T*, governing all matters of credit on stock transactions.

In the case of a Monthly Investment Plan account or similar plan, the broker has no credit problem. The customer makes his payment in advance of the purchase.

If your first transaction with a brokerage firm involves the sale of some stock that you already own, instead of a purchase, you will still be required to open an account. The brokerage firm must still comply with the stock exchange rule that compels every broker to know his customer in order to protect himself against fraud or other illegal practices. For one thing, the routine of opening an account provides the broker with some assurance that the securities you offer for sale are really yours.

A bearer bond, for instance, can be sold by anybody who holds it. The broker doesn't know it's not a stolen certificate. Even a registered bond or a stock with your own name on it can present a problem to the broker. It may be made out in the name of John Smith, and John Smith may bring it to a broker to sell it. But if John Smith hasn't done business there before, how's the broker to know that he really is the John Smith named on the security?

Many husbands and wives prefer to open *joint accounts* with a broker, just as they have joint checking accounts. In case one of them dies, the other can generally sell the securities without waiting for the courts to unsnarl the legal problems involved in settling an estate. But because of tax considerations and variations in state law, a married couple may want to consult an attorney before opening a joint account. Joint accounts are also used by individuals who are not related but have pooled their resources in a cooperative investment venture, often just for the sake of reducing commission costs on their trades.

People frequently want to open accounts for their children or for the children of relatives. Historically this has presented a thorny problem to brokers. In the absence of state legislation specifically authorizing such gifts to children, brokers have incurred a measurable risk in selling stock that was registered in the name of a minor. A minor is not legally responsible for his acts. And if brokerage transactions were carried on in the name of a minor, that minor could, on coming of age, repudiate them, and the broker would have no redress.

Beginning in 1955, the various states began enacting laws permitting an adult, acting as a custodian without court appointment, to handle investments for a child. Such a custodian can buy stocks as a gift for a minor. He can sell them for a minor and he can collect any dividends in the child's name. With the New York Stock Exchange and the entire brokerage fraternity plumping vigorously for the enactment of such statutes, all 50 states had passed laws permitting gifts of stock to minors by 1961. Subsequently, stock ownership among minors increased at a faster rate than in any other age group. In 1962, 450,000 minors owned stock. By 1970, the number had increased to 2,221,000.

It has, of course, always been possible for parents or other relatives to buy stock for children by setting up a trust fund. They just had to get a court order appointing them as trustees so they could legally buy or sell stock for the children. This is an expensive and cumbersome procedure, however, although it does permit wealthy people to realize important tax savings. It is generally much simpler for parents or other relative or friends to give stock to minors under the provisions of the states' laws.

If you want to open a *margin account* instead of, or in addition to, a regular cash account, so that you can buy securities by paying only a portion of their cost, the broker will want to be especially sure of your financial solvency. After all, when you pay only part of the cost, the broker has to pay the balance, and that money may be on loan to you a long time with interest payments coming due regularly.

Once you have opened an account — cash, joint, or margin —

you can buy or sell whatever you want simply by phoning your representative — or by writing or wiring him. Probably 90% of a broker's business comes to him by phone.

If you live outside New York and give an order for a Big Board stock to a registered representative in your local office, that order is teletyped into the New York headquarters of the firm. There it is either switched automatically to the booth on the exchange floor nearest the post where it will be executed, or it is phoned to that booth. In either case the order is executed as promptly as possible by the floor broker. Then the floor broker gives his clerk in the booth a report on the order and the price at which it was executed. This information is then transmitted instantly back to your representative — and then to you.

The entire operation can be accomplished literally while you are still on the phone talking to your representative about other matters. On a market order for immediate execution, one involving an actively traded stock, the round trip from California to the exchange and back again, including the transaction on the floor, can be made in about one minute. Actually five minutes is more like par for an average transaction. If the stock you are buying is one that doesn't trade frequently, or if the market is very active and your broker's wires are flooded with traffic, it may take longer.

In any event, once your order is executed, your representative should report to you. But whether you get the information by phone or not, you'll know within the next day or two just what price you got on the order, because then you will receive in the mail your broker's formal *confirmation* of the transaction.

If you have bought stock, this will be your bill, unless you have bought and paid for the stock in advance as you would under the Monthly Investment Plan.

If you have sold stock, the confirmation will be a report on how much money you realized from the sale. The proceeds will automatically be credited to your account on the *settlement date,* five business days after the transaction.

Instead of having the proceeds credited to your account, you can, of course, ask that payment be made directly to you by check. In very special circumstances, you might be able to arrange for immediate payment, instead of waiting for the settlement date. Brokers are extremely reluctant to make such advance payments, however. After all, they don't get their money from the other broker involved in the transaction till settlement date. Furthermore, advance payment can open the door to sharp practice by unscrupulous customers — a practice known as *free-riding*.

A free-rider is a person who places a purchase order for a stock with one broker and then, if the stock goes up before he is forced to pay, sells the stock through another broker. He then demands immediate payment for some ostensibly good reason ("I can't get my wife out of the hospital till I pay the bill"), and uses the proceeds of the sale to pay for his original purchase. Thus he has realized a profit without putting a cent of his own money at risk. He has had a free ride. If the stock goes down, chances are he will attempt to repudiate the original order ("I said sell — not buy") or simply vanish and leave the broker holding the bag. This is one good reason for the exchange rule that every broker must know his customer.

Of course, if you sell stock in a regular cash account, you must see that the stock is delivered to the broker. Since you have an account with him, he will know what stocks you own, and he will sell any of them for you on your instruction, even if he does not have the certificates in hand. But he expects you to deliver the certificates, properly endorsed, immediately after a sale, because he in turn must settle within five days with the broker who bought the stock.

Many security owners find it more convenient to leave their stock certificates with their brokers. Then the certificates are right there when the owner wants to sell. Such securities are carried in the customer's account just as cash might be. Every month he gets a statement showing exactly what securities and what funds are credited to him.

On stocks that are left with him, the broker will collect all the dividends and credit them as cash to the customer's account. Similarly, on bonds, he will see that the interest is collected, and credit the payments to the customer's account. Brokers will also mail to the customer the regular financial reports of the companies he owns, as well as all proxies, official notices of meetings, dividends, stock rights, and conversion privileges, as those materials are supplied to him by the individual companies.

When the customer leaves his securities with his broker, the actual shares of stock are sometimes physically segregated, much as they might be if he rented a safe-deposit box. As a general rule, however, this kind of *custodian account* is available only to those who own large amounts of securities. In all other cases, when a customer leaves his securities with his broker, they are held in *street name*. This means that all the shares of a given security owned by all that broker's customers are lumped together and held in the broker's name. The broker keeps his own records of just what each individual customer owns. Thus, a broker might hold 100,000 shares of U.S. Steel for 2,000 or 3,000 individual customers. The shares would be made out in the broker's name — not the name of the individual stockholder unless he requested it. But the broker would send each customer a monthly statement showing just how many of those shares belonged to him. Shares held in street name and those held in the stockholder's own name must be kept separate, under federal law.

There is one big advantage to leaving your stocks with your broker. If you want to sell any of them, all you have to do is phone him and give him instructions. You don't have to bother with delivering or endorsing the certificates.

But is it safe to leave your securities with your broker, as you might leave cash with your banker?

The answer is that it's probably safer to leave them with a broker than it is to try to take care of them yourself, unless you rent a safe-deposit box. The broker handles all the safekeeping, storage, and insurance problems. When securities are left with him, they can't be lost or misplaced, and the risk of loss by fire or theft is probably much less than it would be if you kept them in your home or office.

Furthermore, the broker cannot borrow money on those securities, nor can he sell or lend them except on your express authorization. Those securities belong to you. The surprise *audits* that are sprung on all member firms at different intervals by the New York Stock Exchange further help to ensure that brokers are faithful to their trust. Every single share of stock held in street name and every dollar in customers' accounts must be accounted for.

To ensure financial solvency the exchange insists that member firms have substantial capital reserves. Thus, the amount of money owed to a brokerage firm, principally on margin accounts, can never be greater than 15 times a firm's capital. The exchange may even require a member firm to reduce its business if its *net capital ratio* should exceed 12 to 1. It may prohibit a member firm altogether from trying to expand its business if the ratio exceeds 10 to 1.

In 1970, the S.E.C. put the full weight of its authority behind these capital requirement rules and undertook to see that the 15-to-1 ratio also applied to nonmember firms which had previously operated on a 20-to-1 standard.

But what if a broker goes under, despite all the regulations of the stock exchange and the S.E.C.?

For years, an adequate answer to that was that brokers simply didn't go bankrupt. Despite the debacle of 1929, member firms of the New York Stock Exchange boasted a solvency record over a 50-year period that was around 99% — better than the solvency record of state and national banks.

But in 1963, an event took place that shook the brokerage fraternity's confidence in its financial stability to the very foundations. In November of that year, one of Wall Street's most respected houses, Ira Haupt & Company, went under to the tune of almost $10 million. A second firm, J. R. Williston & Beane, was bailed out only in the nick of time and absorbed by another firm.

The Haupt bankruptcy was brought on by the inability of Anthony De Angelis, a big speculator in soybean oil, to meet an obligation to the Haupt firm in the amount of $18 million. Haupt's doom was sealed when it was discovered that warehouse receipts De Angelis had given the firm as security were fraudulent. The receipts were supposed to prove that millions of gallons of soybean oil were stored in tanks in New Jersey. But the tanks were empty.

Ironically, Haupt's relations with its securities customers conformed impeccably to all requirements of the law and of the exchange. These customers were the people — people in no way involved in Haupt's commodity mess — who stood to get hurt by Haupt's inability to meet its loans from the banks.

To save these customers in particular, and to preserve investor confidence in general, the exchange devised over one critical weekend a plan that obligated *all* members to make good Haupt's loss. After the liquidation of Haupt's assets, the bill, which was shared by members in proportion to the amount of their exchange business, came to $9.6 million.

But Wall Street's troubles were far from over. In fact, they had barely begun.

First, the Street was engulfed by the great bull market of 1968, with volume soaring far above the historic highs of late October 1929. Despite the advent of computers and other forms of mechanized record keeping, many brokers and transfer agents were unable to keep abreast of the operational work load. *"Fails to deliver,"* the inability of one broker to settle his trades with another broker by delivering traded securities, rose to a record high of $4.1 billion.

For many brokers, 1968 was a year of profitless prosperity. They were forced to hire more personnel to handle the volume, and to face the fact that they had failed to control costs in many vital areas.

Then came 1969 and 1970. Stock prices went into a tailspin. Volume contracted sharply, falling to an average of only 11,400,-000 shares a day in 1969. This at a time when the New York Stock Exchange was estimating that the *break-even point* for its member firms was a daily average of 12,000,000 shares.

As prices fell, many firms that had invested their own capital in stocks suffered such losses that they were unable to meet the New York Stock Exchange's capital requirements. Fifty firms closed their doors while they were still solvent. Sixty-five others arranged "shotgun" mergers with stronger firms.

But there was no way to stave off the inevitable. Before the storm abated the New York Stock Exchange had exhausted the $25 million special trust fund it had set up after the Haupt disaster. It had also pumped an additional $43 million into its rescue operations — funds it raised by assessing its hard-pressed members.

All told, the exchange intervened in the affairs of almost 200 brokerage houses. Despite its best efforts, however, fifteen firms went under, including such well-known names as McDonnell & Company, Orvis Brothers, Dempsey-Tegeler, Blair & Company, and Hayden, Stone.

The desperate stopgap measures that the exchange had to take to preserve the integrity of the brokerage business made it clear that some far more reliable machinery was needed to insure investors against any future loss caused by a firm's financial failure. Hence, a proposal was made to create a federal insurance system for investors comparable to that provided by the Federal Deposit Insurance Corporation to insure bank savings.

With Wall Street wreckage standing in plain and tragic view, Congress moved with unaccustomed speed in the last half of 1970 to establish the *Securities Investor Protection Corporation.* Only then could the investor — and Wall Street, too — breathe a sigh of relief. Of course investors could still lose money in the market — and plenty of it in bear markets. But at least they now knew they couldn't lose it because their broker had gone broke.

The Securities Investor Protection Corporation, known as S.I.P.C., will advance up to $500,000 per account in case of the liquidation of any S.I.P.C. member. That includes every member firm of every securities exchange and every nonmember securities dealer, excepting those who do only a mutual fund business. Cash in an account is insured up to $100,000.

S.I.P.C. is empowered to disburse up to $1 billion of federal funds to insure investors. The fund is built up primarily from assessments on the securities business of S.I.P.C. members. In 1979, a uniform member assessment of $25 per year went into effect.

Quite obviously, the federal government could not be expected to insure investors against the collapse of securities firms unless it had some definite say in how those firms were operated. The S.E.C. is the agency that really exercises that power, although theoretically S.I.P.C. writes its own rules. One of the rules requires all securities firms to maintain adequate cash reserves against their customers' credit balance — the cash they have in their accounts. Another rule requires brokers to keep separate all securities owned by customers but held by the firm in street name.

S.I.P.C. is run by a seven-member board of directors. One member is appointed by the Secretary of the Treasury, one by the Federal Reserve Board, three represent the securities industry but are appointed by the President, two represent the general public and are also appointed by the President. Originally, the industry fought to get a majority of their representatives on this board. But it gave up without too much argument when it realized that, regardless of who was on the board, the S.E.C. intended to be the power behind the throne. The industry soon resigned itself to the fact that the S.E.C. was going to be an increasingly tough taskmaster in the years ahead — as the Securities Reform of 1975 certainly gave it the authority to be.

During the first four years of its life only one N.Y.S.E. member firm went into S.I.P.C. liquidation, and this was because of fraud.

This record was all the more remarkable considering that volume on the New York Stock Exchange for much of the bear market of 1973–1974 was substantially below the 17,000,000 to 18,000,000 shares per day member firms needed to break even.

The federal insurance program, supplemented in many cases by private insurance coverage, has obviously lifted a tremendous weight off Wall Street's shoulders. Still, the industry knows that the long-range solution to the problem of financing its own business lies in attracting large chunks of permanent new capital and in restoring investor confidence in the financial community in general.

For generations the brokerage business thought of itself as a business of individuals, or *partnerships* of individuals, who exercised an almost fiduciary responsibility. This — the old "family counselor" approach — was the way brokers felt customer confidence in the investment business could best be built. But with the spread of public ownership of stocks, the adoption of modern merchandising methods, and the arrival of computers, the business rapidly outgrew this old concept of itself. And the exchange membership had to recognize that.

In 1953, the exchange took its first step toward liberalizing its rules by permitting the voluntary *incorporation* of member firms. One advantage of incorporation was that corporations were subject to a maximum federal tax of 52%, while individual partners in a firm might find themselves paying a considerably higher income tax. By incorporating, a firm would be able to retain a much higher proportion of its earnings as capital.

More important, incorporation provided a much greater permanence of capital. In a partnership, a partner can decide to withdraw and take his capital with him. When a partner dies, even if his heirs are willing to leave his capital in the firm, a large part of it inevitably has to be withdrawn to pay estate taxes. With incorporation, a firm can spread its ownership among many more people by selling shares to hundreds of key employees. This technique not only gives the employee a piece of the action, and hence stimulates morale, it also reduces the risk of having large hunks of capital precipitously withdrawn.

In the decade following the exchange's abandonment of partnership rule, more than a third of the member firms, including most of the biggest firms, transformed themselves from partnerships into corporations and thus strengthened their financial positions.

In June 1969 the exchange took a second important step. It authorized member firms to raise additional capital by issuing bonds for sale to the public.

Then a few months later the aggressive young firm of Donaldson, Lufkin & Jenrette, which specialized in institutional business, forced the exchange's hand by applying to the S.E.C. for registration and sale of an issue of its own common stock. The exchange had no alternative. It had to amend its rules to permit Donaldson, Lufkin & Jenrette and all other member firms to "go public" if they wanted to.

It was inevitable that many member firms would do so. It was the only way they could raise the capital they needed to stay in business. In April 1971 the biggest firm of all, Merrill Lynch, Pierce, Fenner & Smith, announced it would go public. It has since been followed by almost all the major brokerage firms in the country.

CHAPTER *20*

What It Means to Speculate

SPECULATING is an inevitable part of the business of buying securities. But then speculating is an inevitable part of just living.

Whenever you are confronted with an unavoidable risk — as indeed you are in many circumstances every day — you must speculate. You must meet the risk; you must take your chances. Often you are presented with a choice of risks. When you make up your mind which one you will take, weighing the good and the bad features of each, you arrive at a speculative decision.

The businessman who *must* be in another city at a given time often has the choice of flying or driving. He can figure on getting there faster if he flies. But there's always the possibility of bad weather, mechanical failure, or other delays. Those risks may be somewhat reduced if he drives. But then he faces other hazards — a breakdown, an accident, traffic tie-ups. Faced with this kind of choice, the man must inevitably speculate.

The manufacturer who must pick Jones or Smith for a key job must speculate on which will be the more able man.

And the farmer's whole operation is one vast speculation. When he puts the seed in the ground, he is speculating on his ability to grow a crop and sell it at a profit despite bad weather, pests, blight, and changing market prices.

When a man takes a risk he cannot avoid, he is speculating. But when he takes a risk that he doesn't have to take, he gambles.

That is one distinction between speculation and gambling. But there is another. Speculation involves an exercise of reason, while gambling involves nothing but chance. The man who speculates can make an intelligent forecast of the hazards of his course. The gambler stands or falls on the flip of a coin or the draw of a card.

In the purchase of any stock or bond, even a government bond, there is an element of speculation. The risk that it might decline in value cannot be avoided. For that matter, there is a risk just in holding money — the risk that it won't buy as much in the future as it will today.

When a man buys securities however, he doesn't have to operate exclusively on chance. He can make a fairly intelligent estimate of how much risk he is assuming on the basis of the record. And he has a wide range of risks to choose from — all the way from a government bond to the penny stocks of companies whose assets are made up principally of hope.

The word investments is applied by many old-line investors only to government bonds, municipal bonds, and first-quality corporate bonds. To an ultraconservative buyer of securities for a bank or an insurance company, all stocks are too risky to be classed as investments, despite the fact that some stocks have proved safer than many corporate bonds over the long term.

Because most preferred stocks and a good number of common stocks have proven so stable, even the conservatives refer to them nowadays as "investment-type" securities. These are apt to be the stocks of utilities, food firms, banks, or chain stores — industries that have shown themselves to be comparatively steady earners, come boom or depression.

Of course, what is one man's speculation is very often another man's investment. Below the level of topflight securities is a vast assortment of stocks that many men of sound judgment consider good investments, primarily because of the liberal dividends they pay.

Often these are stocks of companies whose fortunes rise and fall sharply with the business cycle — companies in the automobile, steel, construction, or clothing industries. When business is good, they pay excellent dividends. When business slumps, those dividends may be reduced or eliminated.

As a rough — very rough — rule of thumb, the degree of risk which you assume in buying one of those "*cyclical*" *stocks* can be measured by the liberality of its dividend. The larger the dividend as a percentage of the selling price, the greater the risk tends to be. This is because stocks that pay high dividends are usually in demand. This demand is generally reflected in the high price of the stock. If the stock's price is not high, this means the high dividend is not being reflected in the price of the stock because some other negative risk factor is acting as a deterrent to buyers.

There are other stocks — thousands of them — that must be frankly classified as speculations. Even here, however, there is a wide range of quality. At the top are those stocks that might be described as "good *growth* situations." These are stocks of companies, often paying little or no dividend, that because of their future prospects are regarded as attractive to investors. Sixty years ago, many automobile and radio stocks might have been so classified. More recently, electronic, office equipment, cosmetic, computer, drug, and aerospace stocks have been placed in this category. In recent years, these glamorous growth stocks have been the darlings of the investing public. Such has been the demand for them that aggressive investors have frequently been willing to buy them for prices equal to 40 or 50 times their current annual earnings.

Some speculative securities are attractive not because their future looks so promising but because it looks a lot better than their past. A company may have had to pass some dividends or miss interest payments during a difficult period of reorganization. But once it starts to hit the comeback trail, its securities are apt to take on new life. Many a sizable fortune has been made by buying bonds that were severely depressed because the company had to default on interest payments temporarily. That's also been true of many preferred stocks on which dividend payments have accumulated for a number of years before ultimately being paid off.

Such investments are strictly long shots and must be so regarded.

The most popular kind of speculative stock is the stock issued by small aggressive companies in one of the growth fields. Characteristically, these are over-the-counter stocks selling at relatively modest prices, unseasoned securities issued by companies that are so new they have no record of consistent earnings. These companies are long on hopes, short on cash. Rank speculations though they be, they attract interest because everyone knows that Xerox, Polaroid, and IBM — and Rod & Reel — were just such stocks not so many years ago.

Finally, there are the outright penny stocks. A few of these may be the listed securities of old-line companies that have fallen on evil days. Their business has declined steadily, and their stock seems virtually worthless. But a significant number of these low-priced stocks, selling at 50¢, $1, $2, maybe as high as $5, are the newly issued stocks of questionable oil or mining companies. These are peddled by high-pressure salesmen who expect to make as much as 50¢ on every dollar's worth of stock they sell. Often by direct mail and even long-distance phone, the prospect is told that a block of 100 or 300 shares has been reserved in his name at a special bargain price. But he must buy within 24 hours or lose his chance of a lifetime. People who have charge accounts at expensive stores and professional people are particular targets for this kind of promotion. Their names and addresses are bought from direct-mail firms.

Occasionally these glamorous sales stories have an element of truth to them. The men who put their money in the oil property "right next to our land" may actually have made 1,000% on their investment already. But the fact remains that anyone who takes a flyer on this kind of deal is much more apt to lose everything he puts into it than he is to make a whopping profit.

Although there is an obvious difference between this kind of rank speculation and the solid investment that a government bond represents, it is also true that the distinction between investing and speculating frequently gets hazy as soon as you move away from either of these two extremes. Actually, the difference between investing and speculating is not so much a matter of the individual security's merit as it is the motive for which that security was bought.

The investor is a man who puts his money in a company in the expectation of earning a reasonable and regular return on it over the long pull, both in dividends and price appreciation. The speculator takes a short-term view. He is not interested in dividends. He is interested in making a quick profit on his money and selling out whenever he can get it. Often he takes a big risk in the process. But if he hits it right, he stands to make a lot of money.

Furthermore, under present federal tax laws he may be able to keep more of that money than he would if he made the same amount of money in dividends, salary, or other income.

Risk capital — the money that a man puts at risk when he buys or sells almost any kind of property — has played such an important role in building this country that Congress for more than a quarter of a century has given favored tax treatment to profits realized in such ventures. These are called *capital gains,* and they include the profits realized on the purchase and sale of securities.

For many years our federal tax law provided that a man who made a profit by selling any security he had owned for more than six months — a *long-term* capital gain — would not have to pay a tax of more than 25% of that profit. That was the absolute maximum. Actually, the tax might be considerably less, for instead of paying 25% on the entire gain, he could, if he chose, pay a straight income tax on only half the gain at whatever regular income tax applied in his case. Thus, if a stockholder's maximum tax bracket was only 40% on regular income, the effective rate he would pay on a long-term capital gain would be only 20%.

In recent years the minimum amount of time a stock had to be held to qualify as a long-term capital-gain candidate was extended to one year. And the Economic Recovery Tax Act of 1981 reduced the maximum tax on capital gains to 20% for taxpayers in all brackets.

Short-term gains — those realized on securities owned for less than one year — are taxed at full regular income tax rates.

Furthermore, the government has always offered another special advantage to investors or speculators. It permits them to offset *capital gains* with *capital losses*. Thus, if a person realizes capital gains of $5,000 and suffers capital losses of $4,000 in a given tax year, he pays the capital-gains tax on only $1,000.

Any tax reduction on capital gains, as opposed to ordinary income, is favorable to investing. But many businessmen and some economists argue that the present tax treatment is not favorable enough. They contend that new-venture capital — speculative capital — should be made more freely available to business. This could be accomplished by reducing taxes on long-term capital gains further or by permitting taxpayers to classify profits as a long-term gain after a shorter period of time. There are many who argue that the capital-gains tax rate should be reduced as the holding period lengthens.

It obviously makes sense for a stockholder to consider the matter of taxes on long-term and short-term capital gains (or losses) in deciding whether, and when, to sell his stock. Thus, it would be ridiculous for a man in a high income tax bracket — say 60% — to sell a stock on which he had a substantial profit if he had owned that stock just a few days short of one year. By waiting those few additional days he could establish his profit as a long-term capital gain, and he would have to pay considerably less tax than he would if he realized a short-term capital gain and had to pay a tax of 60%. Only in the most unusual circumstances would his risk of loss in those few days outweigh the extra tax he incurred by selling his stock early.

On the other hand, too great a concern about taxes on capital gains can seriously warp investment judgment. Many a stockowner has refused to sell and take a profit, because he didn't want to pay even a long-term capital-gains tax. While he complains about being "*locked-in*," his profit may dwindle in a declining market. Stock market authorities call this taxation rigor mortis. It costs stockholders a lot more every year than all the dubious new issues and other outright swindles combined. The person with a 100% profit in a stock will complain bitterly about his long-term capital-gains tax. He forgets that when he bought the stock he would have been more than satisfied with any profit whatsoever.

If you have a profit in a stock, you might as well reconcile yourself to paying a capital-gains tax on it. You can, of course, hold on to the stock — and the profit, if you are lucky — till you die. But then your executors and your heirs will have to worry about inheritance taxes.

Of course, you can sidestep the tax by using a capital gain to offset a capital loss. This provision has served to stimulate a fair amount of speculation. A person with a capital gain will often take a much greater measure of risk than he ordinarily would. If he loses, Uncle Sam will cover a part of the losses.

The capital-gains tax constitutes the biggest paradox in the stock market. It stimulates speculation because it offers the high-income investor a chance to build up capital at bargain rates. But it simultaneously deters speculation, particularly among amateurs, because it is human nature to postpone the payment of any tax as long as possible.

Curiously enough, the professional speculator does not so often try to make a profit — a capital gain — by putting money into a really speculative growth stock, as he does by speculating in the 50 or 60 active stocks — many of them topflight investments — that account for most of the transactions on the Big Board.

There is a reason for this. At any given time the price of a stock or the price of all stocks represents the combined judgments of all the people who are buying and selling. Most times a speculator is staking his judgment against the public judgment.

He may study the stock of a company in minute detail, and on the basis of that intensive analysis may feel that he knows better than the public what it's really worth — or, rather, what the public will sooner or later determine is its real worth.

Again, he may think that he has a better feel for the market as a whole, knows better than the public whether stock prices will advance steadily upward in a *bull market,* or decline in a *bear market.* If he is right, the leading stocks — those that enjoy the widest public following — will probably provide the earliest confirmation of his judgment. Hence, they provide the best opportunity for a quick profit.

On the assumption that his judgment is right, the speculator seeks to augment his profits — or protect them once they are made — by using various techniques of trading.

He may buy on margin.

He may pyramid profits.

He may sell short.

He may buy puts or calls.

Let it be noted that none of these techniques, discussed in the following chapters, constitutes in itself unfair or dishonest manipulation of the market. On the contrary, all are legitimate procedures and make for greater trading activity and a more liquid market. Often, in fact, the average investor would find it difficult to sell stock if the speculator were not willing to assume the risk the investor wants to escape.

Periodically, there is public clamor about the ill-gotten gains of market speculators. People are apt to say that "there ought to be a law" to curb them. In 1905, Oliver Wendell Holmes, Justice of the United States Supreme Court, delivered the definitive reply to all such critics. Said Justice Holmes: "Speculation . . . is the self-adjustment of society to the probable. Its value is well known, as a means of avoiding or mitigating catastrophes, equalizing prices and providing for periods of want. It is true that the success of the strong induces imitation by the weak, and that incompetent persons bring themselves to ruin by undertaking to speculate in their turn. But legislatures and courts generally have recognized that the natural evolutions of a complex society are to be touched only with a very cautious hand. . . ."

CHAPTER 21

How You Buy Stocks on Margin

ONCE a security buyer has assured a broker of his financial responsibility and opened a margin account, he can buy stocks — any of the stocks listed on a United States securities exchange and some over-the-counter stocks approved for margin transactions by the Federal Reserve Board — just by making a down payment on them. How big that down payment must be is governed by a wide variety of rules.

First, the New York Stock Exchange says that no one can open an account to buy its securities on margin unless the down payment is at least $2,000 in cash, or an equivalent in securities.

Occasionally, the exchange may be concerned about the market action of a particular stock because of sharp swings in its price or in its trading volume. In such circumstances the exchange may require those who buy or sell that stock to put up extra margin — a higher down payment. The exchange can also forbid all margin trading in such stocks and has often done so, especially in periods of heavy speculative activity.

In addition to the rules set by the various exchanges you may encounter special margin requirements set by individual brokers. Some, for instance, will not permit a customer to buy any stock on margin unless that stock sells above $5 a share. Other brokers require a larger down payment than the exchange does.

Finally, and most important, there are the regulations of the

Federal Reserve Board, which has been empowered by Congress to say, in effect, just what the minimum *margin requirements* must be. Since 1934, when the board began to exercise its authority, it has set that minimum by saying that the down payment must represent a certain percentage of the total value of the stock that is being bought on margin. The percentage is changed from time to time, depending on the availability of credit, how worried the board is about inflation, and the amount of stock trading that is being done on margin.

The lowest figure that the board has ever set is 40%. That figure prevailed for eight years, from 1937 to 1945. The highest figure has been 100%. While that was in effect, from January 1946 to February 1947, nobody could buy on margin.

In bull markets, the board will raise the rate because it is concerned about overtrading and wants to cool down speculative fever. Conversely, in bear markets, when volume has dried up, the board is frequently willing to provide some stimulus to the market by reducing the minimum margin requirements.

To simplify the explanation of how margin works, suppose the Federal Reserve Board margin requirement at a given time is 50%. This means that you can buy $10,000 worth of some marginable stock with $5,000. Your broker lends you the other $5,000. Naturally, when he does that, he charges you interest on the money he lends. How much interest depends on how much interest he himself has to pay a bank — whatever the prevailing interest rate is on brokers' loans — for the $5,000 he borrows from them to lend to you. He'll generally charge you the prevailing interest rate plus, according to stock exchange practice, at least $\frac{1}{2}\%$ to 1%, and sometimes more, for himself.

With basic bank rates at historical highs, during the late seventies and early eighties, brokers were concerned about violating state usury laws. Some states exempt brokers from their usury laws, but where they don't, brokers argued that since their margin orders were executed in New York, the usury law of New York should apply. In various cases, state courts accepted this argument. However, short of a U.S. Supreme Court ruling, no one could be absolutely sure of its validity.

If you think you can get a better deal from your bank than you can from your broker on a margin account — you can forget about it. Banks are not permitted to lend any more on stock purchases than brokers can lend. It is true that you can borrow a greater proportion of the down payment, up to 90%, from unregulated lenders. But you are not likely to get any break there. Indeed, it is probable you will pay as much as 1% or 2% extra interest a month. And any broker or registered representative who helped you arrange such a loan would run afoul of the S.E.C.

When a broker borrows money from a bank and lends it to you so you can buy stocks on margin, he has to give the bank some security on the loan. That loan security may be the very stock you buy on margin. Hence, when you open a margin account, you must agree to leave your margined stocks with the broker and to let him *hypothecate* them, or pledge them as security for whatever bank loan he may need in order to carry margin accounts.

If you buy $10,000 worth of stock on margin, you naturally pay commissions on the full $10,000 worth of stock. But you are also entitled to all the dividends on those shares. This alone is sufficient to interest some investors in buying stocks on margin, especially when stocks are paying liberal dividends and margin interest rates are low.

Still, virtually all margin customers are interested in margin not because of the extra dividends, but because of the speculative profit they hope to make, for margin is the speculator's number one tool.

Suppose that a man with $5,000 to invest has picked out a stock selling at $50 a share which he thinks will go up. Under a 50% margin rule, he can buy 200 shares of that stock, instead of just 100 shares, with his $5,000. If it goes up five points, he makes $1,000 instead of $500, a 20% profit instead of 10%. Doubling a profit can make even a 20% interest charge on a margin loan look cheap.

But suppose the stock goes down in price? There's the rub.

It's then that the margin buyer may receive a *margin call* from his broker, a request to put up more margin — that is, to increase the amount of his down payment. If he can't put up more money, the broker has the right to sell his stock — or as much of it as may be necessary — to raise the required cash. This presents no logistical problem to the broker, because all margined stock must be left on deposit with him.

How much more money may a margin buyer have to put up if his stocks decline? The answer to this is governed by the *margin maintenance* rules of the New York Stock Exchange and by those of the individual broker. The Federal Reserve Board isn't in the picture at all after the original purchase. If a buyer meets the board's original margin requirements — say, of 50% cash — he is never compelled by the board to put up more margin, even if the board later raises its requirements to 75% or more.

Under New York Stock Exchange rules, however, a broker must ask a customer for more margin whenever the amount that customer would have left if he sold his stocks and paid off the broker's loan is less than 25% of the current value of the stocks. (Some brokers have margin maintenance requirements that are higher than the minimums set by the New York Stock Exchange.)

To illustrate: suppose a margin customer bought 100 shares of a stock selling at $60 a share at a time when the Federal Reserve Board required only 50% margin. In that case he would put up $3,000 and he would borrow $3,000 from his broker. Now suppose the stock dropped from $60 to $40 a share. If he were to sell out now, he would realize only $4,000 on his holdings. After he paid his broker $3,000, he would have only $1,000 left. This would be exactly 25% of the current value ($4,000) of his stock.

If the stock fell below $40 in this instance, the broker would have to ask for more margin money so that the 25% ratio would be restored. Actually, he'd probably ask for a bit more so that he wouldn't have to make another margin call very soon if the stock continued to decline.

If a stock is bought on a 50% margin basis, it can drop a full third in price — from 60 to 40, as in the example above — before a broker must call for more margin. If the Federal Reserve Board's initial margin requirement was 75% instead of 50%, the stock could decline two-thirds in value and the customer would still not have to put up more margin. Here's how that works: The customer buys 100 shares of stock at $60 a share and puts up 75% margin, or $4,500. He borrows only $1,500 from his broker. If the stock drops from $60 to $20, his holdings are worth $2,000. At that point, he could sell out, pay the broker $1,500, and still have $500 left. This would represent 25% of the current market value of his stocks ($2,000).

These examples have assumed that the customer bought only a single stock on margin. Actually, most margin customers have positions in a number of stocks in their margin accounts. In such circumstances, the broker must compute exactly how the customer stands on all of his stocks. He will not send out a margin call on one stock that may have fallen below the maintenance requirements if the customer shows a surplus on his other holdings sufficient to offset the shortages. In short, the broker takes into account the customer's overall position — the shortages and surpluses in each stock — and sends out a margin call only when the customer falls below the minimum maintenance requirements on his total holdings.

Thanks to modern data processing and computing equipment, which wasn't available during the 1929 crash, brokers can compute the exact position of an active margin account almost instantly in periods of rapidly falling prices. At other, more normal times, weekly runs on all margin accounts are sufficient to protect the broker.

Incidentally, when a customer gets a margin call, he doesn't have to pony up cash if he has acceptable securities in a regular or cash account that he can post as collateral.

A margin customer is also permitted to substitute one stock for another in his margin account. But if the stock he buys is higher in price than the one he sells, he will have to deposit funds with his broker equal to the Federal Reserve's initial margin requirement on the difference between the purchase price of the one and the selling price of the other.

Conversely, if proceeds from a customer's sale exceed his purchase cost, the amount that he can withdraw from his account is the amount above the Federal Reserve's current initial margin requirement, provided that his account is fully margined (unrestricted). If his account is restricted (margined below the current initial federal margin requirement), the customer can withdraw at least 30% of the difference between the purchase cost and the sale proceeds.

The strictness of both the Federal Reserve Board's requirement governing the initial margin payment and the stock exchange rule on maintenance of margin explain why margin calls are comparatively infrequent today, except during sharp market dips. In severe slumps the margin buyer can be caught in a bad squeeze and forced to sell at a substantial loss in order to meet a margin call. That's why no one should trade on margin unless he has both the temperament and the resources to enable him to accept his losses with reasonable equanimity. You can't be a margin trader — nor should you be — if you have only a widow's mite.

One other restriction on margin trading should be noted. The exchange has put a brake on the heavy margin traders who move in and out of a given stock several times during one day's trading. Brokers are now required to see that such *day traders* operating on margin, as most of them do, have enough capital in their accounts to cover the initial margin requirement on the maximum position they held at any time during the day's trading — not just on their position at the end of the day.

Not only have these regulations resulted in fewer margin calls than at the time of the 1929 crash, but they have also greatly reduced the proportion of margin accounts in relation to all accounts. In 1929 it is estimated that margin customers represented 40% of all customers. And these customers accounted for a considerably larger proportion of total commission business, just how large a proportion no one knows exactly. But as the market boiled upward in the late twenties, the margin customers were always the big buyers, the people who kept *pyramiding* their *paper profits* and buying more and more stock.

Here's how pyramiding worked in those days: suppose a man bought 200 shares of a $50 stock. Under the lax margin regulations that prevailed then, he might have had to put up only $2,000 of the $10,000 cost — maybe even less if he was a favored customer.

Now let's assume that his stock advanced to $75 a share. His total holdings would now be worth $15,000. If he sold at that price and paid off the $8,000 loan from his broker, he would have $7,000 cash. On a 20% margin basis, this would enable him to buy $35,000 worth of stock. Actually, of course, he didn't have to go through the mechanics of selling out and buying afresh. The broker recognized the expanded value of his original holdings and accepted that added value as collateral on additional margin purchases.

In this instance, the customer would have been able to own $35,000 worth of securities on a cash margin of only $2,000, all thanks to a 50% increase in the value of his original 200 shares. If he continued to be that lucky, he could run his paper profits to a hundred thousand dollars, a half million dollars, a million dollars, many millions of dollars, all on just $2,000 cash.

In the twenties many people did exactly that. But when prices started to decline and the margin calls came, many of them couldn't raise even a few thousand dollars cash, except by selling securities. And when they sold, that very act of selling depressed prices further and resulted in more margin calls. Again they had to sell. And so the vicious circle kept swirling downward into the great abyss.

There's nothing illegal about pyramiding, even today, under the Federal Reserve Board rules. But it can't work very effectively when you have to put up margin of 50%, 70%, or 90% instead of

20%. Then only a substantial increase in the price of a speculator's stock will yield you big enough paper profits to permit a significant increase in your holdings.

Current margin trading accounts for only 10% to 15% of total trading on the New York Stock Exchange. However, because they are apt to trade more frequently and in larger amounts, margin customers today probably account for 30% to 40% of brokers' total commission income. Margin accounts are so well protected today that even if there were a serious decline in the market it is unlikely that it could ever be turned into the kind of rout that made 1929 the debacle it was.

CHAPTER 22

What It Means to Sell Short

WHEN an investor opens a margin account with a broker, he is asked to sign an agreement giving the broker authority to lend his marginable stocks to others. It is this lending or hypothecation agreement that makes it possible for other customers to sell stocks short.

Short selling normally accounts for only 6% to 8% of all the transactions on the New York Stock Exchange. Yet probably no other market technique excites so much public interest — or is so widely misunderstood.

A short sale is nothing but the reverse of the usual market transaction. Instead of buying a stock and then selling it, the short trader first sells a stock he has borrowed, then buys it back at what he hopes will be a lower price.

If it is legitimate to buy a stock because you think it's going to go up, why isn't it just as legitimate to sell it because you think it's going to go down? Why shouldn't you be able to try to make a profit in either direction? It can be fairly argued that the right of a bear to sell, or go short, is just as vital to a completely free market as the right of a bull to buy stocks, or *go long*.

Regardless of the logic of the situation, most people think it just isn't morally right to sell something you don't have.

What about the magazine publisher who sells you a three-year advance subscription to his publication?

What about the farmer who sells his whole crop to a grain elevator when the seed hasn't even sprouted yet?

Both of them sell something they haven't got just on the strength of a promise to deliver. That's all a short seller does.

Furthermore, it isn't really true that the short seller sells something he doesn't have. He has to *borrow* the stock that he sells, and he has to give it back. This he hopes to be able to do by *covering*, or buying it back at a price less than he sold it for.

Where does he borrow his stock? From his broker.

Where does the broker get the stock to lend? Usually from his other margin customers, who signed the lending agreement when they opened their accounts. If a broker doesn't have among all his margin accounts the particular stock a customer wants to sell short, he will borrow it from another broker, or from some individual stockowner who makes a business of lending stock. But the broker *cannot* borrow stock from the account of any of his regular cash customers without specific authorization.

Why should one broker lend stock to another? Because he gets paid for it by the borrowing broker, who retains all the proceeds of his customer's short sale until the transaction is closed out by an offsetting purchase. Sometimes, if the stock is in heavy demand and is difficult to borrow, the broker will even pay a premium to borrow it. Any such premium payment is, of course, charged to the short seller. If the price of a stock on loan increases significantly, the lending broker will expect to receive more money for lending it. If the price drops, the borrowing broker will expect a proportionate refund of the money he has paid. (Sometimes a lending broker will demand return of the shares. If the borrowing broker can't locate them elsewhere, he is forced to buy them back from the customer and close out the short position whether the customer likes it or not.)

A short seller operates under essentially the same rules as a margin buyer. If the Federal Reserve Board has a 50% margin rule in effect, the seller must put up cash equal to 50% of the market value of the stock that he borrows and sells. Under stock exchange rules, the minimum margin cannot be less than $2,000.

Suppose an investor wanted to go short 100 shares of a stock selling at 60. If the Federal Reserve Board margin requirement was 50% at the time, he would have to put up $3,000 cash. If the stock dropped to 50, he could buy it back, cover his short position by returning the stock, and make a profit of $10 a share, or $1,000, less taxes and commissions.

But perhaps when the stock hit 50 he thought it would go lower. He could make more money if it did, but he wouldn't want to lose the profit he already had. In such a situation, he might place a stop order to buy at 52, and thus protect himself against a rising market. If the stock does go up to 52, his stop order to buy becomes a market order to buy at once.

If he buys back in at that price, he will still have a profit of $800, exclusive of all brokerage commissions and taxes. Additionally, he will be liable for whatever dividends have accrued on the stock during the operation, because the lender was entitled to get them during the time his stock was on loan.

There is one important difference between the amount of margin required for margin buyers and short sellers. The minimum requirement of the New York Stock Exchange for maintenance-of-margin is 25% for the long position. But when a customer uses margin — as he must — for going short, the minimum is increased to 30%, or $5 a share, whichever is greater. (If the stock itself is selling below $5 a share, the minimum requirement is 100% of the market value, or $2.50 a share, whichever is greater.)

That 30% maintenance-of-margin requirement on short sales means that the broker will call for more money whenever the amount of the margin that the short seller would have left if he bought the stock back and covered his short position is only 30% of its current market price.

Suppose a man sells short 100 shares of a stock at 60. If the initial margin requirement was 50%, he would have to put up $3,000. Now, instead of declining to 50, suppose the price of the stock goes up to 70. If he were to cover at that point, he would owe $7,000, or $1,000 more than he sold the stock for originally. That means he would have only $2,000 margin left in his account ($3,000 minus $1,000), or a little less than 30% of the current value of the stock ($7,000 times .30 equals $2,100). At that point, unless he decided to take his loss and close out the transaction, he would receive a maintenance call to deposit at least $100 additional margin.

Sometimes a short sale can be prudently used to protect a profit in a stock at a time when the buyer doesn't want to sell it and take his capital gain. Suppose, for instance, you had bought 100 shares of a stock in August — a straight cash transaction — and that it ran up 20 points by the next July. If you were to sell before the one-year time period passed and take your $2,000 profit, you would have to pay a short-term capital-gains tax on that profit at the full tax rate applying to ordinary income. If you were in a 50% tax bracket, you would have to pay out $1,000 in taxes. So you might want to hold on for just another month until your capital gain can be reported as long-term.

But suppose the stock were to drop during that month waiting period and you were to lose a substantial part of your $2,000 profit? You don't want that to happen. And you're willing to forgo the prospect of further price appreciation, a bigger profit, just to protect yourself against the risk of loss. A short sale of 100 shares of the same stock you own offers you just that kind of insurance. When you are both long and short the same number of shares of the stock, your position is stabilized. If the stock rises, you make money on your long position and lose an equal amount on your short position. If it goes down, you make money on the short side and lose an offsetting amount on the long side. Your capital gains and losses cancel each other out.

When you stabilize this way, you don't change the tax status of your profit. You simply defer taking your gain and avoid paying the tax on it as if it were a short-term gain. All you lose are the additional commission, taxes, and interest you pay on the short sale. (It should be noted that under federal tax regulations a short sale cannot be used within a single tax year to convert a short-term into a long-term capital gain in order to reduce the tax. It can be used only when the carryover is from one year to the succeeding year.)

Another good thing about this kind of transaction, known as *selling short against the box,* is that the maintenance-of-margin requirement is reduced from 30% to 10%. This is because when the margin customer is "long stock" in his cash account in an amount that precisely offsets the number of shares he is short in his margin account, any chance of loss is eliminated, regardless of how the market moves.

While it is obvious that there is a legitimate place for short selling in a free and orderly securities market, it cannot be denied that short selling has often been used for illegitimate purposes. Such abuses have frequently led to demands that short selling be outlawed. From the time 350 years ago when buyers and sellers first began to trade in the stock of the Dutch East India Company, the history of short selling has not been a pretty one. It contributed some gaudy chapters to the history of the New York Stock Exchange, particularly in the nineteenth century, when short selling was a favorite tool of such famous market manipulators as Commodore Vanderbilt, Daniel Drew, Jay Gould, and Jim Fisk.

These men frequently tried to catch each other in market corners. A market *corner* is created when one man or group succeeds in getting such complete control of a particular stock that others who may have sold it short cannot cover their purchases by buying the stock back, as they eventually have to do, except on terms dictated by the controlling group.

One of the classic corners is the one that involved the old Harlem Railroad, a predecessor of the New York Central. Vanderbilt got control of the Harlem and then proceeded to extend the road down Manhattan Island. Drew, who was also a stockholder in the road and had realized a handsome profit as the stock advanced in price, now saw an opportunity to make a much larger profit. He induced the New York City Council to repeal the franchise that had been granted for the extension of the road, on the assumption that this bad news would depress the price of the stock. Simultaneously, he sold the stock short.

His maneuver succeeded in driving the price of the stock down, but as Drew sold, the Commodore bought. In the end, Drew and some of the members of the City Council who were associated with him in this notorious exploit found that they had sold short more stock than actually existed. They could not cover their short positions except on terms dictated by Vanderbilt — and the terms were ruinous. That is perhaps when the famous couplet, credited to Drew, came into our literature: *"He who sells what isn't his'n/ Must buy it back or go to pris'n."*

Even when nothing so titanic as an attempted corner was involved, short selling often proved an effective manipulative device for *pool* operators, who would join forces to bid the price of a stock up and then drive it back down again with short selling to make a big speculative profit.

Often such pool operators risked very little of their own capital in the operation. They would stimulate public interest in a particular stock by adroit publicity and creation of considerable activity in the market for that stock. That activity was usually more apparent than real, because it would be generated by *wash sales.* A wash sale, now outlawed by the S.E.C., simply involved the simultaneous purchase and sale of large blocks, say 1,000 or 10,000 shares. Such big volume would attract the public, which inevitably seems to buy whenever there is a lot of activity in a stock. As the public bought and forced the price up, pool operators would wait for the strategic moment when they thought the stock was about as high as it could get, then begin selling it short, hammering the price down to a level where they could buy it back at a handsome profit.

One of the most important reforms introduced by the Securities and Exchange Commission was the regulation that effectively prevented abuse of the right to sell short. The S.E.C. accomplished this objective in February 1938 by a ruling that a stock can be sold short only in a rising market, however temporary that rise may be.

The rule, generally referred to as the *one-eighth rule,* works this way: if a customer places an order to sell short, that order, as it goes to the floor, must be clearly marked as a short sale. The floor broker is forbidden to execute that order except at what is, in effect, a higher price. Thus, if a stock were last sold at 50, the broker could not sell that stock short except at a price of 50⅛ or higher. In this case he would be selling on an up tick.

There is one exception to this rule. The broker may sell the stock at 50, the same price that prevailed on the last sale, provided the *last previous* change in the price had been upward. In other words, there might have been one or two or six transactions that had taken place at the same price of 50, but a short sale could still be made at 50, provided the last *different* price had been 49⅞ or lower. This is called selling on an *even tick.*

With the debut of the *consolidated tape* in June 1975, the S.E.C. had some new problems to solve connected with short selling. The commission wanted to prohibit any short sale at a price that was lower than the last sale reported on the consolidated tape, regardless of where that sale was made. Further, the commission wanted to prohibit a short sale on an even tick and to impose short selling restrictions on all over-the-counter transactions in listed securities.

Such stringent regulations posed serious problems for the exchange specialists, who are responsible for maintaining a fluid auction market in the stocks they handle. So the S.E.C. relaxed its rule, providing that short sales could be made by specialists regardless of the tick, as long as they were made at the last sale price reported on the consolidated tape. Still, the specialists were not satisfied. They argued that the consolidated tape might lag significantly behind the actual market in a given stock, that a price change that might appear on the tape to be a down tick might actually be an up tick in their own market.

So the S.E.C. made another concession, which became effective on April 30, 1976. It gave the exchange the choice of basing short sales on prices that prevailed on the big board, or of using those that appeared on the consolidated tape. The N.Y.S.E., of course, adhered firmly to its own prices.

Most of the short selling that is presently done comes not from the public but from members of the exchange. Does this mean that brokers are up to their old tricks? Not at all.

The specialists account for 55% to 60% of all short selling on the New York Stock Exchange. They often have to make these sales if they are to fulfill their obligation to maintain orderly and continuous markets in the stocks assigned to them. Thus, if a broker wants to execute a market buy order for a customer but there are no near offers to sell, except perhaps at a price that is wholly out of line, the specialist is expected to offer the stock at a better or lower price. He must do this even if he doesn't have that stock in his inventory and has to go short in order to complete the transaction.

Registered floor traders frequently engage in short selling for their personal accounts. When they do, it is not because they are trading on inside knowledge. Often it's because they are cynical about the public's perpetual bullishness. Then too, these traders customarily make fast and frequent trades on both sides of the market, long and short, seeking to make a small profit, even if that profit is only a fraction of a point. They can afford to trade for minuscule profits because they pay no brokerage commission by reason of their Big Board membership. Such rapid-fire operations are very closely scrutinized.

Short selling has been strictly regulated by the S.E.C., but it still remains an important trading tool. As evidence of that, the total number of shares sold short on the New York Stock Exchange, the so-called *short interest,* is reported monthly by the exchange, and continues to reach consecutive highs, each succeeding year.

Paradoxical as it may seem, a big short interest is generally regarded as bullish. This is because as the short interest grows, so does the potential volume of buying orders. Because ultimately every one of those short sellers is going to have to buy back the stock he previously sold short in order to make delivery of the shares. Hence, the short interest represents a cushion of upcoming buying orders, which helps sustain the market.

It is a truism that the public always wants the market to go up and generally believes that it will. Most investors act accordingly. In the light of such perpetual bullishness, who could deny an old bear the right to sell short on the assumption that the public is wrong again?

CHAPTER 23

Options—Plain and Fancy

IN addition to margin trading, pyramiding profits, and selling short, the speculator can execute still another market maneuver that has become increasingly popular in recent years: buying and selling options.

If you think a certain stock is likely to increase in price over the next three months, for example, you can buy a *call* on that stock. This call gives you the right at any time within the three-month period to buy 100 shares of that stock at the price specified in the call contract. Whether or not you exercise that option is wholly up to you. Whether you do or don't depends on the market action of the stock. If its price advances and its increase is greater than the cost of the option that you bought, it can be of advantage to you to exercise your option and buy the 100 shares at the option price. Or you might decide to sell your option, which you can do at any time before the expiration date, and take your profit on it.

Thus, if Rod & Reel was selling at $50 a share on August 1, you might want to buy an October call on Rod & Reel at 50. This would entitle you to buy the stock at the same $50 price, at any time from August 1 until the last option trading day in October.

What would it cost you to buy such a call?

That depends on a variety of factors — what the outlook is for the market as a whole, how stable the price of Rod & Reel has been in the past, what its earnings prospects are, et cetera. But, typically, a three-month option on 100 shares of a $50 stock — a round lot is the standard unit of trading — will cost you $500, plus a commission of about $25. At $500, your option on 100 shares would obviously cost you $5 a share. That is the *premium* you pay. Unless Rod & Reel advances by the amount of the premium — from 50 to 55 — within that three-month option period, you will lose money. Anything over 55 will represent a profit to you, because you have the right to buy 100 shares of Rod & Reel at 50. At 55, you break even. That's called parity. At 57, you would be $2 a share ahead of the game.

At that point you could sell your contract in the options market and net a profit of $200, minus commission on both the purchase and sale of your option contract, commissions that might total $50. But you would have made $150 on a $500 speculation, or 30% on your money.

Now suppose Rod & Reel never goes higher than 53 and you conclude it never will before your option expires. Then you might decide to sell the contract, even if it means losing $2 a share or $200, plus $50 in commissions — a total loss of $250.

The comforting thing about buying an option is that you can never lose more than the amount of your original cost. Maybe Rod & Reel goes up above your option price of 50. But maybe it goes down to 48 or 47 or even lower. Obviously, at such prices, nobody is going to be much interested in buying your call on the stock at 50, assuming that the contract is also about to expire. So your call is worthless, and you end up losing the $500, plus the $25 commission you paid for the option. That's the most you can lose, no matter how low Rod & Reel sinks.

And therein lies the great attraction of options. If you buy one, you can't lose more than the contract cost you. But your profit potential is open-ended. You might make 40% or 100%, or even more — all on just a $500 speculation. In contrast, if you owned 100 shares of Rod & Reel outright at $50 a share and it moved from 50 to 57, you could sell these shares and make a profit of

$700, or only 14%. But if you had bought a $500 option at 50 and the price rose to 57 or two points beyond your break-even point, you would make a 40% profit. You would also have put at risk only one-tenth as much of your capital. Of course, you would have to assume the risk that Rod & Reel would advance at least four points in order to make money — a risk the man who owns the stock outright never has to take.

In all these examples, it is assumed that the value of your option moves up or down exactly the same amount as the price of the stock. But that isn't always the case. Obviously, the price at which an option is traded is always going to be influenced primarily by the price movement of the underlying stock. But, after all, options are traded in a separate market from that in which stocks are traded. And options traders may not have the same idea about the future for any given stock as those who buy and sell the stock itself. As a general rule, when options are selling below parity, the price at which purchases can break even, price swings are not as big, either up or down, for the stock itself. But once an option reaches parity, its price is likely to move up or down by exactly the same amount as the stock itself.

If you have a profit in an option contract, you can sell it in the options market, take your profit, and get out. But an option contract gives you the right to buy that stock at a specified price, and this is a right you might decide to exercise if you think prospects look good for the stock. Thus, if you bought an option on Rod & Reel at 50 (plus $5 per share premium cost) and if Rod & Reel went to 58 during the life of your contract, you might decide to exercise your right to buy the stock outright at 50. In that case, your costs would add up like this: $500 for the option contract, plus $25 commission, plus $5,000 for 100 shares of Rod & Reel at 50, plus approximately $40 commission on that purchase — a total of $5,565 for stock then worth $5,800. So you come out $235 ahead.

Even if you couldn't show a profit on your option deal you might, if you liked the stock, decide to exercise the option anyway and cut your losses. Thus, if you had paid $525 for the right to buy a round lot of Rod & Reel at 50, you might decide to exercise the option when Rod & Reel was selling at 53. Your total cost would, of course, be the same, $5,565. But your stock would be worth only $5,300, resulting in a loss to you of $265. But a loss of $265 is better than a loss of $525, which is what you would be out of pocket if Rod & Reel dropped to 50 or below.

There is nothing new about buying calls. You could have bought a call on any number of popular stocks in the over-the-counter market for many years. Or you might have bought a *put* in the same market. A put is the opposite of a call and gives you the right to sell a stock at a specified price within a given time period on the assumption that the stock named in the contract will decline.

What made trading in options so popular was the establishment in April 1973 of the *Chicago Board Options Exchange* for the sole purpose of providing an organized market for trading in calls. In 1975, the American Stock Exchange also initiated option trading, featuring a different list of Big Board stocks. The Philadelphia and Pacific stock exchanges have since followed suit. The exchanges have been doing a thriving business. Although option trading was restricted originally to calls, trading was extended to puts on all four exchanges in June, 1977.

Meanwhile, in the old over-the-counter market, the old-line options dealers still offer a wide variety of puts and calls on assorted stocks, options of various durations that might expire on any one of the 250 trading days in the stock market year.

On the exchanges, order has been brought out of this chaos. Options are offered there for three-, six-, or nine-month periods — just those and nothing else. Furthermore, options contracts expire on a set date, usually on the Saturday following the third Friday of every month. But there are two different time cycles. Some options operate on a January, April, July, and October cycle. Some terminate in February, May, August, and November.

Hence, there are only eight terminal dates a year when contracts are closed out.

Finally, the prices at which options are offered have been standardized. If a stock sells for under 50, prices are quoted in five-dollar steps. These steps are closely related to the price at which the stock itself is selling. Thus, if Rod & Reel were selling at 30, you might, at any given time, be able to buy or sell Rod & Reel options at 25, 30, 35, and 40. No market would exist for option contracts that were farther away than that from the actual price of Rod & Reel. After all, no one would be interested in buying or selling a contract at 50 or 55 for a stock currently selling at 30, because it would not be realistic to expect such a stock to trade in such a high price range soon. Option contracts on stocks selling from 50 to 200 are quoted in ten-dollar steps, and those above 200 in twenty-dollar steps.

Options on stocks that have rapid price movements, either up or down, usually cost more than contracts on stocks whose price performance is more stable. Typically, on these more stable stocks you might pay 5% or 10% of the market price for an option, while on a real swinging stock, you might expect to pay as much as 15%.

The value of the option as a speculative tool is clearly apparent. Anyone can take a flyer in the option market by risking just a few hundred dollars. He doesn't have nearly as much money tied up in the operation as he would if he traded on margin, even when margin is as low as 40% or 50%. With terminal dates on option contracts often forcing the buyer to take his losses, out-of-pocket costs may be higher for option trading than margin trading. But if there is a significant price advance in the stock, the profit may make this cost look incidental.

The value of using options for protection is not always so clear. But if you had a substantial profit in a stock and you wanted to be sure that that profit was protected against any possible loss for three, six, or nine months, you could buy a put on that stock at the prevailing price. This would guarantee that somebody else would eventually pay you the present price for the stock, no matter how much it had fallen subsequently.

For instance, suppose you had bought 100 shares of Rod & Reel at $20, and the price has risen to $40. You would have a paper profit of $2,000. Now let's assume that this was money you knew you were going to need a few months hence to help pay for your children's tuition at college. You don't want to sell Rod & Reel right then and take your $2,000 profit, because you think there's a good chance that Rod & Reel might run up to $50, maybe even higher. Nevertheless, you can't afford to lose that $2,000 profit you have in hand. To insure yourself against loss, you might buy a six-month put. The cost of the put would depend on the degree of volatility of Rod & Reel, its price at that time, where it was traded, and its previous history.

If the market then took a tumble and Rod & Reel declined to, say, $32, you could exercise your right before the option expired to "put" the stock to the seller of the option and force the seller to accept delivery at $40 a share. You would still be out the cost of the put, not counting commissions, but that's better than being out $800, as you would have been if you hadn't bought the contract. In protecting yourself this way you have achieved the same objective as would a margin trader who sold short against the box.

Of course, if the market rose and Rod & Reel kept going up, perhaps to $47 or $48, you would lose the cost of the put option. But you would be comforted by the $700 or $800 increase in the value of your holdings. In such cases, you might consider the cost of the put a cheap form of insurance.

Instead of buying a put, you could also protect yourself by selling your 100 shares of Rod & Reel at $40 and buying a call on it at $40. If Rod & Reel dropped, the most you could lose would be the cost of the call. But if it continued rising, you would be in exactly the same position as if you still owned the stock, except for the cost of the call.

A speculator who has sold Rod & Reel short could also use options to hedge his position. But he would use them in precisely the reverse fashion. Instead of buying a put to protect himself against a falling market, he would buy a call to protect against a rising market.

Of course, you could accomplish the same objective by placing a stop order to sell with your broker — the short seller would conversely place a stop order to buy — but many people dislike using stop orders to protect a profit because such orders have no elasticity, no "give," to them. For instance, suppose that you had bought Rod & Reel at $20 and it now stands at $40. Being willing to concede some of this twenty-point profit, you place a stop order to sell at $37. Now suppose there was a brisk sell-off in the market on a given day because of some worrisome piece of news and Rod & Reel suddenly dropped to $37. Your stop order would become a market order and you would be sold out immediately. Then, in a few days, when the market had recovered from its temporary shock, Rod & Reel might bound back to $40. But you wouldn't own the stock any longer.

In addition to providing protection against loss, puts and calls can also be effectively used to convert a short-term capital gain into a long-term one, thus effecting a tax saving. Suppose you owned 500 shares of Rod & Reel and there had been a 5-point run-up in its price. You might be quite content to take a $2,500 profit and get out. But if you had owned the stock for anything less than one year, and if you were to sell then, you would have to pay the full tax rate applying to your income bracket on that capital gain. If you could only hold the stock until the one-year mark had passed, your capital gain would be taxed at the much lower long-term rate. But because Rod & Reel might decline in those two months, you wonder if you really should sell then, even if it did mean paying a higher tax rate.

Options offer you a way out. Instead of selling, you buy five three-month puts on the 500 shares of Rod & Reel at $40 and hang on to the shares you own, until the six-month holding period is up. In the interim, if Rod & Reel does indeed decline, you can exercise your puts, the right to sell 500 shares at $40. Your profit will amount to the difference between the price at which you bought the puts and the prices at which they were exercised, less contract costs and commissions. On the other hand, if Rod & Reel advances substantially, your puts will be worthless, but you can satisfy yourself with the increased profit on the stock you own and the fact that you now can pay the gains tax on a long-term rather than a short-term basis.

In any situation where a fair-sized tax saving can be realized by holding stock a little longer than you might otherwise care to, the cost of the option may be considered not very important, in view of the protection it provides and the tax money you can save.

While many individuals buy options on one of the exchanges for trading purposes without exercising their right stipulated in the contract, the bulk of options is sold, or "written," by private individuals or large institutions with substantial capital. Does this mean that these people who sell calls are primarily bearish on the market? Not at all. They are willing to assume the risk they take for several very good reasons: (1) they are well paid for that risk by the premium they receive for the options they write; (2) when they sell an option they have instant use of this money; (3) since they usually own the stock against which they write the option, they collect all dividends on that stock in the interim; and (4) the contracts they write often represent "hedge" insurance against wide price fluctuations in stocks held in their portfolios.

Since an active option writer deals in dozens of different stocks, he can count on the law of averages to absorb a good measure of his risk. Stocks simply do not move in identical price patterns. He will lose on some and win on others. Considering all these factors, the trained and knowledgeable option writer does not carry as large a burden of risk as might appear on the surface. After all, sellers of calls always have that premium working for them. A stock has to advance by more than the amount of the premium before the seller loses any money.

Sometimes a trader will buy both a put and a call simultaneously on the same stock. This is called a *straddle* — a double stock option contract, each for 100 shares and with identical exercise prices. Both options are written at the same price.

The trader's purpose in buying a straddle is usually to try to take advantage of anticipated large fluctuations in the price of the underlying stock, without having to pinpoint either the time or direction of such fluctuations. Thus, a stock might rise sharply in price to a point where it became profitable for him to exercise his call and then drop drastically, enabling him to make a profit on the put.

Options are obviously very volatile, with a high leverage factor — the chance to make a lot of money by placing only a comparatively small amount at stake — while the size of the loss is limited just to the size of the investor's stake.

So popular has option trading become in just a few short years that options on several hundred stocks can now be bought on the exchanges. And they are substantial stocks, because the exchanges where options are traded have set certain requirements that a stock must meet before it becomes eligible for trading:

(1) There must be at least 7,000,000 shares in public hands.

(2) There must be at least 6,000 shareholders of beneficial interest.

(3) Trading volume must have been at least 2,400,000 shares during the previous twelve months.

(4) The price per share must have been at least $10 during the three preceding calendar months. The underlying company must have made after-tax profits of at least $1 million during the preceding eight quarters.

(5) The corporation that issues the stock must also meet certain requirements, quite similar to those that govern the original listing of the stock.

The central market system that the options exchanges have designed for options trading is a microcosm of the central market that the S.E.C. has designed for securities. It includes a consolidated tape for reporting price and volume data, a consolidated quotation system for publicizing the prices at which competing brokers will buy and sell options, and a central clearing system for processing all trades. These and other time- and laborsaving innovations have reduced the many variables formerly associated with options trading to one basic factor: the price of the option.

The computer, too, has been created to estimate an option's value, based on its life span and the degree of risk in the underlying stock. These programs produce a value estimate, which is compared with the price at which the option sells in the marketplace in order to determine if the option is overvalued or undervalued. Additional programs are then employed to establish buying and selling strategies.

The juggling of these various speculative devices — margin trading, short selling, puts, and calls — weighing the risks and the costs of each against the other, makes the business of professional speculation a highly complicated one. This alone can explain why it is probably true that among people who speculate, more lose money than make it.

But an even more important reason lies in the inclination of speculators to act on the basis of a tip or hunch, their unwillingness to study thoroughly all the facts about a company before buying or selling its stock. Bernard M. Baruch, probably America's most successful speculator, made it an inviolable rule never to become involved in a speculative venture until he had mastered all the facts concerning it. As he once explained, successful speculation demands not only courage, persistence, and a judgment unclouded by emotion, but above all it requires an infinite capacity for taking pains — the pains to analyze all the available facts.

CHAPTER 24

How to Tell What the Market Is Doing

WHEN most people buy securities for the first time, they are likely to do so for the wrong reasons. They will buy a stock because they've heard other people, their friends or business associates, talk about it.

It seems to be human nature to believe that the other fellow always knows a good thing, that he has reliable inside information on how a company is doing.

Is there such a thing as *inside information?*

Of course there is.

The officers and directors of a company know more about that firm and its prospects than anybody else could possibly know. And they have relatives and friends with whom they discuss their company's situation. In effect, these people do have what appears to be privileged information — the real "inside." And because they do, the S.E.C. has long kept close watch on the stock-trading operations of company executives and other insiders. The commission wants no recurrence of the pre-1929 situation when many company officials considered the privilege of trading in their company's stock on the basis of inside information simply part of their compensation.

Today, any such insider is required to report to the S.E.C. every purchase or sale he makes of his own company's stock. A list of such transactions is published monthly. An insider is never permitted to sell his own company's stock short. Further, if an insider realizes any profit from buying or selling his company's stock within a six-month period, that profit is recoverable by the company, whether or not it can be demonstrated that inside information was used. And if it can be shown that he masked his transaction in the name of his wife or some other relative or friend, he is just as liable as if he had traded in his own name.

Inside information is, of course, no longer inside when it has been made public. But when can such information be said to have become public? This was the key question in a test case initiated by the S.E.C. in May 1966. The case involved a dozen directors and officials of the Texas Gulf Sulphur Company, which in 1963 discovered valuable deposits of lead, zinc, and copper on its property at Timmins, Ontario. The company acquired adjacent properties and resumed drilling operations in March 1964. On April 16, 1964, Texas Gulf announced its discoveries at a press conference.

The S.E.C. in its suit alleged that various officials profited from their inside knowledge by buying stock in the company before the ore discoveries became public knowledge. It even went so far as to charge one director with a violation, although his purchase of 3,000 shares was not made until an hour after news services in virtually every major bank and brokerage office in the country reported it. This particular charge was dismissed when the first verdict was returned in a federal district court, and all but two of the defendants were exonerated. But American industry was put on notice that the S.E.C. intended to be more vigilant than ever in supervising transactions by company officials and other insiders.

If there was any need for emphasis, the S.E.C. underlined its point in September 1968 when it brought an action against Merrill Lynch, Pierce, Fenner & Smith, charging that the firm had permitted a dozen of its large institutional customers to benefit from inside information that it had obtained in the course of working on a proposed underwriting for the Douglas Aircraft

Company. Specifically, the firm was charged with passing along a report that Douglas earnings for the first six months of 1966 were going to be sharply lower than those reported just a little earlier for the first five months. On the basis of that information it was alleged that a dozen of Merrill Lynch's institutional customers had gone short a total of 190,000 shares of Douglas stock a day or two before Douglas's first-half earnings forecast was made public. Because the firm felt that there would be little profit to it in helping the S.E.C. define more precisely what did and didn't constitute inside information, it accepted the S.E.C.'s minimal penalties and did not contest the action. But some of its institutional customers who were also charged with violating the anti-fraud provisions of the Securities Exchange Act of 1934 persisted in fighting the case. All but one — the Dreyfus Fund — were convicted.

In 1974, a case was brought before a United States Court of Appeals that involved a dispute about whether a brokerage firm could function as investment banker for a company, while operating simultaneously as broker-dealer in that company's securities, without running afoul of insider trading regulations.

Shearson Hammill & Co., a large stock exchange member firm involved in the case, contended that it maintained a "Chinese Wall" between its retail sales and investment banking departments. The plaintiffs asserted that, wall or no wall, the firm's investment department transmitted to its sales force on at least four occasions bullish information about Tidal Marine Co., despite the fact that it also had bearish information about the company that was *not* released to salesmen or the public. However, Shearson maintained that its investment department did not possess this bearish information until several weeks after the plaintiffs had concluded their purchases of Tidal Marine.

Regardless of the ultimate outcome of the *Shearson "Chinese Wall" Case*, as it has come to be called, Wall Street houses then took strenuous steps to sever all lines of communication between their investment banking departments and their retail salesmen.

They were hoping thereby to avoid any charge of violating the S.E.C.'s rules on insider trading. However, the S.E.C. rather tartly suggested that a better way to avoid such problems would be for firms to prohibit their salesmen from recommending the securities of any of the companies with which that firm had an underwriting relationship.

On the basis of these cases, you may rightfully assume that there is, indeed, such a thing as inside information about a company. But you should also realize that the really important inside information is usually so closely guarded that neither you nor any other investor is likely to hear it until it becomes generally available to all investors.

All publicly owned companies are obligated to reveal promptly to the public any and all information that may influence the price of their stock or any investment decision about it. The news, whether favorable or unfavorable, must be disseminated. The stock exchanges maintain strict and detailed policies about disclosure, particularly anything that might be considered inside information. Leaks of reliable information are rare indeed, and that's why anyone who invests his money on what he believes to be an inside tip is apt to be seriously misled.

How, then, should a person set about investing?

If he doesn't know anything at all about the market or the stocks of various companies, where can he turn for information?

Probably the first and most obvious answer to that is the newspaper — one of the big metropolitan daily newspapers that carry complete stock market quotations and comprehensive coverage of financial news, or one of the regional editions of *The Wall Street Journal*.

If an investor is not already familiar with the *stock tables*, probably his first step should be to study them regularly for a period of time. If he reads a morning paper, he will find the stocks traded during the preceding day on the various exchanges listed in alphabetical order under those exchanges' individual headings. The late edition of the evening paper provides similar information for the stocks traded during that day.

In their *consolidated stock tables,* some papers provide much more complete information than others. But if our Rod & Reel were sold on an exchange, or over-the-counter, and if your paper published complete consolidated stock tables, an entry for one day, with the appropriate column heads, might look like this:

Year to Date		Stock &	P-E	Sales				Net
High	Low	Dividend	Ratio	in 100s	High	Low	Close	Change
42½	38¾	Rod & Reel 2	12	17	40¼	39⅝	40¼	+¾

The column headings make much of the information self-explanatory. Obviously, the stock has been traded in a fairly narrow range, having fluctuated only between a low of 38¾ and a high of 42½ all year. A comparison of this price range with the range recorded by other stocks will give you some general idea of whether Rod & Reel might be classified as an investor-type stock or a speculation stock. As a very rough rule of thumb, the greater the price fluctuation, the lower the investment caliber of the stock.

The dividend figure immediately following the name of the stock gives you another clue to the quality of the stock. With an annual dividend rate of $2 and a current price of $40, Rod & Reel is yielding exactly 5%. Very often after the dividend figure there will appear a small letter, which will refer to a footnote. These footnotes can be very important, because they may indicate that the dividend figure includes extra dividends, or that this was the dividend paid last year, or that it represents only the total paid so far this year for a stock not on a regular dividend basis, or any of a number of other dividend payout variations.

The *P-E ratio — price-earnings ratio —* of the stock is computed by dividing the market price by its indicated or actual earnings per share. Thus, if Rod & Reel sells at 40¼ with estimated earnings of $3.50 per share, it has a price-earnings ratio of

11.5 ($40.25 divided by $3.50). This would be rounded out to 12 for reporting purposes.

The figure for the number of shares traded simply shows how Rod & Reel stacks up that day alongside other stocks as far as market interest is concerned. Sales volume of a stock in which there is considerable speculative interest will very often exceed that of some of the better-grade market leaders.

The high, low, and close figures give you a bird's-eye picture of how Rod & Reel moved during the trading day. On any given day, the pattern of price movement will not be the same for all stocks. But this profile of Rod & Reel will show you whether its market performance is generally in line with that of other stocks and of the market as a whole. If Rod & Reel closed at its high for the day, as it did, and if the market as a whole had declined that day, you could conclude that because Rod & Reel ran counter to the downward trend of the general market the stock had demonstrated strength.

On the consolidated tape, which covers all markets, the volume figures and closing prices published in the newspaper are those that prevailed at 5:30 P.M., E.S.T. That is when trading terminates on the West Coast market, one and a half hours after the Big Board shuts down.

The *net change* figure (+¾) shows the difference between the closing price that day (40¼) and the closing price the *preceding day* (which thus had to be 39½).

Occasionally you may notice that the price of a stock is down from the preceding day, but the net change figure doesn't show a corresponding drop. That's because the stock is being sold *ex-dividend.*

Suppose Rod & Reel pays its quarterly dividend of 50¢ to stockholders who are on its books as of the close of business on Friday, September 15. Beginning the previous Monday, September 11, and running through Friday, the stock will be worth 50¢ less, because anyone who buys it during that period will not be eligible for the dividend. This is because five business days are allowed to make delivery of stock on a sell order, and only those people who own the stock as of the close of the markets on Friday, September 8, will be on the company's records on Friday, September 15. On any day on which a stock is sold ex-dividend (in this case Monday, September 11), its price is expected to decline by the amount of the dividend. If that is exactly what happens, the net change figure will show no gain or loss. Sometimes, however, a stock may show outstanding strength and "make up" the amount of the dividend, thus, in this case, closing with a net change of $+\frac{1}{2}$, even though the price is exactly what it was before the stock went ex-dividend.

This five-day interval is also important when a stock goes *ex-rights*. Thus, a company with a new issue of additional stock might announce that stockholders as of Friday, September 15, would have the right to buy new stock in proportion to their present holdings at a price somewhat below the market. But obviously only those people who bought the stock on or before Friday, September 8, would appear on the company's records five business days or one week later. Anybody who bought the stock after that date wouldn't get the rights. When a stock goes ex-rights, it usually sells at a price that is lower by an amount roughly equal to the value of the rights. During the time when the rights can be exercised, they are bought and sold separately and often quoted separately in the stock tables. They fluctuate up or down, generally reflecting strength or weakness in the parent stock.

Obviously, it would be a mistake to draw any positive conclusions about a stock on the basis of one day's trading pattern. But if you watch a stock over a period of time and compare it closely with a dozen or so others, particularly with those in the same field, you will begin to get an idea of how that stock is regarded by the thousands of people whose daily transactions make the market.

Not all newspapers publish anything like complete quotations of Big Board stocks. Nor do many of them use the tables compiled from the consolidated tape. Some of them continue to cover just the transactions on the New York Stock Exchange, ignoring what might have taken place in the over-the-counter market or on regional exchanges and what might have happened to prices on the Pacific Coast after the Big Board closed. In smaller cities, the daily newspapers may list only 100 or so stocks with no details except the closing price and the net change from the preceding day. In big cities, the former practice of publishing the bid-and-asked quotations on listed stocks that did not trade during the day has been abandoned.

The American Stock Exchange stocks don't get nearly as much play in the papers as those of the Big Board, and stocks listed on the regional exchanges are likely to get press notice only in the areas where the parent companies operate and where there is some public interest in their stocks. Much the same standard determines how many unlisted stocks are quoted daily from the national and regional lists supplied by the National Association of Securities Dealers through NASDAQ. Big city newspapers usually publish the full N.A.S.D. national list.

Prices reported in the newspapers for bonds are apt to be a little confusing. Although bonds are usually sold in thousand-dollar units, their prices are quoted as though they had a hundred-dollar denomination. Thus, a quotation of 98 would indicate an actual price of $980. One of $98\frac{3}{4}$ would be $983.75.

Since government bonds sold on the open market are traded not in eighths or quarters but in thirty-seconds, a special price-reporting formula has been developed for them. For example, a printed quotation of 99.16 actually means a price of $995. Here's how you arrive at that: the point in the quote isn't a decimal point; it is only a device for separating the round figure from the fraction. Hence the quotation really stands for $99\frac{16}{32}$, or $99\frac{1}{2}$, or $995. Sometimes Treasuries are sold on a price change of just $\frac{1}{64}$ rather than $\frac{1}{32}$. If a plus sign appears after the published quotation for a government bond, this means that $\frac{1}{64}$ should be added to the published price.

Almost every daily paper publishes, in addition to prices on individual security issues, some report on the average movement of New York Stock Exchange prices.

There are a number of these *averages* that are supposed to serve as barometers of the business. The best known of them is the *Dow Jones average.*

Actually, the Dow Jones average isn't one average but four — one for industrial stocks, one for transportation stocks, one for utilities, and a composite one that reflects the status of the other three. These averages are computed constantly and are instantaneously available on desk-model quotation machines. They are officially announced by Dow Jones at half-hour intervals throughout the trading day.

The utility index is an average of prices for fifteen utilities; the transportation index covers twenty railroads, airlines, and trucking companies; the industrial average is based on the stocks of 30 leading manufacturers and distributors. The composite index includes all 65.

Over the years, these averages (which date back to 1897, except for the utilities index, which was first computed in 1929) have come to be accepted as the Bible of the business. This is partly because Dow Jones & Company, Inc., which originated them, publishes the country's leading financial newspaper, the *Wall Street Journal.* It also operates the ticker news service, known as the *broad tape,* which can be found in virtually every major bank and brokerage office, often projected on a large electronic screen.

But in recent years the suspicion has grown that this Bible is not divinely inspired, that the Dow Jones averages are not an infallible measure of the market. This criticism has been aimed especially at the Dow Jones industrial average, the most important indicator of them all, and is based on two counts.

In the first place, it is argued that the 30 stocks that make up the Dow Jones industrial average are not truly representative of all the industrials listed on the Big Board. Too many of them classify as "blue chips" — stocks such as General Motors, Exxon, du Pont, Procter & Gamble, American Can, Eastman Kodak, General Electric, General Foods, U.S. Steel, and Sears, Roebuck. Moreover, one of its components, American Telephone, is really a utility and not an industrial stock at all.

In the second place, over the years many of these stocks have been split several times, and with each split the price of the stock has dropped proportionately. Thus, if the split were two for one, the price of the stock could be expected to decline about 50%. On a four-for-one split it would decline about 75%.

In order to correct these occasional distortions and to maintain the continuity of the averages, Dow Jones introduced a new system of computation in 1928. Instead of dividing the total of the daily closing prices of stocks used in each average by the number of stocks in the average, the revised system is based upon an artificial divisor, which remains unchanged until a stock is split, its price is reduced substantially by a stock dividend, or another stock is substituted. When any of these changes occur, Dow Jones computes a new divisor, which is intended to compensate for the change.

The inadequacy of the system, its lack of mathematical precision, is evident from the fact that it is possible for the Dow Jones industrial average to go up while the aggregate value of all the stocks that comprise the average goes down. For instance, on one particular day the Dow Jones average showed an increase of about ½ of 1%. But on that same day the actual value of all the shares of the 30 companies in the average dropped from $26.5 to $25.5 billion. The apparent gain in the average was accounted for by a rise in the price of a comparatively few stocks that didn't have nearly as many shares outstanding as those companies whose stocks declined.

In recent years, the premier position of the Dow Jones industrial average has been seriously challenged by the 500-stock index of Standard & Poor Corporation, the nation's largest securities research organization. For many years, Standard & Poor had published other indexes — a 90-stock daily index and a 480-stock weekly index — but it wasn't until 1957, when high-speed computers made more comprehensive indexes possible on an hourly basis, that Standard & Poor decided to lock horns decisively with Dow Jones.

Its 500-stock index, covering stocks that account for 86% of the total value of all Big Board stocks, is unquestionably a more scientifically constructed index than the Dow, and provides a much more accurate picture of what is happening in the market. This is true because the Standard & Poor index is computed by multiplying the price of each stock in it by the number of shares outstanding, thus giving proper weight to the bigger and more influential companies like A.T.&T. and General Motors — and IBM, which isn't even included in the Dow Jones average.

Despite the fact that the Dow Jones industrial average has statistical shortcomings and the Standard & Poor 500-stock index is definitely more scientific, the two indexes do move together with surprisingly little disparity. It is unusual when one ends up showing a plus and the other a minus. This happens only on days when the market has had no clear-cut movement in either direction. On major swings, they move pretty much together, although one or the other may boast that its index gave the first indication of such a move. On balance, the Dow Jones is apt to be more sensitive to short-term movements, while the 500-stock index provides a more reliable long-term perspective.

Although Standard & Poor is proud that its index is used by the Federal Reserve Board and the Department of Commerce, as well as many other federal officials and business economists, Dow Jones — by virtue of its age and its popularity with financial editors of press, radio, and TV — continues to have an iron-bound grip on the public mind, particularly that public that frequents brokerage offices.

There is one significant difference between the two indexes, and that lies in the magnitude of the numbers they use. When the Dow Jones industrial stands at 975, the 500-stock index stands at about 100, and that relationship holds pretty true right up and down the line. The Dow figure is about ten times greater than Standard & Poor's. This results from the calculated effort by Standard & Poor to devise an index figure more nearly comparable to the average dollar price of all stocks traded on the New York Stock Exchange than the inflated Dow figures are.

For years the New York Stock Exchange attempted to persuade Dow Jones to divide its index by 10 or devise another formula that would yield an index figure only a fraction of the present level. But Dow Jones, which regards its averages as sacrosanct, despite the many changes brought about by substituting one company for another over the years, has turned a deaf ear to all such suggestions.

The reason why the exchange would like to see the Dow Jones average fractioned is perfectly obvious. The exchange worries about the effect on the public of front-page headlines proclaiming that the stock market dropped 25 points, as it has often done in a single day. It isn't much happier when the headlines say that the market went up 25 points. The big figures, up or down, give the public an incorrect impression of the volatility of the market.

No matter how you attempt to explain the situation, people will go on confusing Dow Jones points with actual dollars, despite the fact there is no relationship between the two. On a day when the Dow might move 15 points — say from 900 to 915 — the aggregate dollar value of all stocks listed on the exchange would increase only about 2%.

Dissatisfaction with the Dow Jones average was certainly one of the key reasons why the New York Stock Exchange decided in 1966 to begin publishing its own official composite index, as well as four group indexes: industrial, transportation, utility, and financial. The composite index covers all 1,532 common stocks on the exchange, and is computed continuously and publicly announced on the exchange ticker every half hour. No one was surprised to learn that the computation process used in this "official" index yielded a figure close to the $50 average price of all shares then on the exchange. To be sure that the exchange is never embarrassed by its own index, it plans to keep the index in line either by splitting it or by changing the base period whenever necessary.

Another new index made its debut in 1966: the first index of American Stock Exchange securities. But this so-called Price Change Index was replaced in 1973 by the index currently in use — Market Value Index, which aligns the American Stock Exchange more closely with other market value indicators in the industry. The NASDAQ Composite Index was introduced on February 5, 1971.

CHAPTER 25

How to Read the Financial News

ONCE a person starts following stock prices and averages, it isn't long before he or she begins reading the rest of the *financial section* of the newspaper.

Here, obviously, will be found much important information both about business in general and about individual companies — their plans for expansion, their new products, their sales and earnings records. Some of these news stories dealing with individual companies may be a little on the optimistic side, since they are often based on publicity releases furnished by the companies themselves. But every responsible newspaper today makes an effort to be as objective as possible in the handling of financial news.

A standard feature of the financial section of every big-city newspaper is the daily column in which the action of the stock market is reported and often analyzed in terms of various technical factors — the primary trend, the secondary movement, resistance levels, and so on.

While there are *technical factors* in the market that may indicate its direction over short periods of time — the volume of short sales, the ratio of odd-lot transactions to round lots, whether odd-lot customers buy or sell on balance, the number of stocks hitting new highs and the number falling to new lows, et cetera — these are factors that are apt to be of far greater importance to the professional trader or speculator than to the average investor. This is especially true for the newcomer, who may be understandably confused by references to the "double top" or "head and shoulders," chart configurations so dear to the hearts of point-and-figure and bar-and-line technicians.

Nevertheless, all market columns can make interesting reading after one gets used to the jargon. Soon even the neophyte finds himself acquiring some familiarity with such phrases as *"technically strong"* or *"technically weak,"* the "short interest" and the *"Dow Theory."*

The phrases technically strong and technically weak have fairly precise meanings. Suppose stock prices have been moving more or less steadily upward over a long period of time. Inevitably, in such a bull market movement, there are price advances and price reactions, ups and downs in the market. If the volume of sales is heavy when stocks go up and light when they go down during such a bull movement, the market can be described as technically strong. Conversely, if volume is heavy on the down side and light on the rallies, the market is technically weak. This interpretation is based on the theory that the amount of volume usually identifies the dominant trend.

The term short interest refers, of course, to the total number of shares of Big Board stocks that all sellers are short — shares they have sold but must buy back at some future date to cover their positions. Many stock market commentators are fascinated by the short interest figures and take them to be a primary index of the technical strength or weakness of the market. Its fluctuations, often very sharp, are interpreted by many technicians to be bullish or bearish signals. But it is worth remembering that even when the short interest rose to a record high above 89,000,000 shares in December 1981, that figure still represented less than 1% of all shares listed on the Big Board. You might well ask if so small a tail can really wag so big a dog. On the other hand, it's the big operators who account for the short selling, and they are the people who are supposed to be most knowledgeable about the market.

The Dow Theory is at once the most celebrated, complicated, and least understood interpretation of market action. This is probably because neither Charles Dow, who founded Dow Jones & Company, nor any of his various disciples has ever adequately defined the theory.

In essence, the Dow theorists hold that three movements of the Dow Jones averages are simultaneously under way at any given time. There is the primary movement — broad upward or downward trends which may last for several years (the great bull or bear markets). There is the secondary movement — a significant decline in a primary bull market, or a strong recovery in a primary bear market, generally lasting from three weeks to three months. Finally, there is the tertiary movement — day-to-day price fluctuations, which are usually relatively unimportant.

The crux of the theory is that reliable conclusions cannot be drawn about the trend of the stock market until it has been ascertained that the industrial average, consisting of 30 stocks, and the transportation average, consisting of twenty stocks (known as the "rail average" until January 1970, when nine airline and trucking company stocks were substituted for nine railroad issues), are moving upward or downward "in gear." When that happens, the averages are said to be "confirming" one another in whatever direction they are headed.

Forecasts based on the movement of one average, if unconfirmed by the other, are generally wrong — according to the theorists. When successive rallies by both averages exceed previous high levels, and when ensuing declines hold above preceding low levels, the inference is bullish. The averages are then said to be charting a pattern of "higher highs." Conversely, when rallies fail to carry above the old highs and subsequent declines penetrate the previous lows, the implication is bearish — a pattern of "lower lows."

Dow theorists contend that by their somewhat occult formula they have been able to forecast almost every significant movement in the market for many years. Other analysts, looking at the same set of facts, dispute the Dow Theory's record. They say it can be made to look good only when the forecasting has become history. Nevertheless, many financial editors continue to expound the Dow Theory, and various Dow disciples appear in the advertising columns from time to time, offering letter services to explain the market action in terms of their interpretation of the Dow Theory and the Dow averages.

Very often in reading the newspaper the new investor will encounter what appears to be a striking contradiction between the news and the market reaction to that news. For example, a company may announce some good news, such as an increase in its dividend — and its stock drops in price. A prime example of this occurred on January 10, 1962, when Ford Motor stock opened at 1½ points lower and then closed down 4 points on the day, after a two-for-one split and an increase in the dividend were declared — announcements one would expect might have given the stock a sizable boost. Again, news may break that Congress expects to enact a new tax bill lightening the tax burden on business — and that day stocks sell off right across the board.

There is one simple explanation for these paradoxes. The stock market has "discounted" the news before it happened. The big traders, the people supposedly in the know, were sure that a dividend increase was coming at Ford, because profits had been increasing spectacularly. As for the tax legislation favorable to business, these same big traders would have been surprised if Congress hadn't moved to enact it. They had already bought or sold the stock affected by this news in expectation of such developments. When the actual news broke and attracted public interest in the market, the professionals seized their opportunity to realize profits — to sell while others were buying on the basis of the newly published news.

Some people consider the market an infallible barometer of

general business. They say that you can tell what's going to happen to business in the near future by the way the stock market acts over a period of time. Even government economists classify stock market action as a key economic indicator.

Actually, the stock market is far from being an infallible business barometer. Consider just a few of the most glaring exceptions.

For instance, business conditions began to look a little less than rosy in the late spring of 1929. But it was not until late October of that year that the market hit the big slide, with some popular stocks slumping 100 points or more in four successive trading sessions.

More recently the stock market has performed very little better as a guide to our economic health. Since the end of World War II, it has missed the boat on several important turns in business.

Thus, in 1945, business was retarded by the necessity of reconverting from war to peace. But the stock market generally continued its upward course until mid-1946. Then it declined 21% in five months when business had already begun to improve. The economy continued steadily on the upgrade for several years. But the market didn't catch up with this postwar boom until early 1949.

The market did turn down before general business in late 1948, early 1953, and mid-1957. But it gave an utterly fallacious signal in the first six months of 1962, when stocks sold off 25% while business generally continued to boom merrily along, unperturbed by the Wall Street Cassandras. Again, in 1966, the market missed the boat. It declined 25% from February to October while business continued on its steady course with only an insignificant drop of 2% in production. The slow but generally steady growth of American business during the 1972–1982 period has been reflected in the Dow-Jones average, which has fluctuated in the 800–1,000 range. However, like the perennial question "Which comes first, the chicken or the egg?" the question of whether the stock market leads business or business leads the stock market is one that probably can never have an unequivocal answer.

But if the stock market doesn't faithfully anticipate business, it must sooner or later fall into step with the basic business trends, because in the end stock values are determined by our economic health. That's why the investor is well advised to keep an eye on some of the more basic indexes of business — such as the Federal Reserve index of industrial production and various statistics tabulating employment, steel output, electric power production, construction, carloadings, retail sales, unfilled orders and prices, as well as data on credit, bank deposits, and interest rates. These statistics will tell how much America is producing, how rapidly this output is moving into the channels of distribution, what kind of consumer demand there is for it, and the availability and cost of money and credit. In the long run, these are the vital factors that will determine the real values of the stock that you own in any company — how much the company is likely to earn and what kind of dividend it can pay.

But how is the individual investor to keep apprised of all the financial news that affects the economy in general and his specific stock investments in particular? The answer is by reading one or a number of the various newspapers and magazines that specialize in economic journalism, reporting in depth on all the news that might affect the outcome of any individual investment.

The following are the most widely read general business/investment periodicals. They are the most useful sources of clear, concise economic reporting for any investor — beginner or expert.

Daily

The Wall Street Journal: every business day the *"Journal"* contains more market tables, more company news, more indications of industry and economic trends, and more analysis of current market conditions and future market directions than any other periodical published anywhere. It is also justly renowned for the scope and quality of its general reportage. Many journalists consider the *Journal* not only an indispensable tool for all investors and businessmen, but also one of the best daily newspapers of any kind in America. Truly the Bible of the investment community.

The New York Times: for those investors who have neither the time nor the patience to wade through the 40-plus pages of economic news and analysis *The Wall Street Journal* produces every business day, the good gray *Times* provides a more modest serving from the same basic menu. In the late seventies the *Times* began devoting an entire ten-to-twelve-page section of the paper to business news Monday through Friday, augmenting its justly renowned Sunday business section. Now Section D, known as "Business Day," presents the most comprehensive array of market quotes, economic news, and investment analysis this side of *The Wall Street Journal*. It is surely as much information as the average investor needs to keep abreast of current developments. And it is far and away the best economic/investment coverage provided by any daily newspaper in America today.

Weekly

Barrons National Business & Financial Weekly: put out by the Dow Jones Company, which also publishes *The Wall Street Journal, Barrons* is a weekly tabloid that contains an encyclopedically comprehensive history of the week's transactions in a wide variety of financial markets, including a range of minute details even the *Journal* does not bother to record. *Barrons* also contains numerous feature articles, the iconoclastic commentary of its acerbic editor Alan Abelson in his front-page "Up and Down Wall Street" column, weekly chronicles of the various doings in the real estate, commodities, and options markets, hard-hitting profiles of specific companies, and the largest imaginable selection of advertising for concerns offering assorted investment expertise.

Business Week looks like *Time* and *Newsweek;* it delivers its weekly amalgam of "hard" economic news features and soft investment analysis in much the same sort of slick, pithy fashion. *B.W.* is not specifically aimed at investors, although it does have a very valuable weekly-performance financial section. It is meant to be more of a digest of national and international business and economic developments aimed at the average businessman and the marginally sophisticated layman. But the implications many of its stories have for every investor are obvious. As a readable and comprehensive source of general business news it is without peer.

World Business Weekly: published by the *Financial Times* of London, *W.B.W.* is a global version of *Business Week.* Done up in a similarly slick format, it reports on international economic developments as well as specific foreign investment opportunities. With the world growing smaller every day and national business enterprises becoming increasingly dependent on international financial opportunities, even the casual investor can't afford to ignore the implications of the kinds of story *World Business Week* presents so clearly and concisely.

Twice Monthly

Forbes is the most comprehensive of the general magazines for the moderately sophisticated investor. It covers all the markets and the men who make them. Its specialty is the short, punchy profile of changing companies and the dispassionate look at new investment gimmicks. *Forbes's* stable of in-house columnists — Ben Weberman, Heinz H. Biel, John Train, Stanley Angrist, Srully Blotnick, and David Dreman — is among the most realistic in the business. The magazine is well edited and entertainingly written.

Financial World: a smaller version of *Forbes, F.W.'s* scope is less comprehensive than its crosstown New York rival, but its stories tend to treat their subjects in greater depth, complete with detailed explanations of their implications for the slightly less sophisticated investor.

Monthly

Dun's Monthly: until 1981 *Dun's* was almost a carbon copy of *Financial World*, with very much the same format, style, and editorial concerns. Late that year, however, the editors transformed the magazine from a semimonthly to a monthly, in the process adjusting both its substance and its personality to reflect its new twelve-issue-a-year schedule. Now *Dun's* looks like a cross between *Forbes* and *F.W.*, as it attempts to cut out a niche for itself in the investment journalism marketplace by combining the best features of both those exceptional magazines.

Fortune is the most prestigious of the general business magazines. Famous as the arbiter of bigness in American commerce with its renowned "Fortune 500" listings, a comprehensive ranking of the largest companies in the country, *Fortune* tends to take the long view of things, with massive in-depth looks at significant economic issues and business developments. Its coverage of personal investment decisions is minimal. But the weight of its opinions and the implication of its researches are things any investor ignores at his peril.

Money: published by Time, Inc., *Fortune's* parent company, *Money* is the financial journalism success story of the eighties. It tailors its editorial policies to deal with the complete financial/ investment needs of the average middle-class American family — from stock selection advice to tax shelter, vacation home buying, and franchised business investing tips. *Money* differs from the other general-interest investment magazines in that it concentrates as much on the changing needs of the individual who makes the investments as it does on the specific characteristics of the vehicle he or she is investing in. In doing so it has scored by far the greatest increase in readership among investment magazines during the past decade.

Changing Times: traditionally less an investment magazine than an editorial advisory service geared to the consumer needs of the average American, *Changing Times* has found itself writing more about municipal bonds and less about can openers of late as the investment awareness of the common man increases dramatically. It has adopted these new duties with its traditional thoroughness and dispassion.

Television

"Wall Street Week" (Friday, 8:30 P.M., PBS): nowhere is the increasing hunger of Middle America for a broad range of investment information more apparent than in the investment-advice community's increasing presence on the nation's television screens. "Wall Street Week" is the granddaddy of all televised investment roundups. Every Friday night on Public Broadcasting channels across the country, host Louis Rukeyser spends a half-hour summarizing the week's general economic news and specific investment happenings, drilling his assorted panelists on their interpretation of the current scene, and interviewing one guest expert on his or her assessment of stocks, bonds, or any of a wealth of other investment vehicles. It's a one-stop video quick fix on the current market picture, which has deservedly become one of public television's most popular weekly fixtures.

"The Business Report" (daily, 6:30 P.M., PBS): the latest entry into the economic video marketplace, this Miami-based, three-anchor-person broadcast looks just like the other three networks' seven o'clock news, except that it concentrates exclusively on business and investment topics. Attempting to be a sort of abbreviated television version of *The Wall Street Journal,* "The Business Report" delivers a nightly roundup of the day's financial activities and market results to its growing audience of viewers, both veteran and beginning investors alike.

All of these publications and shows are extremely useful resources of detailed economic and investment information. But in the final analysis, they leave the investor to work out his own destiny by himself. They give him basic information, but they can't tell him precisely what he should do about it.

CHAPTER 26

Financial Advice—at a Price

DO you want more specific help with your investment problems: information, advice, recommendations?

You can get it — at a price. Whether it's worth the price you pay is something else again.

Maybe you want something more than advice. Maybe you don't want to worry about your investment problems at all. If that's the case — and if you have at least $100,000 to invest, preferably a good deal more — you can turn your entire investment problem over to an *investment counselor.* His sole business is guiding the investment destiny of his clients — making all the buying and selling decisions for them, and seeing that they are properly executed by a brokerage firm. In New York City alone there are hundreds of these counseling firms. They spend their full time investing other people's money — for a sizable fee, of course. This fee is tax-deductible. There are many other such firms in all the other major cities, from coast to coast.

In the main, these investment counselors do a sound job for their clients, which include many institutions. But their services are obviously beyond the reach of the average investor.

Many big-city banks will be glad to take your investment problems off your hands. But again, they will do this only at a price that most investors can't afford. One service such banks offer is the *investment advisory account,* for which they charge an annual management fee, usually ½ of 1%. That may not sound like much. But the minimum annual fee is at least $500, often much more. So again, unless you have at least $100,000 to invest, or unless some unusual circumstance, such as a long-term absence from the country, justifies payment of the bank's supervision fee, such a service may not be for you.

Under another type of bank service the depositor agrees to let the bank withdraw a fixed amount of money from his checking account each month to buy shares or fractional shares of stock in a company, or companies, selected from a list prepared by the bank. The bank then combines the funds allocated by all its customers for specific stocks and makes bulk purchases, thus saving a good deal on commission costs.

Apart from investment counselors and banks, where else might the average investor turn for help?

The answer is that there are dozens and dozens of *investment advisory services*, all of them only too willing to help, regardless of how competent they are. They offer the investor a bewildering array of publications and services. Some are simply compilations of statistical information. Some undertake to review business conditions as they affect the investment outlook. Some provide recommendations about hundreds of different securities — what to buy, what to sell, what to hold.

Some are perennially bearish, but the majority are usually bullish. Some, believing that good investment advice can't be turned out on a mass-production basis, undertake to provide a kind of tailor-made service. They offer to answer specific investor inquiries and to permit occasional consultation with their experts. Some even offer a reasonably well-rounded counseling service at a negotiated fee to the smaller investor, perhaps the man with only $25,000 to invest.

Some of the financial advisory organizations sell many of these different kinds of services. Others offer only one kind.

Most controversial of all are those services that undertake to give advice about the general "market," usually in a weekly letter sold on a subscription basis. Many of these publications offer the subscriber their own rating service, covering hundreds of different stocks. These publications tell the subscriber whether to buy or sell, and most of them maintain *supervised lists* of those investments that they consider particularly attractive. In effect, these supervised lists represent model investment programs.

Many of these services are more concerned with the short-term outlook — what the market is likely to do in the next couple of months — than they are with the problem of long-term investment. A few of them even limit themselves exclusively to a discussion of technical factors affecting the market.

Regardless of their different approaches to the investment problem, these services generally share one common characteristic: they will tell you how successful they've been in calling the turns in past markets and in recommending good buys and good sells at just the strategic moment.

The S.E.C. has the authority to compel investment advisers to conform with strict and detailed standards of advertising. Failure to meet these standards is considered fraudulent conduct in violation of the antifraud provisions of the *Investment Advisers Act of 1940*. But there are those who feel this is an area in which the S.E.C. has not yet done the policing job it might.

In trying to bring these services to heel, the commission has been admittedly handicapped by not having an industry organization like the New York Stock Exchange with which to share the regulatory responsibility. It has tried to induce the advisory services to form some kind of an organization, but the services, realizing how much easier it would then be for the S.E.C. to bring pressure to bear on them, have turned a deaf ear. Then too, such highly ethical and responsible organizations as Standard & Poor's and Moody's Investors Service have an understandable reluctance to be associated, on any basis whatsoever, with the obvious quacks in the business.

In the absence of an industry organization that could pursue a program of self-regulation, the S.E.C. has accomplished most of its housecleaning job on a piecemeal basis by bringing legal action against palpable offenders. This course has been time-consuming and expensive. But the commission has won some landmark decisions in the courts and has brought a number of the services sharply to heel.

The first and most important action was that brought against the Capital Gains Research Bureau. The S.E.C. charged that officers of this advisory service were guilty of price manipulation by buying stock, touting it in their service, then selling out when the price advanced. The U.S. Supreme Court held that such *scalping* practices were a "fraud and deceit upon any client or prospective client." It said that the S.E.C. could enforce compliance with the Investment Advisers Act by obtaining an injunction to halt such practices.

Under this act, designed "to protect the public and investors against malpractices by persons paid for advising others about securities," all investment advisers who receive compensation in any form for their service must register with the S.E.C. They must state the name and form of the organization, names and addresses of the principal officers, their education and business affiliations for the past ten years, the exact nature of the business, the form of compensation for their services, et cetera.

In addition, the services must keep accounts, correspondence, memorandums, papers, books, and other records and furnish copies of them to their clients or to the S.E.C. at any time upon request. Banks, lawyers, accountants, engineers, teachers, newspapers, and magazines are exempt from this registration — an exemption not entirely saitsfactory to the S.E.C.

Brokers are also exempt, as their advisory service is presumed to be incidental to their execution of orders, for which they receive only commissions. However, brokers who perform an advisory service for which they are paid by clients are not exempt.

It is the S.E.C.'s responsibility to see that there is no conflict of interest in the service that investment advisers offer the public. In other words, an adviser cannot offer advice about a stock if there is any possibility of his making money from what he reports, unless he reveals that this is the case.

Significantly, it is *not* the S.E.C.'s responsibility under the Investment Advisers Act to guarantee the competence of any adviser or the quality of his service. Of course, the original Securities Exchange Act does prohibit "any person" from distributing information that is false or misleading. But it's not as easy for the S.E.C. to prove a case against an investment adviser under this board but somewhat nebulous grant of power as it is to establish a case of fraud or deceit.

The S.E.C. has proposed legislation that would increase sharply its authority over investment advisers and make them subject to the types of professional and responsibility standard that apply to brokers and dealers.

The S.E.C. has been so shorthanded, and the field it must supervise has become so vast, that many publishers of market letters have been plying their trade with little interference from regulatory authorities. However, in 1972 the S.E.C. established an Advisory Committee on Enforcement Policy and Practices, which recommended that the S.E.C. double the size of its staff. The S.E.C. accordingly was granted about $45 million more in 1975 in order to augment its staff by some 385 people in the succeeding three years.

How good is the advice that investment services provide?

There's no answer to that, because there is no way accurately to compute and compare all their batting averages. Some make flat-footed recommendations. Others hedge their suggestions with all kinds of qualification. However, one stock market analyst who did keep check on sixteen services for a period of years found that if an investor had followed all their 7,500 different recommendations during that period, he would have ended up just 1.43% worse than the market averages.

Here are some of the most reputable companies whose investment services are in no way to be compared to the many market letters with their "get-rich-quick" recommendations.

Companies Rendering a Comprehensive Research and Advisory Service

The biggest firms in the financial research business are Standard & Poor Corporation, 25 Broadway, New York, NY 10004, and Moody's Investors Service, 99 Church Street, New York, NY 10007.

Known primarily as publishers of financial data, these two firms supply the entire investment business, including all the other advisory services, with the basic facts and figures on all securities sold in the public market and on the companies that issue them. Many of their publications, such as those dealing exclusively with bonds, are too specialized to be of significance to the average investor, but both investor and broker would be utterly lost if it were not for the complete and detailed information that these organizations supply on stocks, both listed and unlisted.

Much of the research material supplied by one firm is also supplied by the other, but they use different methods of organizing and publishing it.

Most fundamental of all the reference books are Standard & Poor's *Corporation Records* and Moody's *Manuals*. In these massive volumes, running into tens of thousands of pages, you'll find a brief history of virtually every publicly owned company in the United States and full financial data running from the present back over a period of years — the figures on assets, income, earnings, dividends, and stock prices.

Standard & Poor's *Corporation Records* consist of six loose-leaf volumes in which reports on over 7,500 individual companies are arranged in alphabetical order. These reports, providing all the basic financial data, are revised whenever a company issues new reports or other important developments alter a company's prospects; supplements are issued every two months summarizing news bulletins on a company-by-company basis. Standard & Poor's also has a special service reviewing conditions by industry, called *Industry Surveys*. It provides economic and investment analysis of 65 leading U.S. industries and 1,500 individual companies. For each industry group an annual basic survey is published, supplemented by current surveys updating the basic information.

Moody's presents its financial information on publicly owned securities in six publications covering municipal bonds, banks and finance, industrials, public utilities, and transportation. It also publishes weekly news reports on over-the-counter industrial stocks. Subscribers to each of the publications receive an annual bound volume containing basic descriptions of these companies and investment situations at no extra cost. Moody's is also the publisher of the authoritative twice-weekly *Dividend Record.*

Standard & Poor's subsidiary, Daily Stock Price Record Services, provides a broad spectrum of computerized financial and corporate data relied upon by security analysts, researchers, and corporate financial executives.

These services, keeping abreast of all corporate facts and figures, are far too costly for most individuals. Nor is it necessary for an investor to spend several hundred dollars a year on them, since they can usually be referred to in a public library or broker's office. A registered representative can also get the information for the client.

Even more condensed information is provided in the *Stock Guide,* a pocket-size manual published by Standard & Poor. Here, in tabular form, the investor can find the high-and-low prices over the past few years, current data on assets, earnings, and dividends, figures on institutional holdings, and Standard & Poor's own quality ratings for 5,100 common and preferred stocks, listed and unlisted. A new edition of the *Stock Guide,* complete with lists of stocks recommended for different objectives, is issued monthly.

For the individual investor, both Standard & Poor and Moody's have special services and letters that comment on business developments as they affect the outlook for individual stocks and industries.

Chart and Statistical Services

M. C. Horsey & Co., Inc., P.O. Box H, Salisbury, MD 21801, issues *The Stock Picture* bimonthly, which provides price charts on more than 1,900 stocks for periods of time ranging from five to fifteen years. Charts show earnings, dividends, and present capitalization. Sample pages are sent upon request.

Trendline, 25 Broadway, New York, NY 10004, which is owned by Standard & Poor, publishes three major stock market services. *Daily Action Stock Charts*, covering 754 companies and 14 market indicators, is published weekly. Each company chart shows the daily high, low, close, and volume and the 200-day moving average (for the previous seven months), as well as the yearly range for ten years. Earnings figures, with comparisons for eight quarters, dividends, and capitalization data, are also provided. There is also a monthly edition. Trial subscriptions are available. *Current Market Perspectives*, published monthly, includes charts of 1,476 individual companies, showing the weekly high, low, close, and volume for the last four years, along with historical price-earnings ratios. A three-week trial subscription is available. Trendline also publishes the bimonthly *OTC Chart Manual*, which includes charts of 840 leading over-the-counter stocks. Each chart includes weekly high, low, and closing bid prices, and volume for up to three years, annual price ranges for eight years, and an earnings-dividend record for six years.

American Institute for Economic Research (AIER), P.O. Box 567, 50 Stockbridge Road, Great Barrington, MA 01230, is an independent scientific and educational organization conducting economic research and publishing the results of that research whenever it considers that the public interest would thus be served.

AIER publishes a weekly bulletin entitled *Research Reports*. The issues analyze current economic developments. Important factors such as industrial activity, prices, and money-credit trends are depicted in an unusual series of charts.

It also publishes monthly *Economic Education Bulletins,* which are studies of such basic topics as property problems, financial relationships, insurance, investment trusts, taxes, estate problems, business cycles, commercial banking, and the role of gold. Its publications are sent free to all sustaining members.

In order to retain its tax exemption, in 1963 AIER transferred its investment advisory activities to *American Institute Counselors, Incorporated,* which contributes all of its income after taxes to AIER. This service publishes a semimonthly report entitled *Investment Bulletin,* which covers business and monetary developments and analyzes their significance for investors.

The bulletins do not advise on margin trading and do not attempt to forecast short swings or technical movements of the stock market. They are intended primarily to assist those who wish to follow long-term investment programs.

Babson's Reports Inc., Wellesley Hills, MA 02181: the Babson organization, founded in 1904 by Roger W. Babson, offers investors four different advisory services — an annual consultation service, an investment advisory (with supervisory option), a quarterly appraisal and review service of the client's portfolio, and a complete investment management service. The company's *Investment and Barometer Letter* is supplied as a supplement to all three services.

Published by a subsidiary of the company that publishes *Forbes* magazine, *Forbes Special Situation Survey,* 60 Fifth Avenue, New York, NY 10011, is for the more sophisticated investor interested in "high-potential" situations and willing to assume the risk. The subscriber receives twelve recommendations a year. Each recommendation covers a stock that the service believes has a potential to perform substantially better than the market in a period of roughly one to two years. Subscribers are kept informed by periodic reviews and, where necessary, suggestions are made about when to get out of stocks previously recommended.

United Business and Investment Service, 120 Newbury Street, Boston, MA 02116: each issue of its comprehensive *Weekly*

Report contains a review of the business outlook, a report on Washington developments, a forecast of commodity prices, an appraisal of the stock market, and specific recommendations for buying or selling different stocks. Regular reports are made on all stocks that are kept on supervised lists. Periodic features include analysis of individual stocks and groups of stocks, a report on bonds, various statistical indexes of business and a summary of opinions and recommendations of other leading advisory services.

Chartcraft, Inc., 1 West Avenue, Larchmont, NY 10538, publisher of the *Chartcraft Weekly Service, Chartcraft Weekly Option Service, Chartcraft Weekly Commodity Service, Chartcraft Technical Indicator Review,* and the *Chartcraft Monthly Point and Figure Chart Book,* offers services devoted to point-and-figure charting and analysis. The *Weekly Service* and the *Monthly Chart Book* cover every stock on the New York and American stock exchanges. The *Technical Indicator Review* deals with point-and-figure analysis of market trends.

Dow Theory Forecasts, Inc., 7412 Calumet Avenue, Hammond, IN 46325: general market projections are based upon the Dow Theory, which this service has undertaken to interpret and apply since 1946. The Dow Theory does not deal with the selection of individual stocks, but seeks to determine and project overall market trends. However, this service does provide monthly buy-sell-hold advice on more than 700 issues. Clients may call at any time for specific advice on their individual problems; unlimited consultation privileges are provided. Its publication appears weekly, 52 times a year.

Value Line, 711 Third Avenue, New York, NY 10017, publishes three comprehensive analytical services. The *Value Line Investment Survey* reports on, and evaluates systematically, on a preset schedule, about 1,700 stocks in 92 different industries. Each report analyzes how the company's business is progressing and how the stock's future is perceived by Value Line analysts. Each stock's prospects are objectively forecast in terms of timeliness and safety. The *Value Line OTC Special Situations Service* (twice monthly) pinpoints emerging stocks with above-average potential for growth-oriented investors willing to undertake some financial risk in the hope of realizing exceptional capital gains. *Value Line Options and Convertibles* (first four Mondays of each month) is an all-in-one service concentrating on listed options, convertibles, and warrants.

In addition to these comprehensive analytical services there exists a number of publications whose primary function is to either reprint or distill in digest form the current thinking of the world's foremost financial advisers. Chief among these are the following.

The Wall Street Transcript, 120 Wall Street, New York, NY 10005, is an enormous tabloid-style newspaper which reprints verbatim the weekly market and technical letters of a wide variety of Wall Street brokerage firms, as well as numerous brokers' analyses of various industries and recommendations of specific stocks. The *Transcript* also reprints corporate news, publishes lengthy round-table discussions of various industries and their stocks, written by analysts of those industries, profiles investment professionals and their current stock selections, and contains weekly options and collectible columns. It is an indispensable tool for investors interested in a wide variety of original market research and specific stock recommendations.

Newsletter Digest, 2335 Pansy Street, Huntsville, AL 35801, provides capsulized versions of current comments by a wide variety of analysts in a broad range of investment fields — stocks, bonds, gold, commodities, real estate, interest rates — and the general economic picture. It also comments on some of these opinions from its own editorial perspective and appears semi-monthly.

Market Consensus Letter, Suite 383, 9333 North Meridian Street, Indianapolis, IN 46260, provides a meaningful selection of current quotes from a wide variety of market analysts, but differs from *Newsletter Digest* in that it concentrates solely on stocks and offers a considerable amount of its own opinion, including the recommending of specific stocks for capital appreciation. It, too, appears semimonthly.

Wall Street Digest, 120 Wall Street, New York, NY 10005, provides a monthly digest of excerpts from the current opinions of the world's leading financial advisers. *WSD* also gives its own precise investment recommendations for the stock and bond markets, gold, silver, the best money market funds, plus a comprehensive general economic survey.

The Hulbert Financial Digest, 8 East Street SE, Washington, DC 20003, is the only monitor of investment advisories that generates no opinions or recommendations of its own. It exists solely to track the advisory records of the various newsletters it surveys. In addition to providing a healthy smattering of opinion on a wide range of investment vehicles from the various advisories it monitors every week, Hulbert provides an objective performance of its subjects' recommendations. Hypothetical model portfolios are constructed according to each letter's advice, and each issue reports on the values of those portfolios as it goes to press. It comes out monthly.

And, finally, of course, we have the specific stock market advisory newsletters themselves. Most major brokerage houses issue periodic investment summaries, which comment on general economic conditions and particular stocks they are currently recommending for purchase. These brokers will be more than happy to send you copies of their letters if you request them. But, in addition, a number of independent market letters, written and published by a wide range of market "gurus" using a confusing array of forecasting techniques, have sprung up in recent years. Many have become so popular that they have come to wield a strong influence on the performance of the very market they have set out to predict. Among the most widely read are the following.

The Granville Market Letter, Drawer O, Holly Hill, FL 32017, is the most widely known financial newsletter in the world. "Joe"

Granville is a pure technician who interprets the "tale of the tape" to tell his many subscribers when to buy and sell. Critics charge that he is as often off target as on, but he goes blithely on making dramatic predictions that are watched by analysts as much for the effect they have on the market as for the accuracy of their prognostications. The letter appears semimonthly.

The Zweig Forecast 747 Third Avenue, New York, NY 10017: a regular panelist on the "Wall Street Week" television program, Martin Zweig topped the *Hulbert Financial Digest* 1981 stock market advisory survey with a 36.3% gain for his model portfolio versus a 1.2% decline for the broadly based Standard & Poor 500-stock average. Zweig screens over 2,000 stocks in an effort to select the potential top performers according to insider trading, yields, price earnings ratios, and a wide array of more obscure technical measurements. The *Forecast* appears every three weeks.

The Professional Tape Reader, Redcap, Inc., P.O. Box 2407, Hollywood, FL 33022, is a technical stock market letter that uses 46 indicators to forecast both the short-term and long-term market trends and recommend specific individual stocks. It comes out semimonthly.

Personal Finance — The Inflation Survival Letter, Kephart Communications, Inc., 901 North Washington Street, Alexandria, VA 22314, emphasizes hard money and alternative investments, and covers gold, silver, hard currencies, foreign bank accounts, real estate, collectibles, commodities, strategic metals, precious gems, foreign stocks, insurance, money market funds, barter, and financial privacy matters. It generates its own articles and quotes from a wide array of varied expert opinion. It appears semimonthly.

Harry Browne's Special Reports, Box 5586, Austin, TX 78763: the best-selling author of *How You Can Profit from the Coming Devaluation* and *Inflation Proofing Your Investments* offers sage advice on the current state of a wide range of investment topics from money market funds to Swiss bank accounts.

The Wellington Letter, Suite 1812, 745 Fort Street, Honolulu,

HI 96813, analyzes and forecasts for the sophisticated investor, all the major financial markets, with particular emphasis on interest rates, commodities, and the stock market. It is a monthly.

International Moneyline, 25 Broad Street, New York, NY 10004, writes commentary and provides general strategy and specific buy and sell recommendations on stocks and currency. It appears twice monthly.

Market Logic, The Institute for Econometric Research, 3471 North Federal Highway, Fort Lauderdale, FL 33306, publishes general stock market timing advice and specific equity purchase recommendations based on econometric forecasting models. *Market Logic* also includes a review of market indicators, mutual fund recommendations, option timing, and a digest of other advisories' commentary. Norman G. Fosback, the editor, and Glen King Parker, the publisher, produce two other innovative newsletters: *The Insiders*, which rates and recommends all listed stocks based on recent sales and purchases by corporate officials of the companies in question, and *New Issues*, which gives analysis and buy recommendations on pending initial public stock offerings. *The Insider* is published twice monthly. *New Issues* and *Market Logic* are published monthly.

The Professional Investor, Lynatrace Inc., 2593 SE Ninth Street, P.O. Box 2144, Pompano Beach, FL 33061, monitors 55 stock market indicators and 100 market letters to arrive at a composite forecast. It appears twice monthly.

The Cabot Market Letter, Cabot Heritage Corp., P.O. Box 1013, Salem, MA 01970, features the Cabot Model Portfolio, an actual working portfolio with stocks of twelve smaller companies possessing high potential for rapid long-term growth. Stock selection and monitoring are based on Momentum Analysis, a unique approach that evaluates stocks' relative strength. The *Letter* comes out twice monthly.

Ruff Times, Target Publishers Inc., 1451 Danville Boulevard, P.O. Box 2000, San Ramon, CA 94853: the charismatic author of *How to Prosper during the Coming Bad Years* offers advice on stocks, hard money, real estate, and inflation. (It appears twice monthly.)

The Holt Investment Advisory, T. J. Holt & Company, 290 Post Road West, Box 909, Westport, CT 06881, provides a complete analysis of the economy and the stock market, supported by numerous charts detailing trends in precious metals, money, credit, and the leading economic indicators. It includes specific recommendations and follow-up reports. It appears twice monthly.

Most investment advisory newsletters will send a sample copy (usually a back issue) of their publication to prospective subscribers who request one.

The most complete listing of investment newsletters, reporting services, and journals available is *The National Directory of Investment Newsletters*. The 1982 edition cost $12 plus $3 postage and handling. It lists hundreds of advisories and newsletters, giving a brief description of their aims and methodology, along with addresses, subscription rates, and frequency of publication. The *Directory* is available from Idea Publishing Corporation, 55 East Afton Avenue, Yardley, PA 19067.

CHAPTER 27

How Your Broker Can Help You

IN the last analysis, the best answer that any investor can find to the question of what stocks to buy is likely to be what he works out for himself through study and investigation.

But where, you ask, can the average investor who is willing to do his own investigating turn for the information he needs? The answer to that is — his broker, preferably a member firm of the New York Stock Exchange.

Perhaps you think this is dubious advice. After all, isn't a broker interested in selling securities? Yes, a broker is a salesman. But that doesn't mean that your interests and his are completely opposed. Quite the contrary. Any salesman of any product wants his customer to be satisfied, because that's the best way of building his own business. That's especially true of the broker.

Then, too, there's an important difference between brokers and other salesmen. The automobile salesman wants to sell you a particular make of car. The insurance salesman wants to sell you a policy in his company. The salesman for a financial advisory service wants to sell you that service and nothing else.

The broker, as a general rule, doesn't care which stocks you buy. Professionally he has no ax to grind. He stands to make about the same commission on the same total investment no matter how that investment is appointed. When it comes to over-the-counter stocks, admittedly, he could have an ax to grind if his firm makes a market in a particular stock, but most securities dealers realize that such a self-serving policy can be bad business in the long run.

All this is not intended to imply that the brokerage business is wholly without sin. Any business has a certain number of sinners in it. And if that business involves the handling of large sums of money, as the brokerage business certainly does, it is likely to have an even greater than average number of sinners, despite all efforts to exorcise them.

Over the years, the brokerage business has done a good job of policing itself, of trying to rid itself of all unprincipled elements. In recent years it has redoubled its efforts. That increased effort can be traced directly to the publication in 1963 of the S.E.C.'s final report to Congress on its study of the securities business. This report led to the enactment of the 1964 Amendment Acts, and to the even more sweeping revisions and regulations imposed by the Securities Reform Act of 1975.

The S.E.C. has made it unmistakably clear with each passing year that it intends to supervise strictly and thoroughly all member firms all over the country and every man in every office. Furthermore, the commission has made it equally clear that unless the New York Stock Exchange, which it has always accused of treating disciplinary matters too tenderly, did a more competent policing job, it would hold the exchange and its member firms responsible.

As a result the exchange has increased the efficiency of its own police force. This force schedules surprise calls on branch offices of member firms all across the country, checking customer trading records and the character and performance of the registered representatives. And the member firms have followed suit. Some initiated policing of their own offices as early as 1965 to forestall trouble with the S.E.C. and customer lawsuits.

What are these policemen — or *compliance officers,* as they are euphemistically called — looking for? In general, they are looking for any abuses of public confidence.

In particular, they are looking for evidence of churning, the overstimulation of customer's trading in order to build commission revenues.

They are looking for high-pressure salesmanship — telephone calls at night, undue persuasion of widows, attempts to prey on the unsophisticated and the unsuspecting.

They are looking for misrepresentation. "The stock is bound to go up . . . you can't miss."

They are looking for abuses of the discretionary authority that a customer may give a broker to manage an account, to buy or sell whatever and whenever he thinks best.

They are looking for margin trading by customers who plainly lack the resources to undertake the risks involved.

They are looking for the flagrant incompetence or the willful malfeasance that could result in the recommendation of a clearly unsuitable investment — a highly speculative penny stock for a retired couple to whom safety of capital is paramount.

They are looking for situations in which securities firms, or even individual partners or salesmen, seek to further their own undisclosed interest in a stock by promoting its sale in order to enhance the value of their own holdings.

In summary, they are looking for any abuse of what is known in Wall Street as the S.E.C. *"shingle theory"* — the theory that when a broker hangs out his shingle he guarantees to the world that he will deal fairly and honestly with his customers.

The S.E.C. holds the home-office executives of member firms wholly responsible for supervising their branch offices. If there ever was any doubt about this, it vanished quickly in the mid-sixties, when the S.E.C. and the N.A.S.D. emphasized their intent by instituting action against several leading firms. Those actions resulted not only in the expulsion of individual employees and branch office managers, but in fines and suspensions levied against the firms' top officials.

The public furor stirred up by these headline cases was actually disproportionate to the problem involved. Admittedly, there were some sharp operators, utterly lacking in moral scruples, among the 25,000 registered representatives then employed. Admittedly, also, top management among the member firms had been lax in exercising supervisory responsibility. And, admittedly, the exchange had been less than stern in its disciplinary actions.

Still the fact remains that the securities business as a whole adheres to a standard of ethics and a concern for the public good that few other businesses can match.

And the fact also remains that the vast majority of registered representatives are honest, scrupulous, and sincerely concerned with the welfare of their customers.

But even if the reliability of your broker can be taken for granted, what about his ability? How competent is he likely to be when it comes to giving you sound advice about your money and how to invest it?

Obviously, that's a question to which there is no absolute answer. Nobody could possibly contend that all the thousands of brokers in the securities business are preeminently well qualified to give investment help. Some are and some aren't. But thanks to the training programs that many leading brokerage firms have been operating for years, the standards of professional ability have been steadily raised. Most of these programs last six months, with half that time spent in the classroom, eight hours a day. Graduates can be considered to be pretty knowledgeable about the investment business, even before they start to work in it.

Certainly this much can be said: as a general rule there isn't anybody who is apt to be as well qualified to advise you about your investments as your broker. After all, the registered representative works at the job of investing at least eight hours a day, five days a week. And he has been doing it for years. He has facts, figures, and information at his fingertips that nobody else can easily lay hold of. He has easy access to the basic reference works — Standard & Poor's *Corporation Records* or Moody's *Manuals* — and he can get detailed data on almost any publicly owned company in the United States.

"Investigate before you invest" is still one of the soundest pieces of advice anyone can give you. And you might start your investigating by thumbing through either Standard & Poor's monthly *Stock Summary* or the *Monthly Stock Digest*, published by Data Digests, Inc. Either of these two publications will give you an idea of the kind of information you should have about any stock before you buy it.

If your preliminary investigation leads you to develop an interest in several specific stocks, most brokers can supply you — within reason, of course — with reports on these companies. They buy these reports from accepted research services or they are prepared by their own *research departments* and often made available to customers without charge.

Research has become vitally important in the brokerage business, and its quality can give a firm a genuine competitive advantage. No member firm can buy a listed stock for you for a cheaper price than another firm. They all must pay the same price for a given stock on the exchange at any given moment. But not all firms can give you the same well-qualified advice about how good a particular stock may be for you in your particular circumstances and with your particular investment objective.

This, plus variable commission rates and service charges, makes a decision about which brokerage firm to use almost as important as deciding which stock to buy. How can you form an opinion about which broker might best be able to help you? Well, you might visit three or four different ones and ask them about the same stock. That would give you some idea of how well informed each one was, what kind of research service each one provided, and the cost, if any.

If brokers charge for research advice they'll tell you. Then you can decide whether you want to pay the fee or not. On the basis of the replies you get from the brokers you contact, you can make a reasonably informed judgment about the quality of their research — provided, of course, that you have leveled with them about how much money you have to invest, what your financial situation is, and what you want most out of your investments: safety of capital, dividend income, near-term price appreciation, or long-term growth. The more complete the information you provide about your circumstances, the more pertinent the broker's recommendations are apt to be.

And you need not feel that you are imposing on a broker for this service. After all, that's part of the job for which he and his firm get paid — by you. Many brokerage houses advertise their willingness to set up a program for the new investor, or to review the holdings of present shareowners, making suggestions about what to buy or what to sell — and why.

A good research department is staffed with *analysts,* who spend all their time following developments in certain assigned industries. By reading countless business and industrial publications and some of the more reliable financial advisory services, an analyst keeps up with the published information on his industries, including the reports of competing brokers. He also tries to establish and maintain contact with key officials in all the major companies he covers, and visits them as often as possible. This is one way in which a brokerage house analyst determines the quality of a company's management, the key factor, after all is said and done, in determining a company's success.

Over the years, officials in companies covered by such research have come to respect the qualified securities analysts. Still they are likely to maintain strict silence about anything that could possibly be construed as inside information.

Publicly owned companies are obligated to reveal promptly to the public any information that may influence the price of their stock. The news may be favorable or unfavorable. It still must be disseminated. But it definitely should not be disseminated through the medium of a securities analyst who telephones a company executive to inquire if an earnings estimate of so much per share is "in the ball park." Casting around for information in this manner has become generally outmoded anyway; not only by much tighter and more rigidly enforced disclosure regulations, but by the increasing unwillingness of executives to cooperate. As a result, when trying to estimate earnings, many analysts depend more these days on what is known as the *mosaic theory.*

By his intimate knowledge of a company's past record, its balance sheet, and the performance of its stock, an analyst today can come pretty close to making a reliable earnings estimate by piecing together the myriad parts of a corporate mosaic — size of inventories, labor conditions, plant cost, capacity, new product development, order backlog, quality of management, and other related data.

Yet the analyst at any given time may still lack one vital piece of information — perhaps the status of a labor contract or facts about inventory — that would complete the mosaic. If he could obtain that, he would be much more confident about his earnings projection. In such circumstances, he has absolutely no qualms about calling his closest contact in the corporation and asking for the information. And the official normally doesn't have to worry about answering the question, since it doesn't really constitute inside information.

In addition to contacting the company itself, an analyst can usually pick up valuable information to complete his mosaic by checking that company's principal competitors. Very often he might even get from the competitor an earnings estimate he can compare to his own.

It is the analyst's responsibility at all times to see that his firm's registered representatives are fully informed about all important developments affecting the companies he follows. Periodically he prepares reports on these companies for distribution to the firm's customers and the public. Many firms also prepare much longer and more detailed reports for their institutional clients.

These research reports are a far cry from the old *"broker's letter,"* a catch-as-catch-can commentary on the stock market, liberally interspersed with tips on what to buy or what to sell. Today, the typical research report on a company, prepared and distributed by a member firm, is a substantial piece of factual and honest work. So that the customer may allow for any possible bias, many firms go so far as to disclose in such reports any special interest the firm or its owners might have in the stock in question as a result of their own holdings, representation on the company's board of directors, or a long-standing underwriting relationship.

In recent years securities analysts have found a valuable new tool to aid them in their complicated studies, the high-speed computer. Since the early sixties, Standard & Poor has made available to them, as well as to banks, mutual funds, and other big financial institutions, its *Compustat* service. This service consists of reels of magnetic tape on which are recorded virtually all the essential accounting data that an analyst needs. These Compustat tapes include millions of figures from the financial reports of thousands of corporations listed on the major exchanges for each company. The tapes provide annual data back twenty years on 60 different items that can be vital in measuring a company's wealth. Quarterly data for the past years is available on 40 of these items. Even brokers who cannot afford the tremendous expense involved in installing their own data processing systems can have access through time-sharing to vital data such as that provided by the Compustat tapes. This is an arrangement that permits brokers to submit specific problems or questions to a central computer and get an answer back by telephone or teletype.

As a consequence, securities analysts no longer have to work endless hours digging the figures they need out of old corporate reports to arrive at a reliable statistical analysis of a company's performance as compared with its competitors. The computer does much of their work for them, and it does it instantly.

Although computer-oriented research is still relatively young, brokerage firms have found data processing machines useful in several other areas: information retrieval, security screening and selection, and basic research into the nature of securities prices and price movements.

It is in the field of portfolio management and evaluation that computers have made their most significant contribution in recent years. This development was spurred by the enactment on Labor Day 1974 of the *Employee Retirement Income Security Act,* one of whose primary requirements is that pension fund trustees evaluate the performance of their fund managers. Several major brokerage firms have created highly sophisticated computerized techniques for the diagnostic evaluation of fund performance. These programs not only calculate the rates of return earned on the assets under management; they also determine the amount of risk taken, the degree of diversification, and the impact of the fund manager's attempts at stock selection and timing.

Finally, each pension fund that is evaluated is compared with hundreds of other professionally managed portfolios, so that the relative performance of the fund manager can also be gauged. Several thousand pension funds are now evaluated by these computer-based performance measurement systems. A continuing record of their investment results is stored in the computer's memory. Other computer programs verify that custodians of securities have paid required interest and dividends into the appropriate account and determine whether each trade occurred between the high and low prices for the day.

Several large firms have computer systems that give branch-office representatives direct wire access to the main-office computer, allowing them to retrieve instantly the latest opinion of the firm's research department on several thousand different stocks. The individual registered representative could not be expected to have valid information on anything like that many stocks to satisfy a customer who wants to know what he thinks about this company or that one. Now, if he works for a firm with a computer-operated retrieval system, all he has to do is punch a few keys and instantly, no matter how far away he is, he gets a printout of the analyst's latest thinking about the stock, complete with his projections for earnings, dividends, and future price range. It is, of course, the responsibility of the research department at headquarters to see that the information file in the computer is kept constantly up to date.

In the area of security selection, the vast capacity of the computer makes it possible to screen rapidly an almost unlimited number of securities in order to find those that will match some predetermined set of standards — stocks that have shown consistent growth of earnings over some specified period, or stocks whose price performance has exceeded some established yardstick, or stocks that match some particular standard for dividend payout in relation to earnings. In using computers in this fashion, the analyst establishes the criteria and lets the machine survey the field to find those that meet his standards. The ultimate objective of this kind of computer research is to find stocks that are undervalued or overvalued in relation to the market as a whole or to any specified segment of it.

Portfolio management by computer is really only a further development of the techniques used in stock selection, although it is infinitely more complicated because the computer must be asked to deal with a wide variety of criteria. Stocks must be chosen not only to satisfy the individual investor's circumstances — cash available for investment, income requirements, tax considerations, and the like — but also to keep the degree of risk that the investor assumes in reasonable relationship to his investment objective. Computers can apply new analytical methods to differentiate between that element of risk in a given portfolio attributable to general market action and that portion inherent in the specific securities included in the portfolio. In tailoring a portfolio to an individual investor's needs the computer is used to review a vast number of alternative investments — a far greater number than an individual analyst could review in months or years. Because of the computer's high speed, the job can be done in a matter of minutes.

The technical market analyst who is interested in trying to predict long- or short-term swings in the market on the basis of such factors as the volume of short selling, the ratio of odd-lot to round-lot transactions, cyclical and random variations in price movements, and other esoteric data finds in the computer the answer to an infinity of mathematical problems he has wrestled with for years. In addition, with the improvements in data communication and the development of video screens, a technical analyst can command the computer to create instantly at his desk a wide variety of charts — trend lines, moving averages, volume data, and high-low-close figures — to help him in his predictions for the market as a whole or for individual stocks.

The computer has had one interesting effect on the analyst himself. Accustomed over the years to generalizations about the probable price action of a stock — "although short-term prospects are not promising, there is appreciable potential for long-term growth" — the analyst now finds it necessary to express his opinion in specific figures if his projections are to be used in a computer program. He must say, for instance, that over the next three months he expects no more than a 1% increase in the price of a given stock, while over a five-year period he anticipates a 12% price appreciation. The necessity of replacing qualitative judgments with quantitative predictions has had the salutary effect of sharpening the analysts' evaluations and even improving their accuracy.

How much you lean on your broker for help is up to you. In special circumstances you may wish to open a discretionary account and give the broker power of attorney to make all buying and selling decisions for you. Most brokers are loath to accept such complete responsibility for an account because losses, no matter how small or infrequent, breed trouble and discontent. Most brokers prefer to act on your specific instructions. Some won't even accept discretionary accounts. One thing you can be sure of: lacking concrete instructions to do so, no reputable broker, no member firm of the New York Stock Exchange, is going to "put you into" some stock or "sell you out" of it. As a general rule, the registered representative today wants you to assume responsibility for managing your own investments — with his help.

Your broker will provide you with the facts and figures you need to make specific investment decisions and to help you to interpret them, but he prefers that the decisions about what to buy and what to sell be yours. Not only will you be less inclined to blame the broker for whatever might go wrong if you determine your own investment course, but, more important, in the long run you will be a better and more successful investor if you make your own decisions. You'll have a greater interest in the problem, and you'll be more willing to work at the job of investing.

Many investors have already learned the ropes in the investment business on a cooperative basis through the medium of an *investment club.* Typically, an investment club will be composed of a dozen or more neighbors, business associates, fellow commuters, or social organization members who meet together once a month, put ten or twenty dollars apiece into a common pool, and spend an hour or two discussing the best possible investment for their money. These are serious sessions in which the pros and cons of various stocks are ardently debated.

Despite the bookkeeping problems and the occasional legal complications such club business creates, most brokers' representatives are more than willing to provide the clubs with company reports and meet with them to answer questions and guide the discussions. The commission return for the time and work involved is negligible. But the opportunity for valuable missionary work, for educating club members in the techniques of investing, is tremendous. And many a worthwhile individual brokerage account has been generated by participation in an investment club.

Information on how to start an investment club is available from the National Association of Investment Clubs (1515 East Eleven Mile Road, Royal Oak, MI 48067).

One thing is sure: investment club members get a good

grounding in the investment facts of life. They learn, as every investor must, that difference of opinion is what makes the market.

If you as an investor can arrive at buying or selling decisions that are better grounded in fact than other individual's, you are going to be right more often than he is. It's just that simple — and that complex.

CHAPTER 28

Can You "Beat the Market"?

ISN'T there any system to "beat the market," any system that will protect you against price fluctuations and virtually guarantee you a profit over the long pull?

Yes, there are such systems, and some of them work pretty well. They are far from foolproof, but at least they do point out some important lessons about successful investing. They are called dollar cost averaging and formula investing.

Dollar cost averaging simply involves putting the same amount of money — $200, $500, $1,000 — into the same stock, regardless of its price movement, at regular intervals — say, every month or every six months — over a long period of time. The Monthly Investment Plan is built on precisely this basis.

Following a system of investing a fixed sum of money in the same stock at regular intervals, you could have made a profit on 90% of the stocks listed on the New York Stock Exchange over almost any period of four or five years you might want to pick in the last quarter-century.

Dollar cost averaging works simply because you buy more shares of a stock with your fixed amount of money when the stock is low in price than you do when it is comparatively high. When the stock rises again, you have a profit on the greater number of shares you got at low cost.

Suppose you bought $500 worth of a particular stock when it

was selling at $10 a share, another $500 worth three months later when it was $9, another $500 worth at $8, and so on, while the stock fell to $5. Suppose it then rose to $15, and settled back to $10. If you then sold out, you would be able to show a profit of about 10%, ignoring both dividends and commission costs, despite the fact that you had paid an average price of $10 and sold out at exactly that same price. You don't believe it?

Don't bother to figure it out, because the proof is in the table below.

Price per Share	Number of Shares Purchased	Cost of Shares	Number of Shares Owned	Cumulative Costs of Shares	Total Value of Shares
$10	50	$500	50	$ 500	$ 500
9	56	504	106	1004	954
8	63	504	169	1508	1352
7	71	497	240	2005	1680
6	83	498	323	2503	1938
5	100	500	423	3003	2115
6	83	498	506	3501	3036
7	71	497	577	3998	4039
8	63	504	640	4502	5120
9	56	504	696	5006	6264
10	50	500	746	5506	7460
11	45	495	791	6006	8701
12	42	504	833	6505	9996
13	38	494	871	6999	11323
14	36	504	907	7503	12698
15	33	495	940	7998	14100
14	36	504	976	8502	13664
13	38	494	1014	8996	13182
12	42	504	1056	9500	12672
11	45	495	1101	9995	12111
10	50	500	1151	10495	11510

To avoid the complication of fractional shares of stock, it is assumed that at every different price level the buyer purchased whatever number of whole shares would cost the amount nearest $500.

All told, you paid $10,495, and your holdings would be worth $11,510, a gain of $1,015, or almost 10%. Exactly the same results — again exclusive of all dividends and purchase costs — would be achieved if the stock first rose steadily from $10 to 15, then dropped to $5, then came back to $10. The table below shows the figures on that.

Price per Share	Number of Shares Purchased	Cost of Shares	Number of Shares Owned	Cumulative Costs of Shares	Total Value of Shares
$10	50	$500	50	$ 500	$ 500
11	45	495	95	995	1045
12	42	504	137	1499	1644
13	38	494	175	1993	2275
14	36	504	211	2497	2954
15	33	495	244	2992	3660
14	36	504	280	3496	3920
13	38	494	318	3990	4134
12	42	504	360	4494	4320
11	45	495	405	4989	4455
10	50	500	455	5489	4550
9	56	504	511	5993	4599
8	63	504	574	6497	4592
7	71	497	645	6994	4515
6	83	498	728	7492	4368
5	100	500	828	7992	4140
6	83	498	911	8490	5466
7	71	497	982	8987	6874
8	63	504	1045	9491	8360
9	56	504	1101	9995	9909
10	50	500	1151	10495	11510

There's only one significant difference between the two tables. Note that you are considerably better off all the way along the line until the very end if your stock drops first and then comes back. Thus, in the first table, after the stock had fallen to $5 and recovered to $10, you could have sold out and made a profit of $1,954, or about 35%, on your money.

So if the stock you buy drops in price and you have the confidence to believe that it will come back, as stocks in general always have, you would do well to continue buying it as it slides on down. This is called *averaging down*. It's a technique the investor worried about the decline in price of some stock he owns should keep in mind.

While no stock is likely to follow the precise patterns set forth in the tables, these examples do serve to demonstrate the validity of the dollar cost averaging principle.

There's only one big catch to this system of beating the market. You've got to have the cash and the courage to buy the same dollar amount of your stock at whatever interval of time you've fixed on, be it every month, every three months, or every year.

And if it drops, you've got to keep right on buying, in order to pick up the low-cost shares on which you can later make your profit. Unfortunately, when the stock market is down, the average person's bank account is likely to be down too. So he often can't afford to buy at just the time he should. If instead of buying he should have to sell at such a time, he might even have to take a loss. This will always be true if a person has to sell at a price lower than the average cost of the shares he owns. In such circumstances, the dollar cost averaging technique will have provided no protection. Most times, however, dollar cost averaging works over the long pull because the long-term trend of the stock market has been upward.

The stock of the RCA Corporation offers a dramatic example of the way dollar cost averaging works most of the time to the advantage of the investor. Let's assume that back at the beginning of 1929 you had a lump sum of $23,000 and you decided to invest it all in RCA stock. RCA was a popular stock then, highly regarded for its growth possibilities. It was selling early in 1929 in the price range of $375 to $380 per share. So for your $23,000 you would have been able to buy about 61 shares. Over the years, thanks to splits in the stock, those shares would have increased in number to 1,087 and you would have received a total of over

$16,700 in dividend payments. But 46 years later, at the end of 1974, when we will assume you had to sell, your stock would have been worth only $11,685 because of the 72% drop in price that RCA sustained during the bear market of 1973–1974. This means that, together with your dividends, you would have had a net gain of only $5,400 on your $23,000 investment after 46 years.

That's pretty bad, especially considering the fact that if you had sold only two years earlier, at the end of 1972, you would have had a net gain of $33,800 on your $23,000, counting both dividends and price appreciation.

Now consider how much more you would have made if you had followed the dollar cost averaging plan and put that same $23,000 into RCA stock at the rate of about $500 a year over the same 46 years. Here it is assumed that the number of shares purchased (at the opening of the market each year) was that number that you could have bought for an amount closest to $500 — sometimes a fraction of a share less, sometimes a fraction more.

At the end of 1974 you would have owned 5,476 shares of RCA, figuring in splits, and you would have had a net gain, after payment of all brokerage commissions on your purchases, of more than $121,000 — this despite selling out at the end of 1974. Of this sum, the $85,000 you would have collected in dividends would have been more than three and a half times the total cost of your investment. This is an impressive record, and it could have been achieved only because of the opportunity you would have had to pick up RCA shares at bargain levels during the half-dozen severe market slumps that occurred in that 46-year period.

However, we would have an entirely different story to tell if we had taken 1933 as our starting date instead of 1929. Then it would have been decidedly more advantageous to have made a big lump-sum purchase of RCA than to have acquired RCA stock in units of $500 a year over the 41-year period 1933–1974.

If you had put $20,500 into RCA at the beginning of 1933 (the equivalent of $500 a year for 41 years) your investment would have been worth almost $372,000 at the end of 1974, counting both price appreciation and dividends. If you had bought the stock at the rate of $500 a year throughout that 41-year period, on the other hand, you would have realized just a little more than 36% of that figure — a bit over $136,000.

Because few people have large sums they can put into a stock at any one time, and because most stocks fluctuate quite widely from time to time, it is generally more prudent and more profitable for an investor to follow the dollar cost averaging plan. It's a plan that makes it possible to capitalize on price fluctuations, rather than to take one big plunge.

The table below (page 258) shows how you would have made out by June 1975 if, beginning in 1929, you had put roughly $500 a year into RCA and nineteen other stocks that proved especially popular with M.I.P. investors.

Of course, this is history, and no one can guarantee it is the kind of history that will repeat itself, but it does provide a convincing demonstration of the value of accumulating shares on a dollar cost averaging basis over a period of time. This accumulation feature is one of the most persuasive aspects of the Monthly Investment Plan, which makes it possible for the small investor to follow precisely this course in buying most of the stocks listed on the New York Stock Exchange.

Formula investing is not so much a system for beating the market as it is a mechanical means of enforcing prudence and caution. There are many different formula plans — almost every expert has his own. Stripped of their technicalities, however, all of them hold that an investment fund should be balanced between stocks and bonds, and the ratio of one kind of security to the other should be changed as the market rises and falls. You buy bonds and sell stocks when the stock market rises — on the assumption that the market becomes increasingly vulnerable as prices advance. You reverse the procedure when the market drops.

Even if it is granted that the premise is basically sound, the

$500-a-Year Investment Program
January 1929–December 31, 1975

	Total Cost of Shares Purchased	Shares Owned	Market Value	Total Dividends Received	Total Dividends Plus Market Value of Stock	Net Gain
Aluminum Co. of America	$23,689	2,283	$88,181	$55,975	$144,156	$120,467
American Tel. and Tel.	23,552	744	37,851	40,877	78,728	55,176
Caterpillar Tractor	23,780	9,263	646,094	199,244	845,338	821,176
Consolidated Edison	23,793	1,283	19,245	43,410	62,655	38,862
Dow Chemical	23,951	8,386	768,367	141,317	909,684	885,733
duPont (E.I.) de Nemours[a]	23,981	453	89,805	97,645	187,450	163,469
Eastman Kodak	23,757	5,858	621,680	133,729	755,409	731,652
Exxon Corp.	23,533	1,706	151,407	126,504	277,911	254,378
General Electric	23,569	2,384	109,962	71,075	181,037	157,468
General Motors	23,613	1,897	109,315	154,775	264,090	240,477
Goodyear Tire & Rubber	23,856	12,590	273,833	190,628	464,461	440,605
Gulf Oil	23,672	6,152	126,116	137,561	263,677	240,005
Nabisco Inc.	23,916	1,208	46,506	47,338	93,846	69,930
Pacific Gas & Electric	23,706	1,683	34,922	53,065	87,987	64,281
Phillips Petroleum	23,600	4,547	246,675	127,612	374,287	350,687
RCA Corp.	23,532	5,523	105,627	90,682	196,309	172,777
Sears, Roebuck	23,863	4,738	305,601	128,614	434,215	410,352
Union Carbide	23,817	1,263	77,201	61,151	138,352	114,535
United States Steel	23,629	1,404	91,260	81,690	172,950	149,321
Westinghouse Electric	23,235	2,985	39,924	56,353	96,277	73,042

[a] Results for duPont include the market value of General Motors shares distributed to holders of duPont stock, as well as the dividends subsequently paid on those shares.

theory is one that the average investor can't apply very effectively. His investment fund is rarely large enough for a formula plan to operate without distortion. This is because all formula plans assume that that portion of the fund which is invested in stocks will perform as the market average does. Obviously, the fewer stocks you can afford to own, the less likely they are to perform in line with the general market. Again, the only bonds a small investor can generally afford are government savings bonds. He can't expect to achieve the same interest return on these bonds as he might earn on other government or corporate bonds, particularly since the return on savings bonds is measurably less in the early years. Savings bank deposits can, of course, be substituted for bonds.

Basically, there are three kinds of formula plans — the constant dollar plan, the constant ratio plan, and the variable ratio plan. The *constant dollar plan* assumes that a fixed dollar amount of stocks will be held at all times. Thus, if you had $20,000, you might decide to keep $10,000 — no more and no less — invested in stocks. If the dollar value of your stock portfolio rose — say, to $11,000 — you would sell $1,000 of stocks and put the proceeds into bonds. If your stocks declined $1,000, you would sell $1,000 of bonds and buy stocks. One objection to the plan is that over any long period of time stock prices are likely to advance — at least they have advanced historically. If your stock investments are frozen at any specified level, you won't keep up with the parade.

The *constant ratio plan* works like the constant dollar plan except that you determine to keep 50% of your investment fund in stocks at all times and 50% in bonds. You don't use fixed dollar amounts. The constant ratio plan is obviously more flexible, can be adapted more readily to the shifting cycles of the stock market, and assures you of at least partial participation in the long-term growth of common-stock values.

The *variable ratio plan* operates like the constant ratio plan, except that you decide to vary the ratio invested in common stocks as the market rises or falls. Thus, you might start out on a 50–50 basis, but decide to keep only 40% of your funds in common stocks whenever the market, as measured by one of the accepted averages, moved up 25%. When the market advanced 50% you would cut back your common stock holdings to 30% of your total funds. If it went up 75%, you would have only 20% invested in stocks. If the market fell, you would reverse the operation, buying stocks at the designated market levels and selling bonds. There are dozens and dozens of variations on the variable ratio theme, many of them involving complicated mathematical formulas and using a variety of economic indexes as well as the market averages. They are designed to permit the investor to take maximum advantage of interim fluctuations in the market while simultaneously protecting his long-term position.

But these formulas don't always work as well as they might. Thus, anyone investing on a formula plan which called for reducing his commitments in common stocks as the market advanced would have lost out on the big bull market in most stocks that began in 1950 and has continued with only occasional short-lived slumps until today. That's why even many big, conservative institutions have either abandoned or modified extensively the formula plans they initiated twenty or thirty years ago. Of course, a shift into bonds, such as these formula plans would have dictated at bull market peaks, would have paid off handsomely during all subsequent corrective phases.

While the average investor may not be able to apply any neatly devised mathematical formula to his own situation, he can profit by paying heed to the one basic precept of all these formulas. Keep an eye on the market averages and, as they rise, let them act as a brake on your buying enthusiasm. Remember, no bull market lasts forever. And neither, for that matter, does a bear market, although it wasn't until 1954, a quarter of a century after the great crash, that the Dow industrial average and Standard & Poor's 500-stock price index surpassed their 1929 highs of 381.17 and 31.92 respectively.

CHAPTER 29

Should You Buy a Mutual Fund?

THINKING is always hard work. Thinking about an investment problem is doubly hard because it frequently involves dealing with words and ideas that are somewhat strange, so it's understandable that you might want to let somebody else do your investment thinking for you. That's just what more and more new investors are doing all the time. They are turning to the *investment trust* — especially the *mutual fund* — as the answer to their investment problems.

There's no special magic about an investment trust — nor anything mysterious about its operation. Suppose you and some of your friends — twenty of you, all told — each have $1,000 to spare. Instead of investing the money individually, you might decide to pool it. Then instead of forming an investment club and arriving at collective investment decisions, you turn the whole sum over to one individual, or manager, to invest for you.

In that situation, the twenty of you would constitute an investment trust, or *investment company*, in miniature.

Now let's assume you're lucky and that at the end of the first year the manager of your trust is able to report that he has made money for you. The value of the stocks that the trust owns has risen from $20,000 to $22,000. Each of your shares in that trust is now worth $1,100 ($22,000 divided by 20).

You've been so successful, as a matter of fact, that some of your other friends would like to join your little trust. The twenty of you must now make one of two decisions.

You may decide that you're going to restrict the trust to just the original members and their original capital, thereby creating a *closed-end trust*. There will be no new members or shareholders in your company, unless, of course, one of the original twenty wants to sell his share to somebody else for whatever he can get for it, a right every member has.

The alternative plan would involve a decision to expand your trust and take in new members. Since your own shares are now worth $1,100 apiece, you decide to allow others to buy in on that basis — $1,100 a share. That $1,100 would represent the *net asset value per share* at that time — a figure determined by taking the current market value of all the shares held in your trust or fund and dividing it by the number of shares outstanding. Net asset value per share is a constantly changing figure for two reasons: (1) the total value of your fund's holdings fluctuates as the prices of the stocks that it owns change in the stock market; (2) the number of shares outstanding changes, too, as additional shares are sold to new or present participants in the fund and as the fund redeems shares for those who want to sell.

If you decide that your fund should be operated in this manner, you will have transformed your company into an *open-end* trust, or what is known more popularly as a mutual fund.

This, in theory, is the essential difference between the closed-end and open-end trusts. In actuality, there are other differences.

Closed-end trusts are stock companies whose shares are bought and sold just like other stocks. The business of these trusts is investing, instead of manufacturing or merchandising. But they are operated just like any other company by officers and directors responsible to the shareholders. These shareholders stand to make or lose money as the value of the stocks owned by the trust goes up or down and as the dividend paid on those shares increases or decreases.

Some of these companies, like Lehman Corporation and Tri-

Continental Corporation, are listed on the New York Stock Exchange. Anything from one share to hundreds of shares of their stock can be purchased through a member firm, at the commission rate that firm charges. The stocks of some smaller, less well-known closed-end trusts are sold over-the-counter.

Sometimes the stock of a closed-end investment trust will sell at a premium price, a price greater than its net asset value per share. Other times it will sell at a discount or below that value figure, particularly during a bear market. Closed-end trusts usually compute and publish their net asset value per share just once a quarter.

In contrast, shares of an open-end trust, or mutual fund, are always bought and sold on the basis of their exact net asset value. Mutual funds usually compute and announce the net asset value of their shares every day. This value determines the price dealers will charge a buyer, or what the owner will get if he sells.

Mutual funds pay dividends, if earned, and these are taxed at regular income tax rates. They also distribute long-term capital gains when they are realized on the sale of their holdings. Since these distributions of capital gains constitute a return on capital, the individual owner of mutual shares pays a tax on such distributions in accordance with his own individual tax situation, just as he would on any other long-term capital gain. Fund shareholders can generally elect to have dividends and capital distributions reinvested if they wish.

The two kinds of trust do much the same type of business. But the difference in their setup makes for a difference in their operation. A closed-end trust cannot increase its original capital at will. An open-end trust not only can, but usually wants to. The more shares that are sold, the more the trust grows, and the more its salesmen and investment advisers stand to profit.

There were more than 675 mutual funds in existence at the end of 1981. It is these funds, not the almost-forgotten closed-end trusts, that have been getting all the play in recent years.

Their growth has been little short of phenomenal — from a half-billion dollars in 1941 to nearly $250 billion in 1981. The half-dozen market slumps since 1941 have naturally been rough on the mutual funds. In these periods their net asset value declined to about the same extent as stock prices generally. But over the long haul they have managed to maintain a fairly steady and impressive growth record. Some funds have grown to gigantic size. Currently, there are seven funds with assets of more than a billion dollars each, sixteen top the half-billion figure, and 112 funds boast assets exceeding $100 million.

This growth has meant that a lot of new shareholders have been created by the mutual funds, people who never had previously ventured into the stock market. As a matter of fact, mutual funds *must* attract a lot of new shareholders every year to offset those who sell their shares. In bad years, they are often called upon to redeem more than they sell. The same situation prevails sometimes even in good years.

In recent years, however, many large institutional investors have turned to mutual funds because the funds relieve institutional managers of responsibility for managing the institutions' investment portfolios. These big investors now hold 37.7% of the total assets of all mutual funds, and they account for a major portion of the big-unit sales. Sales to employee pension funds and to corporation treasurers, who must employ a company's idle funds, are also fast-growing areas of the mutual fund business.

Why have mutual funds enjoyed such spectacular growth? One answer is that the mutual fund has obvious appeal to the person who seeks a ready-made answer to investment problems. It is easier to trust another individual's judgment about the market, especially one who is supposed to be an expert, than it is to make up your own mind about whether to buy stock X or stock Y, whether to sell A or B.

Mutual fund salespeople are paid commissions that can be substantial. It was the big commission that attracted a lot of "moon-lighters" into the business many years ago, but in recent years, as the business became more professional, moonlighters have been replaced by the registered representatives of member firms, salespeople for over-the-counter houses, and, to some extent, by the mutual funds' own trained sales forces.

An individual buying one type of mutual fund typically pays a commission or, as it is more commonly known in the fund business, a *loading charge*, of around 5.6% of the price of the fund. The rates are set by the funds themselves, and some charge up to 8½%, the maximum permitted by law.

To realize just how great a sales incentive the loading charge is, look at the situation from the point of view of a brokerage firm which is a member of the New York Stock Exchange. Suppose one of its sales representatives sells a $5,000 investment in a mutual fund. An 8½% loading charge (the maximum) on such a sale would amount to $425. Since the loading charge is deducted first, that means that only $4,575 of the $5,000 would actually be invested in the fund's shares. Thus, as far as the purchaser is concerned, he is really being charged a sales commission of 9.3% — not 8½% — on the amount of money actually invested. Of the $425 loading charge that the brokerage firm collected, it would typically be permitted to keep 75%, or $317. The balance would go to the fund itself to cover operating costs.

But if the same brokerage firm sales representative sold his customer $5,000 worth of a stock listed on the New York Stock Exchange, the commission the firm would realize would be considerably less. How much less would depend, of course, on that firm's rate schedule. But before Mayday 1975, when rates were fixed, the commission on 100 shares of a $50 stock was just $71.50.

Mutual funds, as a general rule, make no charge when the customer redeems or sells his shares, so the broker doesn't stand to make anything more than his original $317 commission on the mutual fund transaction. In contrast, the customer who buys the listed stock may sell it someday, giving the broker a chance to make a second commission. Still, even the commission on a *round-*

trip trade — the purchase and the sale — would be distinctly less than the mutual fund loading charge. And anyway, a commission in hand is worth two in the bush.

While the average investor in a mutual fund might pay 5.6% on a $5,000 order, big orders do get big concessions. Thus, on orders of $100,000 the rate might be only 1%. On million-share orders, the loading charge might be as little as ½ of 1%. But then, the big institutions also pay much lower commission rates on their big volume exchange orders.

During the sixties, the most aggressively promoted and rapidly growing mutual funds were the *front-end load funds*. The buyer of such a fund agrees to make uniform periodic payments to the fund, usually over a ten-to-fifteen-year period, and in exchange acquires whatever number of fund shares such payments will cover. When a salesman sells such a front-end load fund he collects 50% of everything the purchaser puts into the fund the first year. Thus, if the customer signed up for a $50-a-month plan and paid in $600 the first year, $300 would be paid out immediately as a commission to the salesman. Only $300 of the customer's payment would actually be invested for him. With a sales incentive like that is it any wonder that sales of front-end load funds zoomed in the sixties, while the number of such funds grew from ten to more than 70?

Over the life of a front-end contract, the sales cost may average out to a 5%–6% loading charge. But the advantage to the salesman of such a fund is that he gets the lion's share of the total commission right away. He doesn't have to worry that the buyer might cancel his contract in a couple of years.

If the buyer of a front-end load fund wants to cancel his contract and redeem his shares, he can't normally expect to recover the sales cost and break even until he has been in the plan for about three years, unless, of course, there's been a spectacular increase in the value of the fund's shares. If the stock market is slumping, it might be five or six years before he can break even.

Maybe he never will. Meanwhile, the salesman has his take, all tidily sewed up.

In contrast, the buyer of a noncontractual or *level load* mutual fund might put the same amount of money into the fund and pay the same 5%–6% commission. But he would never be in the hole, assuming the value of his fund shares didn't decline. He wouldn't have to keep buying in order to recover a whopping big commission paid in advance. He could quit when he wanted to.

In 1966, the S.E.C. asked Congress for legislation to curb many mutual fund selling practices. Specifically, it wanted an outright ban on front-end load contracts. In defense of such contracts the funds argued that investors needed some form of compulsion — such as the threat of loss if they backed out of a contract in its early years — to keep them saving and investing regularly. But the S.E.C. pointed to its studies, which showed that 20% of all those who bought front-end contracts were forced to sell at a loss because they couldn't keep up the payments. In general, these were the investors, buying plans at ten or twenty dollars a month, who could least afford such a loss.

When Congress finally passed the *Investment Company Amendments Acts of 1970*, the industry heaved a sigh of relief. The front-end contractual plan had survived, even if subjected to new restrictions. Under the 1970 law such funds may still pay a sales commission equal to 50% of the buyer's first-year payments. But the law stipulates that the buyer can cancel his contract any time in the first 45 days and get back the full commission paid. It further holds that any time in the first eighteen months the buyer can cancel the contract and get back 85% of the commission — plus, of course, the value of the shares at that time.

The law further provides that the buyer shall receive a statement at the time of purchase setting forth the commissions that will be deducted from the purchase price and informing him of his right to withdraw from the fund and obtain a refund. And if the buyer misses three payments in the first fifteen months or one payment from the fifteenth to the eighteenth month, the fund is obligated to notify him again of his right to withdraw and the terms of the withdrawal.

If a front-load fund wants to escape these specific provisions governing the purchaser's right to withdraw, it can do so only by limiting its sales commission to a maximum of 20% in any one year and 64% in the aggregate for the first four years.

Apart from the commission, mutual funds offer brokers still another incentive to push fund sales. As the funds grow, they are constantly buying additional stock, big blocks of stock. Furthermore, they keep changing their portfolios, selling 5,000 or 10,000 shares of this stock and buying 5,000 or 10,000 shares of that one. The funds obviously tend to give this highly lucrative block business to those brokers who do the best job of selling their shares.

All through the sixties and very early seventies the in-and-out trading activity of the funds grew apace, as competition forced them to become increasingly "performance-oriented." Sometimes, in striving for speculative gains in a rising market, a fund would turn over half of its entire portfolio in a year or less.

Since the funds themselves are not permitted to be members of the big exchanges, they execute their orders for listed stocks through established member firms. In the halcyon days of the late sixties bull market, when the funds were setting a feverish trading pace, member firms competed vigorously for this big-ticket business. *Reciprocity* reigned. "You scratch my back, and I'll scratch yours" was the order of the day. Brokers and dealers intensified their fund-selling efforts in order to get more of the fund's commission business.

With the abandonment of fixed commission rates in 1975, however, reciprocity faded measurably. What now became important to the funds was not what a broker's record was on fund sales, but how much he would cut his commission to get the fund's block business.

While mutual funds may be aggressively sold, that does not mean that they are not good things to buy. Quite the contrary.

One great investment virtue all investment trusts, close-end and open-end alike, have is their diversified holdings in many different companies and industries. There is obviously less risk (but less hope of making a killing, too) in owning an interest in 50 or 150 different companies than in owning stock in just one company.

This is the argument, the protection provided by diversification, that mutual fund salesmen stress. It's an argument with significant merit. However, the importance of diversification as a protective device is minimized or magnified by your choice of a specific mutual fund. And there are many different kinds of funds.

The most popular type of fund is the *common stock fund*, a fund whose assets are wholly invested in a diversified list of common stocks. Most put no more than 10% of their assets in any given industry. But even so, there is a wide diversity of investment policy among them. Some accent income. Some aim at the twin objectives of growth and income. And some, probably the greatest number, emphasize long-term capital growth.

Still other common stock funds take an opposite tack. They invest all their assets in the securities of companies in a single industry: chemicals, drugs, electronics, et cetera. Some of these *special purpose funds* concentrate their investments in specific geographical areas. Still others seek to cater to a particular class or type of investor, such as farmers, airline pilots, even cemetery owners.

Then there are the *"go-go" funds*, whose assets are totally invested in aggressive growth situations, and the *hedge funds*, which operate still farther out in a speculative orbit all their own.

Originally, hedge funds were comprised of groups of wealthy men who operated their funds as private partnerships. But as speculative fever rose and the market boiled to its peak in 1973, many of these privately owned and privately operated hedge funds were offered to the general public. If you wanted to become a partner in such a fund, it didn't matter whether or not you could afford to speculate. And hedge funds are nothing if not speculative. They buy on margin and sell short — trading techniques forbidden to regular mutual funds. They deal in warrants and options. They put money into "special situations," even buying the stocks of companies so small or so new that their stock does not enjoy a public market.

In addition to the all-common-stock fund, there are the *balanced* funds, whose assets are divided among common stocks, preferreds, and bonds. Most of these highly conservative funds operate on some kind of a formula investing plan. As common stocks rise into high ground, more and more of the assets of such funds are shifted into preferred stocks and bonds to protect against a break in the stock market. In a falling stock market, they sell bonds and begin buying stocks in anticipation of an upturn there.

In addition to these various types of mutual funds, there is one wholly different species — the *no-load fund.* Your broker is not apt to be interested in arranging for you to buy such a fund direct from the management company of the fund, because he doesn't make a penny on the deal. He'd prefer to sell you a fund that yields him a good commission.

All mutual funds employ the services of a professional management firm to direct and guide their investment policy. One of the proudest boasts of fund salesmen is that such management can invest your money for you better than you can yourself. That's the way mutual funds justify the *management fee,* usually $\frac{1}{2}$ of 1%, that they uniformly charge the buyer.

Very often the men who comprise the management company are the same men who guide its sales destiny. Since they wear two hats they collect two incomes — often very substantial incomes. The law does provide, with some exceptions, that no more than 60% of a mutual fund's directors can be connected with its advisory or management company. But there are still quite a few mutual fund executives who take a double dip out of a fund's earnings.

If professional management is worthwhile, if it's worth $\frac{1}{2}$ of

1% a year, it might seem logical to assume that mutual funds would show a performance record over the years superior to the average action of the market.

Have the funds beaten the average?

There can be no clear-cut, categorical answer to that question. The answer depends on what period of time you are measuring and what kind of fund you are talking about out of the many different types that exist.

In a sense the meteoric growth of the mutual fund industry can be traced to an inadvertent mistake the S.E.C. made when the original Investment Company Act of 1940 was passed. At that time mutual funds were almost unknown. In approaching Congress with a request for legislation in the investment company field, the S.E.C. sought a law that would enable it to regulate the closed-end investment trusts that had boomed as the market roared to its 1929 high.

In those days many of the trusts played fast and loose with investors' money. Trust fund managers paid themselves large fees and bonuses for their somewhat questionable services. They split commissions with accountants and lawyers. Enjoying almost complete freedom to invest trust funds as they saw fit, the managers placed themselves too willingly at the service of investment bankers anxious to market new and dubious stock issues. They resorted to all kinds of speculative practices. They bought on margin. They pyramided paper profits. And they used the trusts to obtain control of whole industrial empires, often with only a paltry outlay of actual cash — cash furnished, of course, by investors in the fund. When the crash came in 1929, 700 trusts collapsed with virtually no show of assets.

The 1940 law was drafted to prohibit such practices, require full and open disclosure, and drive the manipulators from business. But it also sanctioned, however unintentionally, all the selling practices that permitted mutual funds to prosper. Specifically, the act approved loading charges, front-end load contracts, and management fees.

There was only one thing the funds would have liked, but didn't get, in 1940. That was freedom to advertise. Since mutual funds are constantly issuing new stock, they necessarily fall under the prospectus provisions of the 1933 act, which applies to all new stock issues. This means that a mutual fund advertisement must either consist of the full offering prospectus or be limited to a "tombstone" announcement, consisting of the name of the fund, the offer of a prospectus, and a descriptive sentence or two about its objectives. Although these restrictions have been somewhat relaxed in recent years, mutual funds still regard them as a thorn in their flesh.

When the S.E.C. went to Congress in 1966 to ask for legislation that would restrict many mutual fund selling practices, it wanted an outright ban on front-end contractual plans, a 5% ceiling on loading charges, and a drastic reduction in the standard ½ of 1% management fee. The fee, as the S.E.C. pointed out, was considerably more than banks charged for their investment advisory services.

What the S.E.C. got from Congress four years later was distinctly less than half a loaf. Front-end load contracts were not disallowed. They were simply altered to permit buyers to withdraw from such plans without losing all the money they'd put down as a commission. The maximum loading charge was fixed at 9%, not 5%, although the N.A.S.D. was empowered to see that loading charges were "reasonable." Finally, the management fee went unchanged, subject only to the provision that the S.E.C., or any fund shareholder, could bring suit against a fund charging that the management fee was so excessive that it represented a breach of "fiduciary duty."

Behind all the demands for reform of the mutual fund business was a concern that even the Securities and Exchange Commission was reluctant to express. What might happen if the market went into a real tailspin — a prolonged downturn? That would be the time when people who owned shares in mutual funds would be most tempted to cash them in. For that is when they, as individuals of generally modest means, would be most likely to need their savings. And yet that is precisely the time when it would be most difficult for a mutual fund to redeem its shares.

Funds, of course, always have a substantial cash reserve to meet redemptions. But if there should be a persistent demand for redemptions, a fund would have to sell off sizable blocks of stock to raise cash and swallow whatever loss it sustained in these forced sales. Additionally, those very sales might further depress the market and make it even more difficult for the trust to meet the next round of redemptions as prices fell further.

Although fund selling was blamed in some quarters for deepening and protracting the 1969–1970, 1973–1974, and 1978–1979 market slumps, the funds as a whole suffered through those difficult periods about as individual shareholders did. Despite sharp declines in total assets, the funds have always met the redemption bill up until now.

All things considered, if you want the protection of diversification on a relatively small investment and if you want somebody else to assume the responsibility of making investments for you at a modest fee, buy a mutual fund. But be sure it's a good one and be sure it's right for you. There are hundreds and hundreds of different funds, and it can be as difficult to pick the right one for you as it is to select one right stock out of all those listed on the New York Stock Exchange.

As a general rule, the following pointers should be followed by any investor seeking the right mutual fund for his individual objectives.

(1) Recognize your investment goals. Spectacular year-to-year gains, dividend growth, total returns figures: all these provide an excellent measure of an individual fund's merits. But they don't tell the whole story. You want a fund that most closely approximates your own individual investment objectives. If you're looking for high, steadily increasing dividend income you want a fund that emphasizes that particular market aspect. If you want growth you should buy a fund that emphasizes

small emerging companies. If you're interested principally in conserving your capital you should avoid all funds that concentrate assets in a few fields and employ narrow speculative methods. There is a fund for every temperament, for investors of all ages, means, and ambitions. Spend some time finding out if the fund you're thinking of buying has the exact investment goals you do.

(2) Check the fund's performance record. Just because a fund has done well for its investors in the past is no guarantee that it will do as well, or even particularly well at all, in the future. But, all things considered, you'd probably rather be investing in a fund which gained 50% over the past three years than one that lost 50%. Performance records for all mutual funds are tracked on a regular basis by the Lipper, the Wiesenberger, and the United Business Service mutual fund services. Copies of their publications are generally available from most large city libraries and all brokerage house offices. For an idea of which funds have performed best during recent selected periods of time, consult page 276.

(3) Look for consistency. The best funds do well, or at least slightly outperform their competitors and the general market, just about every year. There is nothing quite so discouraging for the neophyte as jumping on the bandwagon of a fund or an individual stock, which rose spectacularly during some unrealistically short period of time, only to have its bubble burst during the subsequent market reevaluation. Some funds have quirky investment philosophies, which work very well for a short period of time under unusual market conditions. Just be sure you don't buy in at the tail end of one of these atypical performance periods. In fund picking, as in most areas of endeavor, it's slow and steady that wins the race — as long as the slow movement is steadily upward.

(4) Be sure management hasn't changed. There's no point in picking out a good-performing, solidly managed fund whose investment goals perfectly match your own if it turns out that both the goals and the performance record really belong to a portfolio manager who left your new fund's employ the week before you made your purchase. A mutual fund, like most other

businesses, is only as good as the people who run it, so that just as when you pick a stock broker you are really picking an individual to help you chart your financial future, when you buy a mutual fund you are buying a managerial team composed of various individuals to buy your stocks for you. Make sure the team you get is the team you paid for.

(5) Read the prospectus to learn fund policies. No two funds operate in exactly the same way in exactly the same areas. Some reinvest dividends. Some pass them on. Some hold stocks for a decade. Some turn over their entire portfolio two or three times a year. If you read every bit of the fund's prospectus before you buy, you won't be brought up short when you find out that the fund you've chosen actually practices as a matter of policy some investment operation with which you have a basic disagreement.

(6) Develop your own investment viewpoint to help you monitor your fund's current purchases. It's your money, after all, that the mutual fund of your choice will be using to pay for the stocks they select. And although your original reason for deciding to invest in stocks through a mutual fund will probably be that you have neither the time nor the expertise to pick your own stocks, there's no reason why this situation should remain permanent. In fact, there are two good reasons why everyone who invests in a mutual fund should carefully monitor his fund's activities. The first is that you want to make sure you are getting the expert management, the philosophical compatability, and the performance that you paid for. If you're not watching your fund closely there's no way for you to know either how it's doing, or, perhaps more important, why it's performing that way. The second reason is that by watching the fund experts invest, you might just gradually, and painlessly, learn enough of the basics to begin a little stock buying on your own.

Above all things, don't just say yes to the first mutual fund salesman who calls on you.

Here's a list of the mutual funds that performed the best since the last edition of this book was published.

Fund	Gain, 1976–81
Twentieth Century Growth Investors	465%
Fidelity Magellan Fund	379%
International Investors	352%
Quasar Associates	344%
Twentieth Century Select Investors	341%
Evergreen Fund	339%
Research Capital Fund	334%
American General Pace Fund	320%
United Services Fund	314%
44 Wall Street Fund	307%
Strategic Investments Fund	302%
Lindner Fund	294%
Sigma Venture Shares	279%
Value Line Leveraged Growth Investors	278%
Weingarten Equity Fund	273%
Explorer Fund	272%
Scudder Development Fund	272%
Oppenheimer Special Fund	270%
Over-the-Counter Securities	266%
IDS Growth Fund	265%
Hartwell Leverage Fund	260%
American General Venture Fund	259%
Constellation Growth Fund	257%
Fund of the Southwest	256%
PLITREND Fund	243%

Nineteen funds that have appreciated each of the past 5 years, ranked in order of their 1981 performance.

Fund	1981	1980	1979	1978	1977
Lindner Fund	32.9%	32.6%	25.1%	21.8%	28.6%
Able Associates	25.6%	56.7%	79.1%	7.7%	6.4%
Delta Trend	23.2%	28.9%	26.5%	0.4%	4.7%
Lindner Fund For Income	19.2%	14.1%	4.6%	7.0%	11.8%
Value Line Leveraged Growth	18.2%	26.9%	26.0%	27.3%	51.5%
American General Pace Fund	16.2%	30.8%	32.6%	23.5%	28.6%

Sequoia Fund	16.0%	12.8%	12.1%	23.7%	19.6%
Fidelity Magellan Fund	13.6%	64.6%	49.8%	29.5%	12.7%
Windsor Fund	13.2%	22.9%	22.9%	8.7%	0.7%
American National Income Fund	12.2%	18.8%	17.4%	2.1%	1.8%
American General Venture Fund	10.4%	28.5%	42.1%	21.4%	25.6%
Value Line Income Fund	10.1%	26.9%	27.6%	10.8%	1.7%
American General Comstock Fund	8.9%	22.7%	47.7%	13.7%	13.5%
IDS Growth Fund	8.3%	76.9%	38.0%	15.7%	7.0%
Nicholas Fund	7.2%	35.6%	31.0%	25.3%	20.3%
Eaton & Howard Growth Fund	6.9%	42.9%	34.6%	14.7%	1.9%
Tudor Fund	6.7%	43.2%	27.4%	20.2%	6.4%
American Ins. & Industrial Fund	6.5%	7.8%	16.1%	3.7%	2.2%
Janus Fund	5.3%	51.7%	34.8%	16.3%	3.5%

CHAPTER 30

Why You Should Invest—If You Can

WHY should a person who has extra money invest it in stocks?

Here is the answer to that question in one chart and one table.

Chart I (page 279) shows the movement of stock prices from 1925 to 1981, as measured by Standard & Poor's Industrial Index.

The table below shows the average annual yield on the stocks included in Standard & Poor's Industrial Index back to 1926, which is as far back as this series of statistics goes.

1926	4.86	1941	6.62	1956	3.95	1971	2.94
1927	4.73	1942	7.04	1957	4.18	1972	2.61
1928	3.93	1943	4.76	1958	3.87	1973	2.79
1929	3.61	1944	4.69	1959	3.11	1974	4.13
1930	4.84	1945	4.13	1960	3.36	1975	3.96
1931	6.40	1946	3.81	1961	2.90	1976	3.79
1932	7.74	1947	4.90	1962	3.32	1977	4.56
1933	4.06	1948	5.47	1963	3.12	1978	4.81
1934	3.37	1949	6.63	1964	2.96	1979	4.87
1935	3.52	1950	6.69	1965	2.94	1980	4.76
1936	3.39	1951	6.17	1966	3.32	1981	4.83
1937	4.83	1952	5.88	1967	3.07		
1938	4.96	1953	5.86	1968	2.91		
1939	3.87	1954	4.92	1969	3.07		
1940	5.51	1955	3.97	1970	3.62		

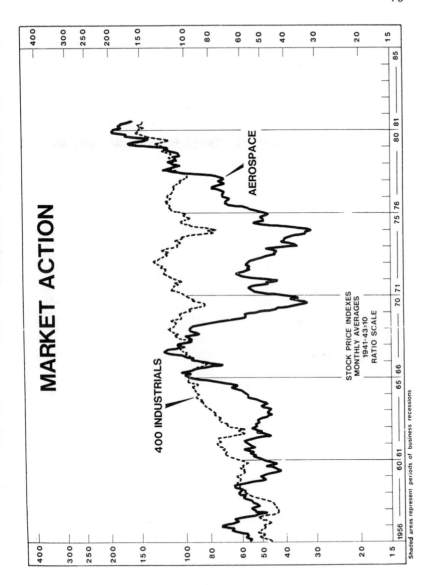

CHART I

In a period like 1973–1974, it was hard for investors to be enthusiastic about investing. After all, the Dow Jones industrial average had dropped 45%, and investors had lost more than $300 billion in that slump. But that's a good reason for looking at the stock market in the long historical perspective — and noting, incidentally, that in the past quarter-century there have been a half-dozen slumps which seemed just as disastrous at the time when they occurred.

The historical record demonstrates the solid fact that the market has always come back and that in the long run common stocks have proved to be good things to own.

But, you might ask, what about that almost steady downtrend in the average return on stocks (see the table, page 278) over the past twenty-five years? Isn't that a cause for concern?

No, it isn't. Because those returns are percentage figures arrived at by dividing dollar dividends by dollar prices for the stocks included in the index. Hence, any decline in the average return could be the result either of an actual decrease in the dollar dividends paid — or an increase in the price of the stocks. The latter explanation is clearly the right one as far as the last two and a half decades are concerned. The average return may have dropped from 6.69% for the year 1950 to 4.83% in 1981, but during this same period, as Chart I shows, per-share prices rose from an average index number of about 20 to over 150. As a result of that great price appreciation, dividends, as a percentage of price, inevitably dropped. But the decline was relative, not absolute.

To illustrate, suppose you had bought a stock at $20 a share in 1950 and received the average dividend of 6.7% on it that year. On this basis, you would have received a dividend of $1.34. If that stock behaved like the average of all stocks, it would have been selling at about $150 a share at the end of 1981 and yielding a return of 4.83%. This would mean that your actual dollar dividend would have increased to $7.23. Furthermore, it would mean that on your original investment you would be earning a return of 35.15%, since you would be getting a dividend of $7.23 on your $20 original investment.

The return that an investor realizes from a stock is not affected in any way by changes in its price *after* he buys it. The return is affected only by a change in the dividend. Thus, if you pay $100 for a stock paying a $5 dividend, you realize 5% on your money, as long as the $5 dividend is paid, regardless of whether the stock drops to $80 or goes up to $120. If the dividend is increased to $6, you make 6%. If it is reduced to $4, you make 4% — regardless of what happens to the price of the stock.

Now let's take another look at the chart. It shows that stock prices have moved generally upward for the past 50 years in a fairly well defined path. One notable exception is that precipitous drop from the 1929 peak to the 1932 bottom.

Isn't that an alarming exception?

No, it isn't. The character of the market in recent years differs markedly from what it was in 1929. It has been more of an investment market, less of a speculative one. Thanks to regulations imposed by the government and the exchange, there has been little of the type of speculative activity that produced the big crash. Certainly, from time to time, glamour stocks like data processing or drug issues have had a big play. But there have been no overextension of credit, no pyramiding, and, most important, little or no manipulation of the market.

Why have people been investing? Why have stock prices been going up over the years?

Because American business has grown steadily. And there is every reason to believe it will continue to grow — continue to develop new products, new industries, new markets, and continue to expand all along the line, despite recessions from time to time.

Figures compiled by the U.S. Department of Commerce on our *gross national product* — the total value of all goods and services produced in this country — tell the story of growth better than any others. In 1929, the first year for which such figures were compiled, gross national product was valued at $103 billion. In the Great Depression, it fell to a low of $56 billion in 1933. Since then, growth has been steady — and little short of phenomenal. In 1960 the gross national product was valued at $504 billion; by 1965 it had advanced to $685. By the last quarter of 1970 it was moving at the rate of about a trillion dollars a year. And by the end of 1981, it approximated $3 trillion.

That's one good reason for investing — for owning a share in American business — but there's a second equally persuasive reason.

When the cost of living goes up and the country is in a period of inflation, prices tend to rise. When the dollar declines in value, it obviously takes more dollars to buy the same amount of food, clothing, virtually everything, including common stocks, because they represent the ownership of companies that produce these goods.

Thus, in periods of inflation, money that is invested in common stocks or other property is not as likely to lose its purchasing power as money that is simply set aside in a savings bank or invested in bonds that have a fixed dollar value. No one can argue that common stocks provide a guaranteed protection against inflation. That such was not the case was all too evident in 1973–1974 and 1981, when the country experienced simultaneous recession and inflation, with business and stock prices both declining, while prices of consumer goods soared. But most times, it is hard to find a better hedge against inflation than common stocks.

For all these reasons — for income, for a chance to see your capital grow, for the protection of its purchasing power — you may decide you want to invest in stocks.

But wait a minute. Maybe you shouldn't. Are you sure that those dollars you plan to put into the stock market are really extra dollars? Remember, there is an inescapable factor of risk in owning stocks, even the best of them. Not only does the market go down from time to time, but even if stocks generally go up, your stocks may go down. That can be a risk worth taking if you aren't going to be seriously hurt in case you lose some of those dollars. But it's not a risk that a person should take if there is going to be a need for those dollars to meet some emergency.

What if there were a serious and expensive illness in your family? Are your savings adequate to meet that situation? What about the other expenses you may have to meet, such as the cost of a new car, house repairs, furniture, college expenses for your children? What about insurance? Have you got enough so that your family would be able to maintain a decent living standard if you were to die?

If you can answer yes to all these questions, you can, and you probably should, consider putting your extra dollars into common stocks.

CHAPTER 31

How Good Are Common Stocks?

PROBABLY the most convincing evidence of the value of investing in common stocks is the data supplied by several studies measuring the rate of return on New York Stock Exchange stocks — dividends plus price appreciation. These studies were conducted by the Center for Research in Security Prices at the Graduate School of Business of the University of Chicago through 1976. (The Center for Research in Security Prices continues the study today.) They constitute the most definitive measurement of the stock market that has ever been made.

Basically, the questions to which the center addressed itself were these: just how good are common stocks as investments? What average rate of return might an investor expect to realize if he simply selected a stock at random — without any professional guidance or research information — from those listed on the New York Stock Exchange? And what would be his average risk of loss?

Obviously, such questions could be answered only in terms of the historical record. And this the center set about compiling. It took five years and $250,000 to put all the essential data on computer tape because of the high standards of accuracy that were established.

First, the center insisted on going back to January 1926, so that it could not be accused of ignoring the 1929 bull market or the consequent crash. It also insisted on covering all the stocks that had been listed on the exchange at any time since 1926 — not just a cross section or sample but all the stocks — good, bad, and indifferent — including those that had been delisted.

Finally, the center wasn't satisfied to work with an annual or semiannual price, but insisted on recording the price at each month's end for each listed stock. Since those prices had to be comparable throughout the whole period, it meant that the prices had to be adjusted to account for every stock dividend, stock split, spinoff, merger, or other change in a company's financial structure. In addition, information on about 150,000 dividend payments was put on the tapes.

The center's file of price and dividend data is unquestionably the most authoritative record that exists.

Because the compiling and recording took almost five years from its 1958 inception, the first study on rates of return was not published until 1963. It told the story of the market only through 1960. But once the data were put on tape and the computer programs written, it became a comparatively simple matter for the center to keep its study up to date. Now it is possible to tell the rate of return on listed common stocks for any period of time from January 1926 right up to the present.

The key table from this study is the one reproduced on pages 286–288. A few words of explanation are in order. The table shows the percentage gain or loss that an investor would have realized over any given period of time if he had invested equal amounts of money in each of the Big Board stocks and had reinvested all dividends that he received.

While it does take account of the varying commissions that the investor would have had to pay in acquiring the stocks over the years, it does not take account of the commission he would have had to pay in selling out his holdings at the end of the period. Nor does it take account of the taxes that the investor would have paid on dividends as received or on any ultimate capital gain he might have realized. In other words, this is the story of how a tax-

FROM

TO	12/ /25	12/ /26	12/ /27	12/ /28	12/ /29	12/ /30	12/ /31	12/ /32	12/ /33	12/ /34	12/ /35	12/ /36	12/ /37	12/ /38	12/ /39	12/ /40
12/26	0.7															
12/27	15.8	30.0														
12/28	23.6	37.6	44.8													
12/29	8.2	9.9	0.6	-29.2												
12/30	-2.1	-3.4	-12.7	-31.4	-37.7											
12/31	-11.2	-13.3	-21.3	-36.1	-40.9	-48.1										
12/32	-10.8	-12.6	-18.8	-30.0	-32.0	-30.7	-9.7									
12/33	-2.7	-3.2	-7.5	-15.5	-11.9	-1.4	37.11	06.0								
12/34	-1.0	-1.4	-5.0	-11.1	-7.0	2.3	28.3	54.4	15.2							
12/35	2.3	2.1	-0.7	-5.6	-0.6	9.2	33.1	53.4	32.1	50.7						
12/36	4.7	4.8	2.4	-1.6	3.8	13.9	35.6	52.3	37.2	50.6	46.8					
12/37	0.7	0.3	-2.3	-6.1	-2.9	3.0	16.2	23.0	8.1	6.0	-11.7	-46.1				
12/38	2.9	2.6	0.5	-2.9	0.8	6.7	18.7	25.0	13.0	12.1	0.6	-16.2	30.6			
12/39	2.7	2.4	0.4	-2.6	0.8	5.7	15.6	20.3	10.3	8.8	0.0	-11.2	13.0	-3.1		
12/40	2.1	1.7	-0.1	-2.9	0.1	4.5	13.0	16.8	8.0	6.2	-1.3	-9.8	6.3	-4.9	-9.9	
12/41	1.5	1.0	-0.7	-3.2	-0.6	3.3	10.8	13.7	5.9	4.1	-2.2	-9.2	2.6	-5.5	-9.0	-9.9
12/42	2.2	1.9	0.4	-1.9	0.8	4.6	11.5	14.1	7.2	5.8	0.6	-4.9	6.2	0.7	1.0	7.5
12/43	3.5	3.5	2.2	0.1	2.9	6.9	13.7	16.3	10.2	9.5	5.2	0.8	12.3	9.3	12.0	22.2
12/44	4.6	4.6	3.5	1.6	4.5	8.5	15.1	17.8	12.3	11.8	8.2	4.5	15.7	13.7	17.1	26.8
12/45	6.2	6.4	5.4	3.8	6.9	11.1	17.5	20.3	15.4	15.4	12.3	9.3	20.4	19.4	23.7	33.7
12/46	5.4	5.6	4.6	3.1	5.9	9.7	15.5	17.9	13.3	12.9	10.1	7.2	16.3	15.0	17.8	24.2
12/47	5.3	5.5	4.5	3.1	5.7	9.2	14.6	16.8	12.4	12.0	9.3	6.7	14.7	13.6	15.5	20.3
12/48	5.1	5.1	4.2	2.7	5.1	8.4	13.5	15.4	11.3	10.8	8.2	5.7	12.7	11.7	13.3	17.0
12/49	5.7	5.9	4.9	3.6	5.9	9.0	13.8	15.7	11.8	11.4	9.0	6.8	13.3	12.4	13.9	17.3
12/50	6.5	6.6	5.8	4.5	6.9	10.2	15.0	16.7	12.9	12.8	10.5	8.5	14.8	14.1	15.6	19.1
12/51	6.9	7.1	6.3	5.1	7.4	10.5	15.1	16.7	13.2	13.0	10.9	9.0	14.9	14.2	15.7	18.7
12/52	7.0	7.2	6.4	5.2	7.5	10.4	14.8	16.4	13.0	12.9	10.8	9.1	14.6	13.8	15.2	18.0
12/53	6.7	6.8	6.1	4.9	7.0	9.7	13.9	15.4	12.2	12.1	10.1	8.4	13.4	12.5	13.8	16.2
12/54	8.0	8.2	7.5	6.4	8.6	11.3	15.6	17.1	14.0	14.0	12.1	10.6	15.6	14.9	16.3	18.8
12/55	8.4	8.6	8.0	6.9	9.2	11.9	16.1	17.5	14.6	14.6	12.7	11.2	16.0	15.4	16.7	19.0
12/56	8.5	8.7	8.1	7.1	9.3	11.9	15.9	17.3	14.5	14.5	12.6	11.2	15.8	15.3	16.4	18.4
12/57	7.8	8.0	7.4	6.4	8.4	10.8	14.5	15.7	13.0	13.0	11.2	9.9	14.1	13.4	14.4	16.2
12/58	8.9	9.1	8.4	7.5	9.6	12.0	15.7	16.9	14.4	14.4	12.7	11.5	15.7	15.1	16.1	18.0
12/59	9.0	9.2	8.5	7.7	9.7	12.2	15.8	16.9	14.5	14.5	12.9	11.7	15.7	15.2	16.2	17.9
12/60	8.8	9.0	8.3	7.5	9.4	11.7	15.1	16.2	14.0	14.0	12.4	11.2	14.9	14.3	15.2	16.8
12/61	9.4	9.6	9.0	8.1	10.0	12.3	15.6	16.7	14.5	14.6	13.1	11.9	15.6	15.1	16.0	17.6
12/62	8.7	8.8	8.2	7.3	9.2	11.3	14.4	15.5	13.3	13.3	11.9	10.8	14.2	13.6	14.4	15.8
12/63	9.0	9.1	8.5	7.7	9.5	11.6	14.7	15.7	13.6	13.6	12.2	11.1	14.4	13.9	14.7	16.0
12/64	9.1	9.3	8.8	7.9	9.7	11.7	14.7	15.7	13.7	13.7	12.4	11.3	14.5	14.1	14.8	16.1
12/65	9.4	9.5	9.0	8.2	10.0	12.1	15.0	16.0	14.0	14.0	12.7	11.7	14.8	14.4	15.1	16.3
12/66	8.9	9.1	8.6	7.8	9.5	11.4	14.2	15.0	13.2	13.2	11.9	10.9	13.9	13.4	14.1	15.2
12/67	9.6	9.7	9.2	8.5	10.2	12.1	14.9	15.7	13.9	14.0	12.7	11.8	14.8	14.4	15.0	16.1
12/68	9.8	10.0	9.5	8.8	10.5	12.3	15.0	15.8	14.1	14.1	12.9	12.0	14.9	14.5	15.1	16.3
12/69	9.2	9.4	8.8	8.2	9.7	11.4	13.8	14.7	13.0	13.0	11.9	11.0	13.7	13.3	13.8	14.8
12/70	9.0	9.1	8.6	8.0	9.4	11.0	13.4	14.2	12.5	12.5	11.4	10.5	13.1	12.9	13.2	14.2
12/71	9.1	9.2	8.7	8.1	9.6	11.1	13.5	14.2	12.6	12.6	11.5	10.7	13.3	13.0	13.3	14.2
12/72	9.3	9.4	9.0	8.4	9.9	11.3	13.6	14.3	12.8	12.7	11.7	10.9	13.3	12.9	13.3	14.2
12/73	8.7	8.8	8.4	7.8	9.1	10.4	12.6	13.2	11.7	11.7	10.7	9.8	12.1	11.7	12.1	12.9
12/74	8.0	8.1	7.7	7.1	8.3	9.5	11.6	12.2	10.7	10.6	9.7	8.9	11.1	10.8	11.0	11.8
12/75	8.5	8.6	8.2	7.7	9.0	10.3	12.3	12.9	11.5	11.4	10.5	9.7	11.9	11.7	11.8	12.6
12/76	9.0	9.0	8.7	8.1	9.4	10.7	12.8	13.4	12.0	11.9	11.0	10.2	12.4	12.2	12.4	13.1
12/77	9.0	9.0	8.7	8.1	9.4	10.7	12.7	13.3	11.9	11.8	11.0	10.2	12.3	12.1	12.3	13.0
12/78	9.1	9.1	8.8	8.2	9.5	10.7	12.8	13.3	12.0	11.9	11.0	10.3	12.4	12.2	12.4	13.0
12/79	9.5	9.5	9.3	8.7	10.0	11.2	13.2	13.8	12.4	12.4	11.5	10.8	12.9	12.7	12.9	13.6
12/80	9.9	9.9	9.6	9.1	10.3	11.6	13.5	14.1	12.8	12.7	11.9	11.2	13.3	13.1	13.3	14.0

Rates of Return on Investment in Common Stocks Listed on the New York Stock Exchange with Reinvestment of Dividends
(*Percent per Annum Compounded Annually*)

FROM

12//41	12//42	12//43	12//44	12//45	12//46	12//47	12//48	12//49	12//50	12//51	12//52	12//53	12//54	12//55	12//56	12//57	12//58
30.7																	
46.7	57.0																
45.5	49.5	38.9															
51.4	55.6	50.5	60.7														
34.7	34.6	26.1	20.4	-9.5													
27.6	26.5	19.1	13.3	-4.2	0.0												
22.5	20.9	14.3	9.2	-3.4	-0.8	-3.1											
22.4	21.0	15.3	11.6	2.0	5.7	8.3	19.7										
23.6	22.6	18.1	15.1	7.9	12.6	16.7	27.2	35.8									
22.8	21.8	17.9	15.4	9.5	13.5	16.5	23.4	25.3	14.8								
21.7	20.6	17.0	14.7	9.6	13.0	15.3	19.9	19.8	12.4	8.9							
19.5	18.3	14.9	12.7	8.0	10.6	12.1	15.2	13.7	7.6	3.6	-3.1						
22.1	21.2	18.4	16.5	12.6	15.7	17.8	21.5	21.6	17.9	18.6	22.8	55.1					
22.1	21.5	19.0	17.3	13.6	16.4	18.4	21.6	21.9	18.6	19.3	22.5	37.9	20.1				
21.2	20.6	18.3	16.7	13.5	15.9	17.4	20.0	20.2	17.1	17.2	18.9	27.2	13.9	6.6			
18.6	17.8	15.5	13.9	10.8	12.6	13.7	15.6	15.0	12.2	11.4	11.5	15.0	3.9	-3.6	-13.6		
20.5	19.8	17.6	16.2	13.5	15.5	16.8	18.9	18.8	16.7	16.7	17.8	22.3	14.9	13.1	16.8	57.9	
20.2	19.5	17.4	16.1	13.6	15.5	16.8	18.8	18.8	16.8	16.8	17.8	21.5	15.4	14.0	17.1	36.0	14.4
19.0	18.2	16.1	14.9	12.5	14.2	15.4	17.0	16.7	15.0	15.0	15.6	18.1	12.8	11.2	12.7	21.9	6.4
19.6	18.9	16.9	15.8	13.5	15.2	16.3	17.8	17.6	16.2	16.2	16.9	19.3	14.9	14.1	15.9	23.7	13.7
17.6	16.9	14.9	13.8	11.6	13.0	13.9	15.1	14.7	13.2	13.0	13.2	14.9	10.8	9.5	10.3	15.2	6.4
17.7	17.0	15.2	14.2	12.0	13.5	14.2	15.4	15.1	13.7	13.4	13.7	15.3	11.6	10.5	11.4	15.8	8.8
17.7	17.1	15.4	14.4	12.4	13.7	14.4	15.6	15.3	13.9	13.8	14.1	15.7	12.3	11.3	12.2	16.3	10.5
17.9	17.4	15.7	14.8	12.9	14.4	15.1	16.2	16.0	14.6	14.6	14.9	16.6	13.5	12.6	13.5	17.7	12.7
16.7	16.2	14.6	13.7	11.8	13.1	13.8	14.7	14.5	13.2	12.9	13.2	14.6	11.6	10.7	11.3	14.8	10.2
17.6	17.2	15.6	14.7	12.9	14.2	14.9	15.9	15.7	14.5	14.4	14.8	16.4	13.7	12.8	13.6	17.2	13.3
17.7	17.3	15.8	14.9	13.2	14.5	15.2	16.2	16.0	14.9	14.9	15.3	15.8	14.3	13.7	14.5	17.9	14.4
16.1	15.6	14.1	13.3	11.7	12.7	13.3	14.2	13.9	12.8	12.7	13.0	14.1	11.6	10.9	11.5	14.0	10.7
15.3	14.8	13.3	12.6	11.0	12.0	12.5	13.2	13.0	12.0	11.8	11.9	13.0	10.7	10.0	10.3	12.5	9.4
15.4	14.8	13.5	12.7	11.2	12.2	12.7	13.5	13.2	12.2	12.1	12.3	13.3	11.1	10.5	10.9	12.9	10.1
15.3	14.8	13.5	12.8	11.4	12.4	12.8	13.6	13.3	12.4	12.2	12.4	13.3	11.3	10.6	11.0	13.0	10.3
13.9	13.3	12.1	11.5	10.1	11.0	11.3	11.9	11.7	10.6	10.4	10.5	11.3	9.3	8.5	8.7	10.3	7.7
12.6	12.1	10.8	10.2	8.9	9.6	9.8	10.4	10.0	9.0	8.7	8.7	9.4	7.4	6.6	6.7	7.9	5.4
13.5	13.0	11.8	11.2	9.8	10.6	10.8	11.4	11.2	10.2	10.0	10.1	10.8	8.9	8.3	8.4	9.8	7.5
14.0	13.5	12.3	11.7	10.5	11.3	11.6	12.2	12.0	11.0	10.9	10.9	11.6	9.9	9.4	9.6	11.0	8.9
13.9	13.4	12.2	11.6	10.5	11.2	11.5	12.1	11.9	10.9	10.8	10.8	11.5	9.9	9.4	9.6	10.9	8.9
13.9	13.4	12.3	11.7	10.6	11.3	11.6	12.2	12.0	11.1	11.0	11.0	11.6	10.1	9.6	9.8	11.1	9.2
14.4	13.9	12.9	12.3	11.2	12.0	12.3	12.8	12.7	11.8	11.8	11.8	12.4	11.0	10.6	10.8	12.1	10.3
14.8	14.4	13.3	12.8	11.8	12.5	12.8	13.4	13.2	12.4	12.4	12.4	13.1	11.7	11.3	11.6	12.8	11.2

12//41	12//42	12//43	12//44	12//45	12//46	12//47	12//48	12//49	12//50	12//51	12//52	12//53	12//54	12//55	12//56	12//57	12//58

Rates of Return on Investment in Common Stocks Listed on the New York Stock Exchange with Reinvestment of Dividends

(*Percent per Annum Compounded Annually*) (*continued*)

TO	12/ /59	12/ /60	12/ /61	12/ /62	12/ /63	12/ /64	12/ /65	12/ /66	12/ /67	12/ /68	12/ /69	12/ /70	12/ /71	12/ /72	12/ /73	12/ /74	12/ /75	12/ /76	12/ /77	12/ /78	12/ /79
12/60	-1.9																				
12/61	12.9	27.5																			
12/62	3.8	5.9	-13.4																		
12/63	7.4	10.4	2.0	17.6																	
12/64	9.7	12.8	7.7	18.6	16.6																
12/65	12.5	15.9	12.9	22.7	23.7	28.5															
12/66	9.6	12.0	9.0	14.9	13.0	10.1	-8.2														
12/67	13.3	16.0	14.1	20.7	21.3	22.4	17.6	51.1													
12/68	14.6	17.3	15.7	21.3	22.0	23.1	20.9	40.1	28.5												
12/69	10.4	12.0	10.1	13.9	13.3	12.7	9.0	15.8	1.5	-20.1											
12/70	9.0	10.2	8.2	11.2	10.2	9.0	5.7	10.1	-0.2	-12.0	-4.5										
12/71	9.8	11.0	9.3	12.1	11.3	10.4	7.6	11.7	4.1	-2.8	6.6	16.8									
12/72	10.1	11.2	9.7	12.3	11.5	10.8	8.3	11.7	5.6	0.8	7.9	13.3	6.6								
12/73	7.4	8.2	6.7	8.6	7.6	6.3	3.7	5.6	0.3	-4.3	-0.6	-1.2	-9.9	-28.1							
12/74	5.0	5.6	4.0	5.4	4.2	2.8	0.2	1.3	-3.6	-7.9	-5.6	-7.4	-14.6	-26.0	-27.3						
12/75	7.2	7.9	6.5	8.1	7.2	6.2	4.1	5.6	1.4	-1.7	1.5	1.7	-2.1	-6.5	6.3	53.7					
12/76	8.7	9.6	8.4	10.0	9.3	8.4	6.7	8.4	4.8	2.2	6.0	7.1	5.0	3.4	16.9	48.3	40.1	0.0			
12/77	8.7	9.6	8.5	10.0	9.3	8.5	6.9	8.5	5.3	3.0	6.4	7.4	5.7	4.6	15.0	34.0	23.9	9.5			
12/78	9.0	9.8	8.8	10.2	9.6	8.9	7.5	8.9	6.0	4.0	7.2	8.2	6.9	6.1	14.8	28.7	20.5	11.7	14.0		
12/79	10.2	11.0	10.1	11.6	11.1	10.5	9.2	10.8	8.2	6.6	9.8	11.0	10.1	9.9	18.0	30.0	24.0	19.1	24.2	35.3	
12/80	11.1	12.0	11.1	12.6	12.2	11.6	10.6	12.1	9.8	8.4	11.5	12.8	12.2	12.3	19.8	30.2	25.4	22.0	26.4	33.1	31.0

exempt individual would have made out in the market over the years.

The resultant figures can be compared directly to the compound interest rates paid by banks on savings in the various periods and to the published yields on most other kinds of investment, since these figures never take account of taxes either.

It is not difficult to read the table. If you want to see how a hypothetical investor would have made out over any given period, select any starting year you like from the columns headed "FROM" and read down till you reach the figure for whatever terminal year you select in the stub at the left headed "TO." That figure, expressed as a compound interest return, shows the rate of return that an investor would have realized had he bought all the stocks on the Big Board at the beginning date and reinvested all his dividends until the terminal date. Since his investment would have covered *all* the listed stocks, the rate of return can be taken to represent the average of what he might have realized on any one stock. On some stocks, the rate of return might have been infinitely higher, while on others there would have been a 100% loss.

Actually, the center computed results in dollars, not in percentages, and these results show how the invested dollar would have increased or decreased (by thousandths of one cent) during each of the time periods shown in the table. The dollar difference between any starting date and any terminal date is simply expressed here in terms of its compounded interest equivalent, either minus or plus.

Probably the most significant figure in the table is that 9.9% at the bottom of the first column. That figure means that an investment of an equal amount of money in each of all the Big Board stocks on December 31, 1925, would by December 31, 1980, with the reinvestment of dividends, have yielded a return equal to 9.9% interest per annum compounded annually.

Other significant findings, as demonstrated by the table, were as follows.

(1) In all the year-to-year periods, January 1926 to December 1980, there are only 91 with negative rates of return — in other words, losses. In the other time periods you would have had a profit. The longest span of years showing losses is the fourteen-year period from 1928 to 1942. The only other periods when you would have had to hold on for as long as six years in order to show a profit were the ones from 1929 through 1935 and from 1936 through 1942. Because of the market declines of 1968–1969 and 1973–1974, you would have been able to show a profit in only 25 of the 45 year-to-year time periods from 1966 to 1975.

(2) The longest period of time in which the rate of return was less than 5% was 1928 through 1950. If you ignore the 1929–1932 crash, the longest period of time in which the return was less than 5% was 1936 through 1944.

(3) In the last 25 years, there has been only one period (1968–1975) of more than three consecutive years in which the rate of return was consistently less than 5%. Furthermore, in this 25-year span there has never been a ten-year period in which you could not at some point have realized a return of at least 10%.

(4) If you had bought in 1932, there was never a year in which you would not have realized a profit of at least 10% — usually much more — until 1974.

The Lorie-Fisher study also reports the results that would have been obtained if dividends had simply been accumulated and not reinvested, and if dividends were completely ignored. Obviously, the rates of return were considerably lower in both cases.

A second study, conducted at the Center for Research in Security Prices, answers the questions of how often and how much an investor might have gained or lost on each of the stocks listed on the exchange from 1926 to 1960. While this study has not been updated, there is no reason to believe results would be materially different.

To arrive at its conclusions, the Center computed results for every possible combination of month-end purchase and sales dates for every stock throughout the 35-year period from January 1926 to December 1960. For any one stock, this would have represented 87,000 monthly combinations. For all exchange stocks, it meant tabulating results on more than 56,000,000 such possible transactions.

Here is the key finding of this study: if one had picked a stock *at random* from the Big Board list, if one had then picked *at random* a purchase date between January 1926 and December 1960, and if one had picked at random any later sales date within those same 35 years, one would have made money 78% of the time. The median return, assuming reinvestment of all dividends and payment of brokerage commissions on purchase and sale, would have been 9.8% per annum compounded annually. At that rate of interest, money doubles in about seven years, and the study showed that the investor would have had a better than 50–50 chance of doing exactly that — doubling his money — with purely random selection. His risk of losing as much as 20% a year on his investment was only one in thirteen, whereas his expectation of making as much as 20% per annum compounded annually was one in five.

The study demonstrated two other points of vital significance to any investor.

(1) If the investor had picked three or four stocks at random instead of just one, the risk of loss would have been considerably reduced, and the probability of a larger profit would have been considerably improved.

(2) If the investor had not been forced to sell during a period of economic recession — if he had been able to hold on for a year or two — his chance of making a profit and the amount of profit would have both been significantly increased.

The value of long-term investing, the value of being able to hold on through a period of weakness in the market, is convincingly demonstrated by the table on pages 292–293. It may look complicated, but it's well worth five minutes of study.

Profit Probabilities on Common Stocks Listed on the New York Stock Exchange, 1926–1960

Sale Period

Purchase Period		Jan. 26 Sept. 26 U	Oct. 26 Oct. 27 D	Nov. 27 July 29 U	Aug. 29 Feb. 33 D	Mar. 33 Apr. 37 U	May 37 May 38 D	June 38 Jan. 45 U
Jan. 26–Sept. 26	U	.46	.60	.77	.37	.38	.44	.48
		−4.2%	18.2%	18.2%	−8.0%	−4.6%	−1.9%	−0.5%
Oct. 26–Oct. 27	D		.58	.59	.32	.33	.40	.45
			10.0%	21.0%	−11.9%	−6.7%	−3.0%	−1.5%
Nov. 27–July 29	U			.75	.15	.21	.27	.35
				10.0%	−29.7%	−13.0%	−7.4%	−1.0%
Aug. 29–Feb. 33	D				.13	.56	.59	.62
					−45.6%	4.3%	3.9%	3.9%
Mar. 33–Apr. 37	U					.69	.49	.55
						21.0%	−0.8%	1.7%
May 37–May 38	D						.13	.55
							−59.6%	2.3%
June 38–Jan. 45	U							.66
								9.1%
Feb. 45–Sept. 45	D							
Oct. 45–Oct. 48	U							
Nov. 48–Sept. 49	D							
Oct. 49–June 53	U							
July 53–July 54	D							
Aug. 54–June 57	U							
July 57–Mar. 58	D							
Apr. 58–Apr. 60	U							
May 60–Dec. 60	D							

Feb. 45 Sept. 45 D	Oct. 45 Oct. 48 U	Nov. 48 Sept. 49 D	Oct. 49 June 53 U	July 53 July 54 D	Aug. 54 June 57 U	July 57 Mar. 58 D	Apr. 58 Apr. 60 U	May 60 Dec. 60 D
.72	.77	.71	.82	.84	.83	.89	.91	.90
4.1%	4.7%	3.9%	5.4%	5.8%	7.0%	6.6%	7.5%	7.3%
.70	.75	.69	.79	.82	.87	.88	.91	.90
3.7%	4.4%	3.5%	5.1%	5.4%	6.7%	6.3%	7.2%	7.1%
.62	.67	.62	.73	.77	.84	.85	.90	.89
1.9%	2.8%	2.1%	3.9%	4.3%	5.7%	5.3%	6.3%	6.2%
.84	.86	.83	.89	.90	.94	.93	.95	.95
8.6%	8.9%	7.3%	8.8%	8.8%	10.0%	9.4%	10.3%	10.0%
.90	.92	.86	.93	.94	.96	.95	.97	.96
9.0%	9.4%	6.4%	9.7%	9.4%	10.9%	10.0%	11.0%	10.6%
.93	.95	.90	.95	.96	.98	.97	.98	.98
11.6%	11.4%	8.5%	10.7%	10.5%	12.0%	10.9%	11.9%	11.4%
.98	.97	.92	.97	.97	.99	.98	.99	.99
24.0%	18.6%	11.5%	14.1%	13.1%	14.9%	13.1%	14.1%	13.4%
.65	.74	.60	.83	.85	.93	.92	.95	.94
16.6%	11.1%	2.8%	9.4%	9.5%	12.3%	10.7%	12.2%	11.6%
	.38	.36	.78	.83	.92	.90	.95	.94
	−7.0%	−5.2%	9.1%	9.3%	12.8%	10.7%	12.4%	11.5%
		.48	.93	.92	.96	.94	.98	.96
		−1.8%	21.7%	15.1%	18.2%	14.3%	15.9%	14.4%
			.73	.68	.91	.88	.95	.92
			11.9%	7.3%	15.8%	11.4%	14.0%	12.5%
				.70	.94	.88	.95	.93
				18.8%	24.8%	12.3%	15.6%	13.2%
					.64	.48	.79	.77
					7.6%	−0.9%	10.5%	8.6%
						.37	.88	.82
						−17.3%	25.6%	13.9%
							.64	.50
							11.8%	0.2%
								.40
								−11.0%

The table shows, by examining economic periods from 1926 through 1960, how you would have made out if you had bought a stock at random from those traded on the New York Stock Exchange, reinvested your dividends, and sold that stock in the same period or in any later period. The boldface decimal figures show you what percentage of the time you would have made money — thus, .46 means you would have made money 46% of the time. The lightface figures on each line immediately below show you the median rate of return (percent per year compounded annually) you might have expected to realize. The periods themselves are all of different lengths, but each one corresponds to a recognized upswing or downswing in business as defined by the National Bureau of Economic Research. The U identifies an upswing, and the D a downswing. The periods listed vertically are for purchases; those listed horizontally are for sales.

Here's how to read the table. Let's assume that you made your random purchase in the first period between January 1926 and September 1926 and then sold out in that same period. Your chance of making a profit would have been only 46%, and your average profit or loss would have been minus 4.2%. However, if you had made your purchase in that first period and did not sell until the last period, between May and December 1960 (the last figure in the first line of the table), your chance of making a profit would have been 90%, and your median profit would have been equal to 7.3% compounded interest for 35 years.

To see how the table proves the value of long-term investing, look at the boldface figures diagonally down the table from upper left to lower right. These figures show your average chance of making money if you had bought and sold within the same time period. Now contrast the irregularity of these figures with the boldface ones in the last column to the right, reading straight down from top to bottom. These show your expectation of profit if you had held your stock and not sold it until the last period covered by this study. Down to 1954, all but one are over 90%.

The table on page 254 shows how the figures look when set down right together.

Certainly these figures demonstrate emphatically the value of long-term investing.

None of these studies guarantees anything about future investment success. But if you are willing to assume that the past is any kind of a guide to the future, their meaning is clear and unmistakable.

One other study conducted by the center throws significant light on the question of how large a portfolio has to be in order to achieve essentially the same rates of return as an investor would get if he owned all the stocks on the New York Stock Exchange. The study calculated results for portfolios, selected at random, that consisted of two, eight, sixteen, 32, and 128 stocks that were held for each of the 40 single years from 1926 to 1965 as well as for the eight five-year periods, four ten-year periods, and two twenty-year periods. The study shows that with eight stocks, performance was raised to a range of 94% to 96%. At 128, the figure was a straight 99% for all time periods. One inference that might be drawn from this study is that if you think you can pick stocks that will perform better than an equal number picked purely at random, you have pretty good assurance of beating the performance record of the stock market as a whole.

Since these studies cover all the stocks listed on the New York Stock Exchange, the results they show are the results you might have expected on the average to achieve with the random selection of any one stock. For this reason they exemplify what is called the *random walk* hypothesis. They have been accepted today in financial and academic circles as establishing the standard yardsticks against which anyone who has a technical theory of his own must measure his performance.

The entry of scholars into the field of stock market research may not guarantee that someday the touchstone to investment success will be found. But it should go a long way toward disabusing the public of its misplaced confidence in those who regularly advertise investment infallibility in the financial pages of our newspapers.

In this connection, the following observations of Professor Lorie are highly pertinent:

Many people have been beguiled by the possibility of buying wealth, believing that it is possible to buy information or formulas which will permit extraordinary high rates of return on capital. As evidence for my statement, one need only look at any issue of the numerous periodicals dealing with the stock market; they are thickly strewn with offers to sell for a few dollars the secret of getting rich. It should be clear that one cannot buy wealth for a few dollars, but this is not the same as saying that research on the stock market is without value or that it cannot provide the basis for the more prudent management of funds.

For many years, it was probably true that formal and quantitative research was not very useful either because of its lack of comprehensiveness or its lack of rigor. It was very difficult to do comprehensive financial research before the availability of high-speed computers. Rigor was frequently or even typically lacking because research was usually the product of persons familiar with the financial markets under investigation but not the canons of scientific inquiry. . . .

As an example of the lack of rigor which formerly characterized much research, I cite the Dow Theory of stock price movements. This theory is based on crude measurements, and in its typical formulation is so ambiguous as to require interpreters, and they often disagree.

It is clear that much of the work done so far [at the center] has had the effect of discrediting beliefs — and even some relatively sophisticated ones — about the behavior of security prices. . . .

For the businessman and investor, it is true that an awareness of ignorance is better than an erroneous belief, if only because it tends to eliminate buying the services of charlatans and attending to the insignificant.

CHAPTER 32

How You Should Invest — If You Can

THE stock you'd like to buy, of course, is the one that just doesn't exist. You'd like a stock that is completely safe, one that pays a liberal dividend, and one that's bound to go up.

There are a lot of good stocks that will probably satisfy you on any one of these counts. But none will accomplish all three objectives.

If you want safety in a stock, you'll have to give up the hope that it will increase sensationally in value.

If you'd like to see your money grow, you have to be prepared to take a considerably greater measure of risk.

Sometimes it's possible to find either a fairly safe stock, or one that seems likely to appreciate in price, that will also yield you a better-than-average dividend. But even here, as a general rule, you can't have your cake and eat it too. If you get a liberal dividend, it will probably be at the expense of one of the other two factors.

Hence, the first step in solving your investment problem is to decide on the one objective you most want to attain by investing. Is it safety of capital? Or liberal dividends? Or price appreciation?

When you start thinking about stocks that might best match any of these objectives, you should first take a look at various industries and their future prospects. Remember, the carriage industry was a thriving business at the turn of the century.

To see how these various factors might influence your own investment selections, consider how seven different people in widely varying circumstances might approach their investment problem.

Mr. Adams is twenty-four years old, unmarried, and, as far as he can see, likely to pursue his course of single blessedness for some time to come. Having received his college degree, he now has a trainee's job as a chemist with a large food-manufacturing company. His income is $20,000 a year, and, thanks to the fact that he cuts living costs by sharing an apartment with two roommates, he can save at the rate of $5,000 a year. With a $20,000 ordinary life insurance policy and a $50,000 group policy issued by his company, he has made a start toward building an estate for himself.

With the savings that he accumulated, he now has about $10,000, very little of which has to be earmarked for emergencies as long as his responsibilities are as light as they are. Then, too, if he really got in a serious jam, he knows he could count on his folks to help him out.

He wants to see his capital grow, so he wants to invest in stocks that have good growth possibilities, even though such stocks may yield only a scant return in dividends now.

Such a young man can afford to take a considerable measure of risk. But before he starts eyeing some of the more speculative stocks, he probably ought to put out an anchor to windward. Marriage has a way of creeping up on a man when he least expects it.

He can probably afford to invest all of his nest egg. Of this, at least $2,000 ought to go into a money market fund so that he can have funds of known amount instantly available to him if he should need them. Another $4,000 might be divided between two solid common stocks — stocks that might be described as defensive in character because they have weathered many an economic storm in the past with an unbroken record of dividend payments. One of these might be a public utility like Pacific Gas & Electric or Tampa Electric, utilities that stand to benefit from the rapid growth of the areas they serve. The other might be a stock like General Electric. Such a stock may fluctuate a little more when business expands or retracts. But it is still essentially stable, because it makes so many different products for so many different markets.

Mr. Adams might then very properly put his remaining $4,000 into stocks of a more speculative nature — stocks with good growth possibilities. Maybe one of the drug stocks that seem likely to benefit the increased number of older people in our population. Maybe something in computers or electronics. But probably first of all a chemical stock — a field in which he should have firsthand knowledge of new and promising developments.

Whatever he buys for long-term growth, it may pay him to comb the list for some "sleepers," rather than simply to fall for some of the well-known glamour stocks that usually sell at very high price-earnings multiples. There are many good solid companies with growth records and further growth potential that can match the glamour stocks but are available at lower price-earning rations. Finding these overlooked stocks can be worth a good deal of study and effort. Don't forget that most of today's glamour stocks were once in the overlooked category themselves.

As for his future savings — that $4,000 he expects to accumulate each year — that money too can go largely into growth stocks as long as his present situation remains unchanged. But he probably ought to start a systematic investment plan with his broker.

Mr. Adams can accomplish his plan in one of two ways. He can open a Monthly Investment Plan account, or similar accumulation plan, such as many large banks and most big brokerage firms have available. That way he can apply his monthly savings toward the regular purchase of some stock. Or he can save his money, and when a sufficient sum has accumulated, he can buy additional shares on an odd-lot basis.

Consider now the case of Ms. Baxter, a capable young woman of twenty-four. As a computer programmer trainee in a large company, she makes $375 a week, about as much as Mr. Adams. She lives alone in a small studio apartment, responsible only to herself. She has no family to worry about, and she doesn't expect her mother and father, who live in a little town out West, to worry about her.

A thrifty person, she has managed to add a little every month to a small inheritance she received from an aunt. Now and again she has supplemented these savings with a special bonus check. Currently, she finds she is able to bank about $200 a month out of her salary. All told, she has about $8,000, a large part of it in savings bonds.

Now Ms. Baxter has decided she wants to invest in stocks. Why? Because every time she cashes a bond, the $100 she gets for it buys less than it did the last time — usually not even as much as she could have bought a few years ago with the $75 she put into the bond. She wants to put her money into some investment where its purchasing power will be better protected and where she'll still get a good return on her money. And if she's lucky, maybe she'll make a profit on her stocks — a big enough profit so that she'll eventually be able to take that trip to Europe she has always promised herself.

But maybe stocks, including hers, will go down. That's a risk she has to take. But fortunately it's one she can afford. If stocks drop, she can probably wait for them to come back without any serious jeopardy, because her job offers her a good measure of security. Quite apart from her own medical hospital insurance, she knows the firm will help her over any rough spots. And as for protection in her old age — well, the firm has an excellent pension program. This, plus Social Security, should take care of her quite handily.

What kinds of stocks should Ms. Baxter buy?

Obviously, she wants to be pretty conservative in her selections. But she probably doesn't have to make safety her sole objective. She can afford to take what's called a businessperson's risk, and she can look for stocks that pay relatively liberal dividends.

Ms. Baxter should put her money into three or four different stocks, each of them a blue chip, each a leader in its own industry — stocks like Sears, Roebuck & Company, Eastman Kodak, Exxon, International Paper, plus one good utility.

Alternately, to benefit from more diversified holdings, she might put her money into one of the big mutual funds that have growth as their objective — funds like Massachusetts Investors Growth Stock Fund, Putnam Growth Fund or Fidelity Capital Fund. None of these funds fared very well during recent dips, but neither did the entire mutual fund industry — nor the stock market. Ms. Baxter's primary interest is in growth; she should be much more interested in their longer-range prospects.

To make these investments she will have to sell her savings bonds.

As for the $200 a month she is able to save, Ms. Baxter might prudently keep half as an emergency fund until it exceeds $2,000. With the other $100 a month she too might open a Monthly Investment Plan, or some other accumulation plan account. As a matter of fact, she might even open two or three such accounts, putting her $100 into one stock one month and into another stock a second month on a regular, rotating basis.

Mr. and Mrs. Chandler face quite a different problem, despite the fact that Mr. Chandler's income as a skilled toolmaker in an auto parts manufacturing plant is about $35,000 a year. To begin with, they live on a very modest scale in a small Ohio town. Still in their thirties, they have been able to raise two children, now eight and ten, buy their own home, and still save a little bit.

They have only about $4,000 in their bank account. But from now on that's going to grow fast. Mr. Chandler was made foreman just last month, and that means $125 a week more in his pay envelope. Furthermore, in just a couple of months the mortgage will be paid off, and they will have another $200 a month free and clear.

What it all adds up to is that they've got $4,000 now, and they figure on having $5,000 to $6,000 a year to invest from now on.

What about protection for his family? Mr. Chandler has a $20,000 insurance policy. He considers that plenty in view of the benefit program which his union sponsors for all members.

He has become sold on stocks. He wants to start buying stocks now in order to build a little estate and finance college education for his children.

That's a program that makes sense, provided it is handled right. He hasn't a lot of money to put into the market, so, to start with, he wants to be sure that money is well protected. What if one of his children has to be hospitalized for a long time?

Where should he start? His local utility — the Ohio Edison Company — might be as good as any. The dividends will help pay his electric bill. That's an idea that has real appeal for Mr. and Mrs. Chandler.

After that, he might buy ten shares of a natural gas company, a stock that offers assurance of a fairly stable price, plus some possibilities of growth as natural gas consumption continues to grow.

His future investments for some time might be of much the same type — fairly stable stocks but ones that nevertheless offer some prospect of growth over the long pull. Nothing as spectacular as computers or electronics, which market analysts might call "aggressive-growth situations," but perhaps something like American Can Company, which stands to grow as our population and food consumption increase, or Federated Department Stores, or General Foods.

Mr. and Mrs. Davenport are even better off financially. But from an investment point of view they're not as well off as the Chandlers. As one of the younger officers in a big advertising agency, Mr. Davenport makes $50,000 a year. But his scale of living is such that after taxes, mortgage payments on his $100,000 house, and premiums on a $50,000 life insurance policy, there's not much left over at the end of the year — just what he might need to pay an unexpected doctor's bill. His equity in the house — the unmortgaged part that he owns — and the cash value of his life insurance policy represent all his savings.

But Mr. Davenport has just received a $20,000 bonus, because he brought a new account into the agency last year. And Mr. Davenport knows exactly what he's going to do with that $20,000. He's going to buy common stocks in two companies he has just read about. One of them is a new small airline serving a growing resort area. The other is a company that Mr. Davenport believes is going to lick the problem of desalting seawater economically.

When Mr. Davenport announces what he expects to do with his bonus, Mrs. Davenport puts her foot down. It sounds altogether too speculative for her. That money, she contends, should be set safely aside to provide a college education for their two children.

How should Mr. and Mrs. Davenport solve their problem?

Probably $5,000 of their $20,000 ought to go into government bonds in case the family meets a real emergency. As for the balance, the stock of a good growth mutual fund or a closed-end investment trust like Lehman Corporation or Tri-Continental Corporation might represent a happy compromise between Mrs. Davenport's conservatism and Mr. Davenport's "all-or-nothing" impulse.

Ordinarily it would not be prudent for a man to put all his investment funds in a single security. But a mutual fund or an investment trust is an obvious exception because of its diversified holdings. Furthermore, shares in a closed-end trust can be bought on the exchange without any loading charge, and are frequently available at a substantial discount — that is, at a price below net asset value per share.

Then too, Mr. Davenport is still only in his early forties and looks like a comer. He's the kind of a man who will get a number of bonuses and salary increases along the way. As time goes by, he will probably be buying other stocks. And he might just as well begin buying in good-sized units.

Mr. Edwards is a Nebraska wheat farmer. For fifteen years life has been good to him. He has had good crops and has received good prices for them. He is completely clear of debt on his farm and on his equipment, and all of it is in excellent condition. Insurance is no worry to him, because his boys, both of them in college now, could take over the farm and make a good living out of it if anything should happen to him.

He has $19,000 in extra capital, over and above necessary reserves for upkeep of the farm. He's beginning to wonder if he's doing the best he can with it. His older son started him thinking about that the last time he was home from college. Mr. Edwards has $4,000 in savings bonds, $4,000 in a building and loan association, $8,000 in a savings account, and about $3,000 in his checking account.

Obviously, he has far more cash than he needs. One thousand dollars in his savings account and another thousand in his checking account should suffice.

Hence, he could prudently put $13,000 cash and savings bonds into securities, and he probably ought to sell his $4,000 worth of building and loan shares and invest that money in stocks too — a total of $17,000. The building and loan shares provide a good yield. But he can get an attractive return, plus growth potential, by investing that money in common stocks. Furthermore, his building and loan shares really represent an investment in real estate. And since his principal asset, the farm, is also real estate, it would seem wise for him to diversify his investments.

Here is a man who can really afford to take a fair measure of risk with his money for the sake of getting a better-than-average growth potential, because he already has a substantial measure of protection — far more than most people have. In fact, he can afford to be a bit speculative in his selections.

First, it would be natural for him to invest in a good farm-machinery stock — something like Deere & Company. But he ought not to put too large a share of his $13,000 into such a stock because if farmers suffer a reverse in their fortunes, as they sometimes do, so do the machinery manufacturers.

He might also properly invest in a company like General Mills that processes the grain he raises.

But he might also be advised to put some money in the stocks of companies that have no relationship to his own business of farming — perhaps natural resource stocks like the Weyerhaeuser Company, or American Natural Gas, or chemical stocks like Union Carbide, Dow, or Monsanto. Other stocks that might suit his situation would be stocks like Minnesota Mining & Manufacturing, or Procter & Gamble, or Eastman Kodak. All these companies operate in fields that show great future promise.

Mr. and Mrs. Frank are a retired couple, both over sixty-five. Social Security and small benefits accruing from a company pension plan are sufficient to provide them with an income of about $600 a month. Their only other assets consist of a home, which they own free and clear in a small town in Kansas where taxes and living costs are a lot lower than in urban centers. They have a good-sized garden plot that helps reduce food costs. They have $85,000 in savings, most of it realized on annuities and life insurance policies in which Mr. Frank thriftily invested through the years.

On the other hand, if their assets are limited, so are their liabilities. Their two children are both married, and their futures are as secure as those of any people with modest incomes and frugal habits can be.

The natural impulse of Mr. and Mrs. Frank is to conserve what they have — to leave their money in the savings bank or invest it in savings bonds. But even with a return of 6% on their money, their income from all sources would amount to only $12,000 a year, or a little more than $230 a week. And in a time of rising prices and increased taxes, $230 a week allows little latitude for luxuries — nothing at all for an occasional trip to visit their children and grandchildren.

Without any appreciable sacrifice of safety, Mr. and Mrs. Frank ought to consider investing at least part of their money — perhaps $25,000 — in corporate bonds, especially in a period of tight money such as 1981–1982, when high-rated bonds could be bought at prices that would yield 15% or 16% on their money.

With the balance of their savings they could afford to take some measure of risk. Two or three good growth mutual funds might seem like a prudent investment for them. But it wouldn't be wholly out of order for them to consider something even more speculative, such as a half-dozen cyclical stocks. Since these are stocks in industries like steel, automobiles, chemicals, paper, metals, and petroleum, which usually follow the business cycle pretty closely, they can often be bought at attractive prices in periods when business slows down, as it did in 1981.

During a business decline, dividends might be reduced, and that could make things a little hard for them. But what if they did have to sell $1,500 or $2,500 of stock in a bad year in order to make ends meet? At their age they can afford to dip into capital if they have to without putting their lives in peril. And consider the rewards they might reap. Dividends of 10%, 12%, or even 14% were not too remarkable on cyclical stocks in 1981. More important, there seems reason to believe that significant capital gains can be had over the years ahead with a careful selection of quality growth stocks.

For rewards like these, Mr. and Mrs. Frank can afford a sizable measure of risk on the bulk of their capital.

Finally, consider the situation of Mrs. Gordon, the fifty-seven-year-old widow of a successful doctor. Her principal assets consist of the family home and $230,000 worth of life insurance. True, the doctor did leave an assortment of stocks. But they proved to have a cash value of only about $20,000, because, like most medical men who have little contact with business and less time in which to study it, Dr. Gordon had bought only the most speculative of securities — Canadian oil shares, stock in a plastic airplane company, and some preferred stocks that must have looked attractive because of big accumulations of back dividends — dividends that were owed but unfortunately never paid.

Mrs. Gordon doesn't want to see her capital dissipated that way. She wants to live off her investments but leave the principal intact, so that she can pass it along to her three children, all of them now launched on substantial careers of their own.

Mrs. Gordon begins her calculations where every investor in such a situation must: "How much income do I have to have?" She figures she needs $25,000 a year to maintain her standard of living. That in turn means that she must get a return of 10% on her $250,000.

Time was when an investor like Mrs. Gordon would have had to put her money into common stocks if she wanted to realize a return of 10%. Thus, in the early 1950s, she could have expected to earn only about 3% on government bonds and 4% or so on corporate bonds and good-grade preferreds. But thanks to the bull market that got under way then, she would have experienced little difficulty in finding top-quality stocks that would have given her a return of 10% or even more, counting both the dividends and the capital gains that she could have realized.

Of course, in the early 1980s, the situation had changed. All Mrs. Gordon would have had to do to realize 10% was put her money into any top-rated corporate bonds and sit back and collect the interest.

But that wouldn't wholly satisfy someone of Mrs. Gordon's temperament. Nor would it protect her against the possible ravages of continued inflation in all the years that might still remain to her. Perhaps, down the road, $25,000 a year wouldn't permit her to continue her present life-style. Perhaps she should have one eye on guaranteed income, and the other eye on long-term appreciation in the value of her holdings.

For all those reasons it would make sense for Mrs. Gordon to divide her $250,000 — to put half into corporate bonds, and the other half into good-quality stocks that pay good dividends and offer prospects of long-term growth.

Most of Mrs. Gordon's stock selections would probably be industrials of the blue chip variety — stocks that have paid dividends consistently for a long period of years and thus offer some compensation for any compromise she may be forced to make temporarily in the 10% income return that she feels she needs.

On the New York Stock Exchange 493 common stocks listed can boast records of consecutive quarterly dividends running back at least 25 years. Most of these can be classified as "the bluest of the blue," because many are also the stocks of companies that have no bonds outstanding, and little or no preferred. Hence, all earnings, or virtually all earnings, are available for dividends on the common stock. This can be very important in a period of bad business. Stocks like J. C. Penney, American Can, Borden, Eastman Kodak, General Electric, American Brands, Scott Paper, and Procter & Gamble should suit virtually any investor in Mrs. Gordon's position.

As a general rule, Mrs. Gordon should not put more than 20% of the capital that she has for common-stock investments into any one industry or more than 10% into any one company.

No one of the programs outlined for these seven investors is likely to perfectly fit your own special situation. But a consideration of their problems and the ways in which they might have been solved can serve to illustrate the kind of sober thinking required of an investor before deciding what stocks or bonds are right for the particular situation. Remember, there is no all-purpose security — no stock that fits ideally into every investor's portfolio. Each person must work out his own investment salvation for himself.

That's why the best advice that was ever given is "investigate before you invest." And the investigation should properly begin with your own financial situation.

CHAPTER 33

When Is the Time to Sell?

THUS far we have been talking almost exclusively about buying stocks — about investing for the long pull.

But just because a convincing case can be made for the fact that it is a good idea to have extra dollars invested, it doesn't follow that it is a good idea to keep them invested in the same securities forever.

Change is the common denominator of all life. And change can, and does, vitally affect the value of all investments.

The intelligent investor keeps in mind two broad kinds of change — change in one's personal financial situation, and change in available investment opportunities.

As far as the first is concerned, it is perfectly obvious that the kind of investment program that is well suited to a young person with no great responsibilities is not the kind of program that same young person should pursue when starting a family. And investments that are geared to that period of life when the heaviest load is being carried are not the kind to be made when the kids are through school and the investor is able — at the peak period of earning power — to branch out again and try to build something of an estate before having to start thinking about retirement.

It is, of course, always later than we think. Changes in an individual's personal situation, in financial circumstances, often come so gradually that the person is rarely shocked into an awareness that it is high time he sat down and took a personal inventory of his situation — where he stands now and where he is headed. Most of us are just too used to drifting with the tide.

This is particularly true as far as investments are concerned because of the strange, irrational attachment that most men and women seem to feel for the stocks and bonds they own. It's no overstatement to say that many a person becomes married to a stock and is apt to talk about it to associates a good deal more pridefully than about almost anything else.

Once a person buys stock in a company he often seems to feel some sort of compulsion to talk it up to others — sell it to them. Thus he seeks from others confirmation of his own good judgment. In such circumstances, he regards the sale of his stock as tantamount to treason.

There is another psychological reason why most people are loath to sell securities. Very often, the original investment decision — the selection of stock A over B, C, or D — was so charged with emotional conflict that the buyer wants to shut the door on the whole episode. The investor doesn't relish the idea of fighting out the issue all over again and weighing the comparative values of the purchased stock against E, F, or G.

Nevertheless, there is the inexorable fact that investment values constantly change and what was a good buy last year may be an even better *sale* this year.

Every investor owes it to himself to take an objective look at his holdings — as objective as possible — at least once a year. And when he tackles that job, he should ask himself at least one simple question about every stock in his list: "If I had the money, would I buy this stock at today's prices?"

If the answer is no, if you own a stock you wouldn't enthusiastically want to buy at that moment, you should consider selling it, even if you have to take a loss on it — or *especially* if you have to take a loss.

If you don't want to make the decision yourself, you may wish to ask your broker for his opinion. In fact, if you don't want to review your whole investment program once a year, as you should, you can submit the problem with all pertinent data to your broker and ask for recommendations and suggestions. Brokers are used to such requests, and in the main they do a remarkably conscientious job on them. They know that suggestions for changes that are made simply for the sake of building commissions are bound to backfire and result, eventually, in the loss of customers.

Of course, there are some investors who approach the job of evaluating their securities with the kind of relish that all of us should bring to bear on the job. These are usually the same stockholders who carefully read the annual and quarterly reports that they get from the companies whose stock they own and painstakingly compare performance with results in other years and other companies.

While only a trained analyst can get the real meat out of a corporate report, there are a few simple points that every investor can check easily to determine if there are any danger signals that might suggest the desirability of a switch to another stock.

If a stock's dividend is cut, even the least sophisticated investor is apt to be properly concerned, but the dividend is actually of less importance in evaluating a stock than the earnings figure. If a company's earnings drop, the stockholder has a right to know why. Often there are legitimate reasons. The company may have decided to put a substantial sum of money into the development of a new product not yet on the market, or it may have embarked on some new program of plant expansion. Such decisions might cut sharply into earnings for any given year, but they may also hold a promise of expanded profits in years to come.

Again, there are times when business in general or a given industry in particular may go through a period of stress. Hence, a company's earnings record must always be considered on a comparative basis. A bad earnings record for your stock is in itself no substantial reason for a switch in holdings if other companies in the same industry are doing no better.

Any cut in dividends or drop in earnings is certain to be fully elaborated on in the company's annual report. Although the management will place the most palatable construction possible on such unpleasant facts, its explanations are apt to be pretty trustworthy, for these reports must pass the scrutiny of trained security analysts in brokerage offices and financial institutions all across the country.

The price-earnings ratio of a stock, which is shown in the stock tables published in big city newspapers and can always be computed from the reported figures, is actually a more reliable measure of investment value than straight earnings per share. This is because the P.E. ratio reflects something of how other investors regard your stock. Suppose your stock sold last year at a price fifteen times earnings, but this year it sells only at ten times earnings. A drop like that would reflect a serious loss of investor confidence in your company, unless, of course, stocks in general had been under heavy selling pressure and price-earnings ratios had dropped all across the board.

A decline in the price-earning ratio of your stock is the kind of danger signal that suggests that a more intensive study of other figures in the annual report might be in order. You might, for instance, look at the *income statement* and see how net sales have fared. Have they fallen off to a disturbing degree? And what about operating costs? Have they risen unduly? Has there consequently been a serious squeeze on profit from operations — net sales less operating costs? How does the margin of profit, obtained by dividing net income by net sales, compare with the figure for earlier years and with margins of other companies in the same industry?

Next, you might take a look at some of the key figures shown in the company's *balance sheet*. You will especially want to look at the *current assets* and *current liabilities*. On the asset side of the ledger you will want to see if there has been any big drop in the company's cash position or in its holdings of government bonds. You might similarly be concerned about any undue increase in *accounts receivable* — what people owe your company — or in inventories. Any big increase in inventories of finished goods is apt to prove risky, for a sharp drop in prices could cause heavy losses. Or it might suggest that the company had a lot of unsalable merchandise on its hands. On the other hand, a big increase in the inventory of raw materials might be regarded more hopefully. At a time when prices are rising generally, an increase in raw-material inventories might suggest that your company had very prudently decided to stock up when prices were low. It could also imply that your company anticipates good sales ahead for its finished products.

As far as current liabilities are concerned, the most important item is apt to be *accounts payable,* for this represents the money your company owes for raw materials, supplies, insurance, and the like.

More important than the total figure for current assets or the total figure for current liabilities is the relationship between the two. Most security analysts figure that current assets should be twice as large as current liabilities. But that is only a rough rule of thumb: in industries like railroads, where inventories are not a major problem and where accounts receivable can easily be collected, lower ratios of assets to liabilities are acceptable. On the other hand, in industries like chemicals or tobacco, ratios of three-to-one or four-to-one are more commonly expected.

The difference between current assets and current liabilities represents a company's *net working capital* — the money it has to grow on. This is the lifeblood of a business. Any serious shrinkage from year to year in a company's working capital is something that should worry an investor and make him think seriously about selling his stock.

For an investor, the payoff figure in the balance sheet is the figure for *stockholders' equity* or *net worth.* This is usually shown on a per-share basis. It is the figure he most wants to see grow because over a period of time that figure will determine not only the book value of the stock but the price he is likely to get for it.

The stockholders' equity is made up of three components: (1) *capital stock*, which is the actual declared value of the company's stock when it was originally issued and which may or may not be identical with its par value; (2) *capital surplus*, which is the amount over and above the declared value that the company might have been able to realize on the original sale of stock; and (3) accumulated retained earnings or *earned surplus*, which is the amount of money that the company has earned over the years, less what it has paid out in dividends.

Of course, even if an investor takes the time and trouble to look at just a few of these key factors in his company's annual report — and there is no question that he should — he is still not likely to have a substantial basis for deciding to buy or sell. This is because the figures for any given year take on real meaning only as they are compared with the same figures for earlier years and for other companies in the same field.

Finally, the most important question of all — how good is the management? — is one to which the investor can find only an implicative answer in any annual report.

In evaluating a company's reports, an investor has the right to look for help and advice from his broker. Within reason, he can expect detailed and specific answers to his questions, reliable data on the basis of which he can make up his own mind whether to buy, sell, or hold.

While brokers are frequently accused of stimulating customers to switch from one stock to another for the sake of building commissions, the blunt fact of the matter is that many don't suggest enough sales to their customers, probably because they fear being accused of churning. And the customer, left to his own devices, goes along with his broker's inaction, holding on to the same old stocks, blissfully ignoring his own self-interest. A few years ago a New York Stock Exchange survey showed that a third of all people who owned stock had never sold any. They had just bought and held on.

This static attitude toward investments is reflected in figures showing the *"turnover rate"* on the New York Stock Exchange. The turnover rate shows the percentage of all the shares listed on the exchange that is traded in any given year. From 1915 to 1920 it was 117%. Although it dropped to 70% from 1920 to 1925, it rose to a peak of 132% in 1928. From then on the trend was almost steadily downward to a low of 9% in 1942. There has been a revival of trading interest since then, but the average figure for 1950 to 1960 stood at only 15%. It dropped back to 12% in 1962 but revived again to 16% in 1965 and headed straight on up to 24% in 1968. Falling stock prices and contracting volume took their toll in 1974, however, and the rate fell back again to 16%, only to recover to 33% by 1981. Of course, the number of shares listed on the New York Stock Exchange has increased steadily over the years, so percentage figures are somewhat misleading. As the number of listed shares increases, trading activity as a percentage of the total listings is almost bound to decrease.

As far as actual trading volume is concerned, it was not until 1963 that the volume of shares traded surpassed the 1,124,800,000 shares that changed hands in 1929. In 1981, it reached an all-time high — up to that point — of 11,850,000,000 shares.

The do-nothing attitude of many stockholders holding substantial profits is unquestionably explained by their reluctance to pay a capital-gains tax on their profits. This is certainly the least defensible of all reasons not to sell.

Because the long-term outlook for American business is a bright and promising one, no one wants to preach a doctrine of "sell . . . sell . . . sell." Nevertheless, if you think you can improve your investment position, it is ridiculous to go along comforted simply by the thought that inflation and an expanding economy will rescue you from your own faulty judgment.

It is a truism of the stock market that there are sell orders to match all buy orders. There have to be. That's something worth remembering. And here's something else worth remembering. The individual who sells a stock — some stock you own, perhaps — very often has done his homework a little more conscientiously than the buyer. He may have a better reason for selling the stock than anybody has for buying it — or than you have for holding it.

CHAPTER 34

The Folklore of the Market

THE cheapest commodity in the world is investment advice from people not equipped to give it.

Many a man who doesn't own a share of stock fancies himself an authority on the market. He's always ready and willing to deliver himself of an opinion about it on the slightest provocation. If he actually owns stock himself, chances are you won't have to ask his opinion. He'll tell you what to buy, what to sell, and what's going to happen to the market. And you can't stop him.

The more a man knows about the market, the less he is willing to commit himself about it. The wisest of them all, old J. P. Morgan, when asked his opinion of the market, always used to reply, "It will fluctuate." He wasn't just being canny. He knew that was the only provable statement that could be made about the market.

Nevertheless, over the years a number of generalizations about the market and about investing has come to be accepted as gospel. Actually, those homespun axioms must be accepted as just that — little more than folklore. Like most folklore, each of them has a certain element of truth about it — and a certain element of untruth.

For instance: *"Buy 'em and put 'em away."*

This would have been a fine piece of advice if you had bought

$1,000 worth of General Motors stock in 1923. By the end of 1981 that stock would have been worth almost $30,000, and you would have collected over $70,000 in dividends. Had you been lucky enough to sell your General Motors before both the gasoline crisis and the 1973–1974 recession had taken their toll, you would have realized more than $100,000 — for General Motors has dropped 50 points since then.

Of course, in the early twenties the car company everybody was talking about was Stutz — not General Motors — and there was a great deal of speculative interest in Stutz stock. You might very well have decided to put your $1,000 into that. How would you have made out on that purchase? The answer is that you would have lost all your money, and, furthermore, you would never have collected a penny in dividends.

Of course, there is a measure of sense in the axiom. If you start worrying about fluctuations of a point or two and try to buy and sell on every turn, you can needlessly pay out a lot of money in commissions and you may end up with less profit than if you'd "bought 'em and put 'em away."

Nevertheless, it's only good sense to remember that securities are perishable. Values do change with the passage of time. Industries die, and new ones are born. Companies rise and fall. The wise investor will take a good look at all his securities at least once a year. And he could do worse than to ask his broker to review them with him then.

"You never go broke taking a profit."

That's obviously true. But you can certainly be badly hurt.

Suppose you had put $50 into Sears, Roebuck in 1906. By 1940, the stock that you had bought would have been worth $1,276 at its high. That would have been a nice profit — and you might have decided to take it.

But look what you would have lost if you had sold. By 1954 your same holdings in that stock would have been worth over $4,300, and by the end of 1981 your $50 investment would have been worth almost $12,000.

Or consider another classic case. In 1914, you could have bought 100 shares of stock in International Business Machines for $2,750, and in just eleven short years you could have sold out for $6,364. Certainly you can never go broke taking a profit of nearly 250%.

But as far as IBM stock is concerned, you certainly would have taken a licking if you had sold in 1925. For by the end of 1981, your original 100 shares would have grown to 291,192 and they would have had a market value of over $17,000,000. A few years earlier, when IBM was selling at $365 a share, you could have sold your IBM for $26,571,270. The government's antitrust action (which was not dismissed until January 1982), coupled with the recession, whittled away over half of that value in the next two years.

Of course, a profit is always a nice thing to have — in the pocket, not just on paper.

"Buy when others are selling. Sell when they buy."

This is a neat trick, if you can do it.

Obviously, you can't make money if you consistently buck the trend of the market. Where, for instance, would you have been if you had been selling stock all through various bull markets since 1950?

So the trick lies in anticipating the action of all the others — in buying just before the crowd decides to buy and selling just ahead of them. This is exactly the trick that the exponents of various formula plans try to turn by hitching their buying and selling operations to various technical declines or advances in the market.

Others, less scientific, simply try to sell at the top and buy at the bottom. But how do you know when the market hits bottom? How far down is down?

Make no mistake about it. Anyone who tries to practice this fine art is "playing the market" in the purest sense of the phrase. He's speculating; he's not investing.

"Don't sell on strike news."

There's some truth to this old adage. Nowadays, labor troubles in any big company or in any industry are apt to be pretty well publicized. Consequently, the market is likely to have discounted the possibility of a strike during the time when it was brewing. The stock will already have gone down in price in anticipation of the strike, and it may even advance when the strike news breaks.

Again, many people think that a strike doesn't really damage a company's long-term profit picture. They contend that while a strike is on, demand for the company's products is only deferred. As soon as the strike is over, the company begins enjoying better business than ever.

But such a theory is often little more than wishful thinking. After all, most strikes end with the company facing higher labor costs. And many times the demand for its products, which the company couldn't fill while its employees were on strike, has been happily filled by a competitor.

"Don't overstay the market."

A fine piece of advice. But how do you know when to sell and take your profit — if that's what you're primarily interested in?

Sometimes you can tell by watching those basic business indicators that show what's happening to production, distribution, and consumption of goods. But sometimes you can't, because the market doesn't always pay close attention to them. Sometimes business looks good and the stock market skids. Sometimes the reverse is true.

Nevertheless, if business appears to be on the skids and the stock market is still boiling merrily upward, sooner or later there's going to be a reckoning.

"Always cut your losses quickly."

Nobody wants to ride all the way downhill with a stock if the company is headed for bankruptcy, as Chrysler — a formerly well regarded stock — seemed to be in 1981. However, at the same time you don't want to be stampeded into a sale by a price decline that may have no relationship to the fundamental value of the stock.

Remember, the price of a stock at any time reflects the supply and demand for that stock, the opinions and attitudes of all the buyers and all the sellers. If a stock is closely held, if its *floating supply* — the amount usually available in the market — is limited, the price of that stock can be unduly depressed if one large holder sells a sizable block of it just because he needs the cash. That doesn't mean the stock is intrinsically any less worthwhile.

The trading market on any given day is made by just a tiny handful of all those who own stocks. On the exchange, 60,000,000 shares may be traded in one day, but that still represents only $\frac{1}{2}$ of 1% of all shares listed on the exchange. The 99.5% of shares which aren't being sold that day are being held on to by investors who have some reason for holding on — or think they have.

Of course, there is much truth in the observation that unsophisticated investors do tend to sell a stock too readily when they have a profit in it and to hang on to a stock in which they have a loss, hoping that it will come back.

"An investor is just a disappointed speculator."

This cynical observation has a measure of truth in it. Every stock buyer hopes for a big fat fast profit, even if he won't admit it to himself. So, when the market drops, he does the best he can to assuage his disappointment by assuring himself and everybody else that he never really expected to make a killing — he was just investing on the basis of his stocks' fundamental values.

This is especially true of odd-lot buyers, who, all too often, finally decide to buy only when the market is already too high.

So often does this happen that some speculators gauge their own actions by the relation of odd-lot buying to odd-lot selling. When that ratio increases — when the proportion of odd-lot purchases rises — the speculators begin to anticipate a reversal of the upward trend.

But in the long run, the small investor often has the last laugh. After all, the stock market has gone up pretty steadily for 50 years. Since the odd-lot man is principally a heavy buyer of the market leaders — the 100 stocks that usually account for two-thirds of the exchange volume — he has made out pretty well over the long pull.

On the other hand, many a big speculator, like Daniel Drew, has died broke.

"*A bull can make money. A bear can make money. But a hog never can.*"

That's one to remember.

The desire to make money leads most people into the market. Call it ambition, or call it greed, but it still remains the prime motivating force behind our whole business system, including the stock market.

But greed is always dangerous. It's an engine without a governor. So you made a killing once in the market. Good. You were lucky. Don't think you can make one every day.

If you own a good stock, one that's paying you a good return on your money and seems likely to go on doing so, hang on to it. Don't keep looking for greener pastures, bigger profits. And forget about the other fellow and the killing he made — or says he made. Maybe he can afford to speculate more than you can.

In short, if you're an investor, act like one.

CHAPTER 35

Who Owns Stock?

IF Wall Street didn't exist, it would be necessary to invent it. In fact, that's just exactly what our forefathers did.

Why must there be a Wall Street?

Because in our economy, capital, like labor, must be free to work where it wants to. If you've got extra dollars, you've got the right in our society to say where you want to put them to work in order to make more dollars.

And that's a right that would be a pretty empty one if there weren't some means for you to switch your funds from one enterprise to another when you wanted to, just as you might switch from one job to another.

Wall Street provides that means. It's a marketplace for money.

And in the past thirty years, it has played an increasingly important role in our economy. It has made it possible for millions of people to put their savings to work in American business. That has been good for them, good for business, and good for the whole country.

Time was when only wealthy people owned stocks and bonds, but that's no longer the case. For one thing, there aren't as many truly wealthy people as there used to be. Death and taxes have taken their toll.

If business is to have the money it needs to go on growing, somebody has to take the rich man's place. That somebody can only be the investor of moderate means — thousands of such small investors, because it takes 1,000 of them with $1,000 each to equal the $1 million in capital that one wealthy man may have supplied yesteryear. And tomorrow it will take many, many more thousands of them, because business is constantly in need of more and more investment capital to build new plants and replace old equipment. From the turn of the century to the end of World War II, business put $218 billion into plant and equipment. But in the next ten years expansion accelerated so rapidly that $232 billion of capital was needed — more than in all the preceding 46 years. And industry continues to invest in new plants and equipment at an accelerated rate. By the early 1980s such expenditures were running over $100 billion a year.

Wall Street bears the primary responsibility for recruiting the new investors who must supply this capital, Wall Street and all its counterparts throughout America.

Wall Street takes its responsibilities seriously. Every year it puts millions of dollars into booklets, pamphlets, and letters to explain securities. It uses educational advertising: newspapers, magazines, television, radio, even billboards. It has taken the story of stocks and bonds to country fairs, department stores, labor unions, and women's clubs. It has even put the story into movies that any group can show free of charge.

How well has Wall Street done with all this educational effort in stimulating new investor interest?

Better than you might think — but not nearly as well as it must.

Not until June 1952 did Wall Street know just how it stood on the job. Strange as it may seem, nobody could say how many stockholders there were in the country until the New York Stock Exchange got the Brookings Institution to find out. American Telephone & Telegraph knew it had 1,200,000 stockholders back then. And 30 other big companies knew they had 50,000 or more apiece. But nobody knew just what duplication there was in those stockholder lists. And nobody knew the grand total for all companies.

The Brookings Institution reported in 1952 that the total was 6,490,000, representing a little more than 4% of all the individuals, and just about 10% of all the families, in the country. Disappointing as that total figure was when it was announced, Wall Street found encouragement in the fact that about one-fifth of the total had become stockholders in the preceding three years.

Four years after the Brookings study, the New York Stock Exchange retained Alfred Politz Research, Incorporated, to make another census of shareholders. Politz reported a total of 8,630,-000 stockholders in publicly owned corporations, an increase of 33% in four years.

Since then, the New York Stock Exchange has conducted similar censuses every four or five years, and until the second last report, published in December 1975, each census showed a steady increase in share ownership. In 1970, the exchange reported that the total of individual stockholders had passed the 30,000,000 mark. In 1972, estimates placed the number at a record 32,500,-000. But the 1975 census showed an 18.3% drop to 25,200,000. This recovered to 32,260,000 million in 1981's census.

Here are some highlights of that study.

The typical American stockholder is a 46-year-old man. Male shareholders had outnumbered women in the 1965–1970 census, but the standings were reversed in 1970–1975, only to revert in 1981. In fact 52.9% of all stocks were owned by men, as against 47.3% for women. The median age declined by over seven years, reflecting the increasing number of young people entering the market.

The 1981 report also showed that the value of the average investor's portfolio was $5,450, down from over $10,000 in 1975. New York replaced Chicago as the city with the largest number of shareholders.

The average investor was a technical or professional worker

with at least four years' college education and an average household income of $29,000 a year, 60% more than the national average of $17,700. In 1975, the average shareholder's income was $19,000, compared with a national average of $11,800 — almost the same percentage variation.

But despite the gains shown in 1981's census, Wall Street still finds itself confronted by the fundamental question that has been nagging it for a quarter of a century.

Why is it that so many people who can afford to invest don't own any stocks?

Why should shareowners represent only about a quarter of all U.S. families while 64% have savings accounts, 62% own their own homes, and more than three-quarters have life insurance?

In short, why don't more people invest?

There's one clear-cut answer to that. Millions of people still don't understand stocks and bonds. And what people don't understand they are apt to be afraid of.

We may be the richest nation in the world, the very bulwark of a modern and enlightened capitalism, but the blunt fact of the matter is that we are still not a financially enlightened nation.

Yes, ignorance is unquestionably the biggest deterrent to investing. But there's another factor in the picture too. Successful investing isn't simple. It means thinking your own investment problems through to a logical conclusion. It means being willing to study all the facts available about various securities. It means checking up on a stock both before you buy it and after you buy it.

That's not easy, admittedly. But it's not beyond the capabilities of any of us. Not if Nicholas J. Harvalis could do it. You're not likely to remember the story in the newspapers about him when he died in 1950. But he was an uneducated immigrant who worked all his life in restaurants for a wage that never exceeded $125 a month, but who still managed to leave an estate of $160,000.

Here is how he did it, as related by his counselor, Max D. Fromkin of Omaha:

Fromkin & Fromkin
Keeling Building
Omaha 2, Nebraska

February 13th, 1951

I give you now the story of Nicholas J. Harvalis, late of Omaha, Nebraska, who departed this life on the last day of the month and year of 1950, to wit, December 31, 1950, shortly after the close of the market for the year.

Nicholas was a friend of mine for over 25 years, and during that time I was his attorney and counselor.

Nicholas came to this country from Greece at the age of 15 years. He was without education and money, and he immediately went to work as a waiter in various cafes and restaurants operated by his countrymen in Omaha at wages which provided a bare living for him.

He was unmarried and lived the many years in Omaha alone in a modest room.

He was thrifty to a point of many times denying himself the comforts of life in order to save from his earnings sufficient to make investments for his security and old age. He employed his leisure hours reading and studying financial papers and books. He also spent many hours in the public library poring over history and philosophy.

On May 18, 1927, he became a citizen of the United States by naturalization. He was a firm and optimistic believer in the opportunities offered the common man in the United States, and he believed that the greatest return in investments was in common stocks of well-managed companies.

Thus, beginning about 1937, he started a systematic purchase of common stocks. His early investments were in National Distillers, Laclede Gas, General Motors, S. S. Kresge, Atlantic Refining, International Nickel, J. C. Penney, General Electric. He bought a few shares in each of these companies and added to them from time to time.

He kept meticulous records of all of his transactions, including dividends received. His dividends, which at first were modest, he would save and reinvest in these same stocks.

He subscribed to the *Wall Street Journal* and avidly read the paper from cover to cover. As a matter of fact, at the time of his death the only thing in his room apart from bare furnishings was a neat stack of issues of the *Wall Street Journal* for the last two years.

In 1943, he began selling stocks for long-term profits when he felt the market was high, and later he began a repurchasing program.

In 1943, his earnings from wages as a waiter and soda jerk in a local drugstore known as the Paxton Pharmacy at 15th & Harney Streets in Omaha were $1,602.00, while his income from dividends of common stocks was $1,825.00.

In 1944, his earnings from wages were $1,525.00, and his dividends from common stocks rose to $2,285.00. In the same year he made from gains in the sale of stocks the sum of $2,600.00.

In 1945, his wages were the same, but dividends from stocks came to $2,785.60. Long-term profits in that year were $7,713.84.

In 1946, his dividends from stocks fell to $1,506.24, but his gains on the sale of stocks were very substantial.

In 1947, his dividends rose to $2,191.24.

In 1948, his dividends were $10,562.98.

In 1949, his dividends were $7,081.24.

In 1950, his dividends were $10,095.50.

During all these years he earned from wages as a soda jerk a sum not to exceed $1,600 per year.

When he died on December 31, 1950, he was the owner of the following common stocks:

1,370 shares Cities Service common
  200 shares Boeing common
  300 shares Rock Island common
  100 shares General Electric common
  200 shares American Bank Note common
   40 shares Hearst Consolidated Publications 7% preferred
  200 shares Great Northern Iron Ore.

The above shares had an approximate value at the time of his death of $160,000.

Nicholas J. Harvalis kept perfect records and had in his room every statement from his broker of every transaction he had ever made.

In addition he made accurate reports for income tax purposes and was proud to pay his government every cent of tax for the privilege of his citizenship and the opportunity that his government gave him. In my association with him as his attorney I found him always to be a very polite, mild-mannered, and courteous individual. He was often asked for advice on the market and was always very cautious to mention only highly rated dividend-paying stocks.

Nicholas amassed this huge sum considering his limitations and in his death he leaves to his brother and sisters (11 of them) in Greece a substantial inheritance, which they will no doubt spend more freely and with less good judgment than the man who earned it.

> Very truly yours
> MAX FROMKIN

Or consider the story of Sam Hamilton, a dishwasher in a mission and a janitor at the Pacific Stock Exchange. The methods by which this shy octogenarian amassed a $300,000 estate will never be known exactly, but according to a spokesman for the Life Line Mission, mentioned in his will, Mr. Hamilton must have gathered some pretty good information in his many years of sweeping and cleaning around the stock exchange.

Few of us would be willing to pay the price Mr. Harvalis or Mr. Hamilton did for their achievement. But then most of us would be willing to settle for just a small measure of their success — the success that can be achieved not by luck, not by "inside tips," not by speculation, but only by prudent and intelligent investing.

CHAPTER *36*

Stock Screens

BY utilizing high-speed computers, Wall Street research firms have been able to examine the total body of all stocks available for investment and ferret out those that meet only various sets of rigorous statistical criteria. Now it is even possible to program the computer to sift through thousands of potential investment-grade stocks and pick out only that handful that meets several sets of these criteria simultaneously — stocks that have similar earnings, dividend payout, cash flow, or capitalization characteristics that make them likely investment candidates for certain specific types of stock buyers.

These computer stock "screens" or "nets" are available from a wide range of brokerage house research departments. They also appear on a regular basis in a number of general financial advisories and magazines, including Standard and Poor's *Outlook,* Value Line's *Investment Survey,* and in Forbes "Statistical Spotlight" columns. The average investor should find these computerized stock screens a tremendous help in narrowing his range of potential investment vehicles, as well as an invaluable aid in determining just what criteria are important in picking a particular stock for him to buy.

The following is a selection of basic stock screens that were applicable in January 1982. They are presented here to give you some small idea of how they work and of the tremendous potential range of their statistical fine tuning.

COMPUTER SCREEN #1: NYSE. Companies That Have
Paid Higher Dividends in Each of the Past Ten Years and
Whose Current Yield Is over 10%

The computer ran through all the stocks listed on the New
York Stock Exchange. First it pinpointed all the companies that
had raised their dividends in each of the past ten years. There
were 162. From these it then selected the 24 stocks whose current
yield exceeded 10%. The rationale for this screen is obvious. It is
for income-conscious investors who seek the stability of a NYSE-
listed company, a higher than average current yield, and a solid
indication based on past evidence that that yield will continue to
rise every year just as the real value of the yield diminishes because of the dollar's gradual devaluation.

This screen can be more finely tuned to pick out companies
whose yield has risen by a certain percent in the past ten years,
stocks whose recent price action does not reflect their rising dividends, stocks with low price/earnings ratios, et cetera. The
beauty of screening stocks with computers is that additional criteria can be added to the program indefinitely, until the only
stocks the computer has left are those that match the individual
investor's needs and wishes perfectly.

Computer Screen #1's results are shown on page 332.

Faced with these 24 dividend-increase leaders, the individual
investor can then decide whether he wants a company with a
larger current yield (Kansas Gas and Electric, Long Island Light-
ing, Niagara Mohawk Power) or one that has raised its dividend
extraordinarily fast (Nevada Power, Florida Power and Light,
Houston Industries). He is also now free to investigate thoroughly the individual companies the computer has selected, to
see if they fulfill his other investment criteria, to see if they stand
up under objective financial scrutiny, and to determine if there is
any negative reason why these particular stocks are the great
bargains they seem to be. In this particular screen, for example,
most of the stocks pinpointed by the computer are utilities. And

Stock	Current Yield (%)	Percentage Increase in 10 Years
Allegheny Power System	13.5	54
Atlantic City Electric	11.8	50
Cleveland Electric Illuminating	13.5	42
Connecticut Natural Gas	12.2	77
Florida Power and Light	10.5	176
Hawaii Electric	11.4	93
Household International	11.0	98
Houston Industries	12.0	140
Idaho Power	12.0	52
Kansas Gas and Electric	14.1	42
Long Island Lighting	13.9	39
Louisville Gas and Electric	12.3	27
Middle South Utilities	12.8	56
Minnesota Gas	10.8	47
Montana Dakota Utilities	11.1	108
Nevada Power	11.6	258
Niagara Mohawk Power	13.7	46
Public Service Indiana	12.4	78
Rochester Gas and Electric	12.6	100
South Carolina Electric and Gas	12.1	33
Southwestern Public Service	11.5	97
Utah Power and Light	12.2	124
Washington Water Power	12.9	66
Wisconsin Public Service	10.9	66

in early 1982, utilities, which need to borrow huge amounts of money to finance their continuing operations, were under great pressure because of the dramatic increases in interest rates on those borrowed funds. This is a dramatic indication of how and why computer screening of stocks should never be the end of the road for investors, but merely a tool for beginning the stock selection process, a process which should always continue with an extensive investigation of the companies the computer has selected out.

COMPUTER SCREEN #2. Companies Whose Dividends
Will Be 100% Free of Federal Income Tax during the
Coming Year

Here the computer has pinpointed stocks whose current yearly dividend exceeded the earnings that it reported to the IRS for tax purposes. The IRS has determined that when that happens, the difference is a return of capital, and therefore not subject to federal income tax. It is important to remember that investors must use the portion of a dividend that is a return of capital to reduce their cost basis for the stock. When they sell the stock either their capital gain will increase or their loss will decrease. It is also important to remember that since the dividends these companies are paying out are greater than the amount of money they are taking in, neither this dividend, nor in some cases the very financial underpinning of the companies themselves, can be considered very secure.

Computer Screen #2 companies are American Family, Apache Petroleum, Boston Edison, Fairchild Industries, Forest Oil Corp., General Dynamics, Green Mountain Power, Grumman Corp., Mesa Petroleum, National Student Marketing, Ohio Edison, Pennsylvania Power and Light, Public Service Company of New Hampshire, Rockower Brothers, Rouse Company, San Juan Racing Association, U.V. Industries Liquidating Trust, Universal Marion.

This screen can further be fine-tuned to reveal which companies have been paying tax-free dividends for an extended period of time, which are anticipating future earnings to offset their accumulated payouts, and which offer a particularly generous yield. (Many of the stocks included in this screen have yields of 10% or more.)

COMPUTER SCREEN #3. Stocks Selling for at Least
an 80% Discount to Their Net Liquidating Value

American International (selling at 51% of its net liquidating
value), Superscope Inc. (53%), Bobbie Brooks Inc. (54%),
Craig Corp. (64%), Sterchi Brothers Stores (69%), Barber-
Greene (70%), Facet Enterprises (71%), Dynamics Corporation
of America (74%), Aileen Inc. (75%), Vista Resources (78%),
Gordon Jewelry (78%): this is a list of stocks whose current per-
share price on the exchange is not equal to at least four-fifths of
its real per-share worth in terms of net working capital (that is,
current assets less all current liabilities, including long-term debt
and preferred issues). Theoretically it offers investors a chance
to buy a dollar's worth of assets for 51¢ to 78¢.

COMPUTER SCREEN #4. Stocks Whose Current Price
Earnings Ratios Are under Three

Pan American World Airways (1.2 price/earnings ratio), Atlas
Corp. (2.1 p.e.), Mesta Machine (2.3 p.e.), Allied Supermarkets
(2.4 p.e.), U.S. Steel (2.4 p.e.), Filmways Inc. (2.5 p.e.), L.T.V.
Corp. (2.6 p.e.), L.F.E. Corp. (2.9 p.e.), Republic Steel (2.9
p.e.): this is a list of stocks whose current per-share price has a
ratio to its current annual earnings per share of less than 3:1. All
other things being equal, it is a screen of stocks selling at bargain-
basement prices relative to the amount of money they made the
previous year.

COMPUTER SCREEN #5. Stocks Whose Total Annual
Return Is at Least 63% of Its Current Per Share Price.

Armada Corp. (total annual return is 93% of its current per-
share price), A.V.X. Corp. (71%), Millipore Corp. (69%), International Harvester (67%), Robintech Inc. (66%), Benguet
Corp. (66%), Atlas Consolidated "B" (65%), Tubos De Acero
(64%), American Quasar Petroleum (63%), Spectra Physics

(63%), Sunshine Mining (63%), K.D.T. Industries (63%), Ranger Oil (63%): for the purposes of this screen a company's annual return is defined as its current yield plus its growth plus its appreciation due to a changing p.e. trend. This screen therefore identifies thirteen companies with stock selling at per-share prices very near to the amount of return they're generating on their capital every year.

COMPUTER SCREEN #6. Stocks Whose Outstanding Shares Have the Greatest Market Value

Such stocks are American Telephone and Telegraph ($44.53 billion total market value), IBM ($33.50 billion), Exxon Corp. ($26.03 billion), Schlumberger ($14.18 billion), Standard Oil of Indiana ($13.40 billion), Standard Oil of California ($12.79 billion), General Electric ($12.70 billion), Shell Oil ($11.28 billion), Eastman Kodak ($11.26 billion), General Motors ($11.25 billion).

One hundred and two publicly traded U.S. corporations had market values in outstanding shares exceeding $2 billion in early 1982. A list of these stocks ranked by total market value would be extremely useful for an individual who placed a great value on either the size of his stocks' stake in the world economy, or in their ability to withstand external economic shocks or internal financial problems by virtue of their very size.

COMPUTER SCREEN #7. Stocks of Companies with Average Growth Rates over 30% for the Past Ten Years and Projected 18%+ Growth Rate for the Next Five Years

Some of these are Wal-Mart Stores (39% average growth rate over the past ten years), Fremont General "A" (37%), Tymshare Inc. (36%), Texas Oil and Gas (34%), Ranger Oil (34%), Church's Fried Chicken (33%), Dome Petroleum (33%), First Mississippi (33%), Natomas Company (33%), Valley Industries (33%), Humanna Inc. (32%), Lennar Corp. (32%), Petro-Lewis

(32%), Waste Management Inc. (32%), Mary Kay Cosmetics (31%), National Data Corp. (31%), Sigmor Corp. (31%), Western Company of North America (30%).

Of course, just because a company has grown dynamically in the past is no guarantee that it will continue the same pattern of growth into the future. But it is a good starting point. And the fact that a company has attained impressive growth over a full decade with no notable negative impact on its financial structure automatically gives it a positive image in investors' minds over companies which have not achieved similar growth. And if you add to this screening process the factor of a low price earnings ratio you can further identify stocks whose dramatic growth has not yet been discovered by the marketplace.

COMPUTER SCREEN #8. Stocks with over 20% Return
on Capital over the Past Five Years, Ranked by Earnings
Retained to Common Equity

Tandy Corporation (40% of earnings retained to common equity), Texas Pacific Land Trust (39%), Intermedics Inc. (37%), Commodore International (32%), Criton Corp. (30%), Teledyne Inc. (28%), Fremont General "A" (28%), Rolm Corp. (27%), Savin Corp. (27%), Brooks Fashion (26%): here is a screen which measures the productivity of a company with its capital relative to how much of that productivity the company uses to invest in its future.

COMPUTER SCREEN #9. Stocks of Companies That
Have Earned in the Past Five Years More than Three Times
as Much Cash Flow as Was Required to Build
Plant and Pay Dividends

Lin Broadcasting (6.34 times the amount of "cash flow" to cash out), Shapell Industries (5.64), Commerce Clearing House (5.01), Presley Construction (4.13), Teledyne Inc. (4.04), U.S. Home Corp. (4.02), Columbia Pictures (3.99), Pulte Home (3.67), Standard Pacific (3.58), Capital Cities Communication

(3.56), Kaufman and Broad (3.46), Loews Corp. (3.26), General Housewares (3.06), Premier Industrial Corp. (3.04).

There can't be a much better test of a public corporation's overall efficiency than the extended record of how much more money it has earned than it has paid out.

COMPUTER SCREEN #10. Stocks of Companies with No Long-Term Debt, 15% Recent Returns on Equity, and Price/Earnings Ratios under Six

American Filtrona Corp., Falconbridge Copper, O'Sullivan, Page Airways, Sturm, Ruger and Co., Tri-Chem, United Keno Hill Mines, Wham-O Manufacturing: here's a screen of companies that don't owe anybody any money, make a lot of money themselves, and haven't had the price of their stock bid up by eagle-eyed bargain hunters — yet.

Obviously the number of different computerized stock screens it is possible to come up with is limited only by the number of different statistical variables it is possible to feed into the computer. And there are so many variables that impact in so many different ways on the varying preferences and needs of individual investors that the number of different combinations is practically limitless. With the aid of screens you can get from your broker, or glean from the financial press, and with the information you get by comparing the historical performances of similar stocks in all kinds of past markets, it should be possible for you to narrow your investment choices down to a handful of stocks that satisfy your own personal financial demands.

CHAPTER 37

The New Investment Areas

FOR the first six editions of this book we limited the investment areas under discussion to the basics: stocks, bonds, mutual funds, and options. We did this not only because these vehicles comprised the principal investment tools in Wall Street's basic inventory, but also because they were the most accessible areas for the average investor and they offered the most tested means of participating in America's present and future growth.

We still believe that common stocks are the best long-term investment tool for the average American. They are truly "shares" in the tremendous accumulated wealth and glowing future prospects of this country's business community. And now, perhaps more than ever before, this is both a present reality and a future hope that is being unrealistically discounted in the marketplace. On June 30, 1976, the day on which the sixth edition of this book went to press, the Dow Jones industrial average stood at 1002.76. As this seventh edition is being prepared, in February 1982, the Dow has fallen to 833.80. In a 5½-year period, during which the price of almost everything else has at least doubled, the price of the average stock, as measured by an assortment of popular averages, has declined 15 to 20%. Publicly owned American companies are making historically high profits, paying out historically high dividends, and their prospects, in both domestic and international markets, have never looked better. Still, stock prices are down. This is not a condition that can continue for very long. We believe common stocks are the last bargain around, and that prudent investors who show their faith in American commerce by buying them now stand to profit more than participants in any other investment area — that is, as soon as the relationship of these stocks' *value* to their *cost* rights itself. As it always has.

Still, because the prices of American stocks and bonds have remained so relatively depressed throughout the seventies and early eighties, because inflation has remained so high, and because investment professionals, including most of the major brokerage houses, have been so diligent in creating new instruments for these increasingly complicated financial times, the investor finds himself now faced with a growing, and increasingly complicated, field of alternatives vying for his investment dollar. Most of the products available in these emerging investment areas can be participated in through your stockbroker. Those that cannot can surely be explained to you by him. What follows is a brief description of all of these alternate investment vehicles, an explanation of how the average investor can participate in each of them, and some suggestions for further reading about them.

Futures: Commodity and Otherwise

Buying futures is very much like buying stock options. When you buy a *future* you are buying the right to purchase a certain amount of a specific thing at a specific price for a specific period of time. For example, you can buy the right to purchase 5,000 bushels of wheat for $4.30 a bushel for any time up to six months. In times of generally rising prices, which, in fact, is most of the time, the "farther out" the option is — that is, the longer it remains possible for you to buy the commodity at that specific price — the more the option costs you. The principal difference between futures contracts and stock options is that in futures contracts the buyer never actually takes physical delivery of the commodity he has bought. There is no equity in buying futures.

It is now possible to buy futures contracts in over 30 different commodities, including soybeans, cocoa, orange juice, cattle, and other edibles; silver, gold, platinum, copper, and other metals; lumber, cotton, heating oil, and other industrial materials; the yen, franc, pound, and other foreign currencies; Treasury bills and bonds and other money market instruments. It is even possible now to buy a contract on the future course of interest rates and the popular stock averages. Futures trading, however, is generally only for speculators. Ninety percent of all individual-futures traders lose money. And aggregate losses are six times aggregate gains. Even the best commodity traders lose money more often than they make it. They stay ahead of the game by taking small losses right away while letting their gains pile up.

It is the staggering potential profit on a small initial cash investment that is the principal appeal in buying futures. The initial cash requirement is generally 5 to 10% of the market price of the commodity. There is no interest charge on the outstanding balance. And commission charges are relatively low. Thus, if the price of a commodity goes up 10% before the future contract on it expires, the investor who bought that contract can double his money or more.

The best solution for the average investor who wishes to participate in the futures market is to do so through a commodity market pool, which acts like a mutual fund for futures buyers. According to the Commodity Futures Trading Commission, there were 827 such pools in 1982, up from 532 in 1979. In a pool, as in a mutual fund for stocks, the investor simply buys shares, usually in minimum amounts of five units of $1,000 each. He pays a one-time commission of $70 per unit. Some pools include cash disbursements, but, more often, gains and losses are simply distributed among the units, to be taken when the investor sells one. Investors in such pools enjoy the high leverage of the futures market without worrying about margin calls or making trading decisions in markets that change from minute to minute. Even during such generally bad years for commodities as 1980–1981, the pools did well. Of the 36 pools monitored by Norwood Securities, a Chicago brokerage house that doesn't handle commodities business itself, half showed net gains in unit value, for an average gain of 26.3%. The other half showed declines averaging 12.8%. Further, of the nineteen funds in existence at the start of 1981, eleven had gains averaging 32.9%; the others had an average loss of 15.3%.

Further reading on futures: Stanley W. Angrist, *Sensible Speculating in Commodities* (Simon & Schuster).

Commodities Magazine, 219 Parkade, Cedar Falls, Iowa, 50613, published monthly;

Tewdels, Harlon, and Stone, *The Commodity Futures Trading Guide* (McGraw-Hill).

Gold

Until the Great Depression of the 1930s, Americans were allowed to own as much gold as they wanted to. Gold coins were legal tender. But in 1934 the Gold Reserve Act made ownership of gold bullion, except for industrial purposes, illegal. It also fixed the price of gold at $35 an ounce. From that point until 1968, as the price of everything else rose dramatically, the price of gold remained static. In 1968 the Gold Pool, formed by the United States and seven other large western governments to trade gold at a stable $35 price, went out of business because of increased demand for the metal from foreign investors. The price of gold was set free. From that point until early 1980, spurred on by President Ford's lifting of the gold sales ban to individual Americans in 1974, the price of gold rose in steady spurts to $875 an ounce. It has since settled back to less than 40% of that price, although gold bugs everywhere predict an eventual rebound to even higher highs.

Gold is the purest hedge investment in the marketplace. It is an internationally recognized medium of exchange. It is portable. And, unlike paper currency, it has legitimate underlying value. In times of political economic turmoil people return again and again to gold as *the* medium of exchange. This is why gold prices rise in times of growing inflation (and falling interest rates) and also why gold always moves upward whenever world peace is threatened. Gold is a crisis commodity. It does well when everything else is doing poorly, or looks as if it is about to do poorly.

There are five basic ways to invest in gold.

(1) Gold futures, which allow you to buy a fixed amount of gold at a fixed price for a certain specified amount of time, like all futures contracts, are basically closed-ended speculations meant only for sophisticated traders.

(2) Gold stocks — shares in U.S., Canadian, and South African mines — are, many of them, traded on the larger exchanges and some, particularly the South Africans, because of the uncertain political climate in that country, pay substantial dividends.

(3) Gold mutual funds buy a wide range of such gold mining stocks.

(4) Gold bullion can be bought through, and both stored and insured by, large brokerage houses like Merrill Lynch.

(5) Gold coins, both antique and freshly minted: these latter are bullion coins sold for little more than the price of the gold they contain. Most weigh one ounce. In February 1982, the American Gold Coin Exchange, a subsidiary of the American Stock Exchange, made gold coins the most accessible gold investment for most Americans when it began trading South African Krugerrands, Mexican pesos, Canadian Maple Leafs, and Austrian crowns at or near the spot-metal price plus approximately 2% commission. Purchasers could avoid local sales taxes by having their coins stored in a Delaware vault operated by the exchange. Again, major brokerage houses are equipped to handle such transactions.

Silver

When Alexander Hamilton was establishing this country's monetary system, he pegged silver at one-sixteenth the price of gold. Since then silver has generally commanded a price reflective of that relationship. In early 1980, however, while gold was climbing to its all-time high of $875 per ounce, silver was staging its own panic buying rally. Fueled by increasing margin buying by the Hunt brothers of Texas, silver shot up in a few short months from $10 to over $50 an ounce. Then the Commodities Trading Commission stepped in and demanded that more cash be put into such speculative margin buys. The price of silver dropped even faster than it had risen, until in mid-1982 it fell below $5 an ounce, at a time when gold was selling for $350 an ounce. The old 16:1 gold/silver ratio, which had been reestablished during silver's 1980 climb, had fallen to an all time low of 60:1.

Silver, like gold, is basically a crisis metal, a natural store of value to which investors automatically turn when the value of paper currency seems to be eroding. But because silver is so much cheaper than gold, it is also much less portable. With silver currently selling for one-fiftieth the price per ounce as gold, $10,000 worth of physical silver takes up 50 times as much space and is 50 times heavier to carry than the same sum in gold. This lack of portability seriously diminishes silver's worth as a crisis investment. Still, silver has a wide variety of industrial uses — in photography, dentistry, and industry — and this fact, plus the chronic shortfall between annual demand and yearly production, leaves most metals analysts feeling that silver is a very good long-term investment indeed at current prices, despite the government's repeated attempts to sell off its massive stockpiles and despite the heavy supplies of hoarded ornamental and coin silver that always seem to appear during any price increase.

Like gold, silver can be bought either on the futures market, in the form of stocks in mines (although as of this writing there exists no mutual fund that buys only silver stocks), as bullion, or as coins. Most large brokerage houses can buy bullion for you in one-ounce, twenty-ounce, 50-ounce, 100-ounce, or 1,000-ounce bars or ingots. All such bars should have international hallmarks. Experts agree that the best way to buy silver coins is to buy U.S. silver coins minted prior to 1976. One hundred dollars in dimes, quarters, and halves weighs about five and a half pounds and contains 71.5 troy ounces of silver. Collector coins, such as Morgan half-dollars, may sell at premiums higher than the meltdown value of their silver. As this is written, several large silver mining companies are planning to manufacture their own one-ounce coins to rival the Kruggerands and other gold coins. There is not yet, however, any official market for the trading of such silver coins.

Other Metals

The only other precious metal that is widely traded on world markets is platinum. It is essential for a large number of industrial processes, and is extremely rare. Over twenty times as much gold as platinum is mined every year worldwide. Platinum is traded on the futures exchanges, as is its sister metal palladium. They are the only other precious metals so traded. Both platinum and palladium are also available, although not readily, in physical form.

Of the nonprecious industrial metals, copper is the most actively and widely traded. Copper futures contracts are traded on most commodity exchanges. Other industrial metals that maintain active markets but that are generally impractical for individual investors to speculate in are aluminum, antimony, lead, pig iron, mercury, tin, steel, and zinc. Daily quotations for all are published in the *Wall Street Journal* and *New York Times*.

During the early 1980s one other family of metals has emerged as a particularly interesting investment area — the so-called strategic metals: titanium, cobalt, chromium, manganese, tantalum, indium, rhodium, vanadium, and several others. All of them have very specific industrial applications and several are critical in the production of defense weaponry. In 1981 President Reagan announced his intentions to increase as soon as possible the supplies in the drastically depleted U.S. strategic metals stockpile. Strategics are mined primarily in South Africa and Russia. Political disruptions and dwindling supplies of these metals could therefore send prices sharply higher at any moment. Individuals can invest in strategics by buying quantities of the metals themselves through brokers, by acquiring stocks in companies that utilize them, or, perhaps in the near future, by joining an investment pool or partnership that will buy the metals for their investors.

The difficulties in buying strategic metals are many: there is no organized exchange or futures market for them; trades are executed through dealers in direct negotiations; prices aren't published in newspapers or any other readily available publication; the metals come in many different grades, complicating matters enormously; markets are thin, and like any other "hot" investment area the strategic field has its share of shady salesmen and marginally viable brokerages. That is why the handful of large brokerage houses that traffic in strategics are so careful about them, requiring of potential customers an annual income of $25,000 or more, $75,000 in net assets exclusive of a house, $20,000 in liquid assets, and the signing of a suitability letter that spells out all the potential dangers. Typically, 25% of the amount of a strategics purchase price must be put down beforehand, with the balance due in two days. Commissions run to about 5% of the purchase price plus insurance and storage fees.

Further reading on gold, silver, and other metals: Donald Hoppe, *How to Invest in Gold Coins* (Arco [paperback]); Donald Hoppe, *How to Invest in Gold Stocks* (Arlington House); *Silver Profits for the Eighties* by Jerome Smith (ERC Publishing); *Get Really Rich in the Coming Super Metals Boom* by Gordon McLendon (Pocket Books [paperback]); "Behind the Hype for Strategic Metals," *Changing Times Magazine* (November 1981); *Gold Newsletter*, 8422 Oak Street, New Orleans, Louisiana, 70118.

Coins, Gems, and Other Collectibles

In addition to the gold and silver coins that are in common circulation or are currently being manufactured to be bought by investors, there is another class of coin — the collectible coin, sometimes of ancient vintage — which by virtue of its rarity sells for a premium above that which most other coins command. These coins can be bought from local dealers, but it is always best to compare prices, condition, and guarantees. Prices for the same graded coin can vary substantially among dealers. Two large, reliable firms that guarantee their coins are Numisco in Chicago and Deak Perera in New York City.

Gems are another hard-asset investment area that has attracted considerable public interest in recent years. Gems can be bought as either rough stones, cut stones, or as components in new or antique jewelry pieces. Diamonds alone constitute one very active gem market. The other two markets are composed of colored precious gemstones (rubies, emeralds, and sapphires) and semi-precious stones (opals, topazes, aquamarines, tourmalines, amethysts, garnets, tsavorites, et cetera). The retail markup for gems is very high, so investors must be prepared to hold on to them for a long time to make a profit. Quality and cut are also of great importance, so that some experience in judging stones is necessary before plunging into the gem market. Until recently individual investors who wished to buy gems had to do so either from a retail merchant or a private party or at auction. Recently, however, there has been talk of several brokerage houses setting up "diamond trusts," permitting small investors to own units of investment-grade diamond collections for minimum investments of $1,000.

The number of collectible investment areas is almost limitless: art, antiques, stamps, autographs, rare books, antique cars, vintage wine, baseball cards. Almost any well-made artifact that appeals to the aesthetic sense or nostalgic sensibilities of a cross section of human beings and is in somewhat short supply is a potential investment collectible. The keys to getting into the collectible market are (1) knowledge — find out as much as is possible about your specific area of investment — (2) passion — if you don't really care about what you're collecting, your time would probably be much more fruitfully spent investing in some

less subjective area — (3) quality — all experts agree that it is
the better examples of any collectible that appreciate the fastest
and the most — (4) knowing where to buy — in collectibles prices
and quality vary more widely than in any other investment area.

Most collectibles, like coins and gems, are bought either from
retail dealers or galleries, or at auction, particularly from the
larger international auction houses like Sotheby's and Phillips,
which started out dealing mostly in art but have rapidly expanded into every imaginable collectible area. During the early
1980s several small regional brokerage houses experimented with
the notion of coin, stamp, and art pools — getting $10,000 from
individual investors, securing the advice of expert consultants in
these various collectible fields, and buying a portfolio, in whose
future appreciation the individual investors would share to the
extent of his financial contribution to the pool. The progress of
such pools lost its momentum during the collectible price decline
of 1981. But because the notion of a "mutual fund" for collectibles
seemed like an idea whose time had come, such pools promised to
make a comeback as soon as collectible and other hard-asset investment prices start rising again.

Further reading: everything the beginning or advanced investor in collectibles is likely to need to know can be found in
current or back issues of *Collector Investment Magazine*, a mar-
velously readable, comprehensive, and concise guide to current
trends in all the collectibles markets (740 Rush St., Chicago, IL,
60611); Bowerd and Ruddy Galleries, Los Angeles, *High Profits
from Rare Coin Investments;* Michael Freedman, *The Diamond
Book* (Dow, Jones, Irwin).

Real Estate

Real estate was the big inflation-hedge investment winner all
throughout the seventies, with prices in some areas of the country
rising by 500 to 600% during the decade. With 9% mortgages
paying for 15% inflation, homebuyers were actually being paid to

buy an investment that they could then both live in and use as a tax deduction. It seemed like the best of all possible worlds. In the early eighties, however, as mortgage rates rose and inflation rates fell, it became extremely problematical whether or not real estate prices, despite the pent-up demand caused by the maturing baby boom and the long-standing inactivity in building, could sustain their previous gains.

Nevertheless, as real estate boomed, the proliferation of imaginative variations on investing in land and commercial and residential property kept pace. At this writing it is still possible, of course, to buy traditional real estate parcels — single-family houses, apartment buildings, commercial parcels, and raw land — through traditional real estate brokers. But it is also possible to buy cooperative and condominium apartments, time-sharing opportunities in resort properties, high yielding second mortgages with capital gain potential in three to five years, real estate investment trusts traded on the various stock exchanges, pooled partnerships formed and marketed by various syndicators and brokerage houses, "rich uncle" partnerships formed by developers to help cash-poor house buyers come up with a down payment. It's even possible to invest in timberland pools, like the one formed in 1981 by First Atlanta Corporation. Yes, there are almost as many ways to invest in real estate today as there are individuals willing to invest. But the wrinkles are endlessly complicated, and the potential for loss heightened by those complications. Real estate investors need to be particularly nimble and well informed.

Further reading: Robert G. Allen, *Nothing Down* (Simon & Schuster); Harcourt, Brace and Jovanovich Newsletter Bureau, *Real Estate Investment Letter*, 747 Third Avenue, New York, NY, 10017 (monthly); Albert Lowry, *How You Can Become Financially Independent by Investing in Real Estate* (Simon & Schuster); George Maier, *Guide to Successful Real Estate Investing* (Prentice-Hall); Maury Seiden and Richard Swesnick, *Real Estate Investment Strategy* (John Wiley).

Foreign Currencies

As the world shrinks faster and faster every year, each individual country's economic condition and inflation rate impacts more directly on its neighbors and trading partners. Thus what kind of money an individual investor holds has come to be almost as important as what sort of investment he puts that money into. Money, after all, is every bit as much a commodity as sugar or wheat, every bit as much a medium of exchange as gold or silver, and, during the late seventies and early eighties, it has come to be as popular a tool of international investment as stocks and bonds. When the Swiss franc appreciates 30% a year compared with the American dollar, while the American stock market is declining 20% during that same period, the investor who bought francs with his dollars rather than shares of General Motors or U.S. Steel has not merely switched the nationality of his monetary holdings; he has made an extremely good investment by selling out of a weak commodity and buying into a strong one.

The average investor is perhaps more intimidated by the prospect of currency transactions than by any other investment possibility. Trading in foreign currencies seems like an exotic undertaking, forbidding because it is supposed to be for only the very wealthy, dangerous because all one gets in return for one's "real money" is a lot of strange-looking paper, which represents an unfamiliar medium of exchange in a very distant place. Yet buying foreign currencies is one of the simplest and most pleasurable of investment activities.

Basically there are four ways to invest in foreign currency. You can buy a futures contract on that currency on one of the futures exchanges. This is a good way to proceed if you think that currency is going to have a pronounced move in a short period of time. Futures trading is generally conducted in Canadian dollars, Swiss francs, Japanese yen, the West German mark, the British pound, the Mexican peso, the Netherlands guilder, and the French franc. You can also buy foreign currency directly from a bank or foreign-currency broker. You can do this either in the form of the notes themselves or in travelers' checks denoted in that currency.

The third way to invest in foreign currency is to open a Swiss bank account. Swiss banks offer an extraordinary array of services: checking and savings accounts in all major currencies; trading and storing of precious metals; buying and selling stocks and bonds on all the world's major exchanges; managed accounts in stocks, bonds, commodities, metals, et cetera; safe deposit boxes; and, of course the Swiss banking community's renowned and inviolable code of secrecy. Opening a Swiss bank account is simple. Just pick the name of a bank out of the many books written on the subject and write them a letter. All correspondence is conducted in English. You can open an account with a personal check, a bank cashier's check, or a money order.

The fourth way to invest in foreign currencies is through the Eurocurrency market. Eurocurrency certificates pay higher dividend rates than Swiss bank savings accounts, are available in a wide variety of foreign currencies, and are available for three-, six-, and nine-month periods.

Foreign Stocks

Most Americans think that the stock market begins and ends on Wall Street. But there are stock markets in London, Paris, Zurich, Milan, Hong Kong — in fact in all the world's major cities. And during the late seventies and early eighties as the American stock market stagnated, many of these bourses flourished, as Japanese and German companies flexed their industrial and technological muscles, as Australian and other Pacific Basin countries began mining and marketing their staggering natural resources, and as the Third World let it be known that the shift of wealth away from the large industrialized democracies was not to be a passing phenomenon.

Today it is almost as easy to buy shares in most foreign stocks as it is to pick up ten shares of IBM. You can open an account with a foreign broker in much the same manner as you do here. Or you can invest in any of hundreds of individual foreign stocks from all over the world that are traded on American stock exchanges as American Depository Receipts (ADRs). Or, finally, and perhaps most conveniently and prudently for the average American investor, you can choose one or more from the growing list of American mutual funds that invest exclusively in foreign stocks. There are now over two dozen such funds, with more being added all the time as foreign investment opportunities and the American economic community's perception of those opportunities increase. Some funds invest in only one geographic area, like Merrill Lynch's Pacific Fund and Japan Fund. Others spread their stock-picking net all over the world, like Templeton Growth Fund or Scudder International Fund. All offer American investors who believe all the growth isn't going to take place at home a chance to broaden their horizons in a geographical and industrial diverse portfolio of international holdings. Contact your stockbroker for more details on specific funds.

Further reading on foreign currencies and stocks: Harry Browne and Terry Coxon, *Inflation Proofing Your Investments* (Warner Books [paperback]); Adrian Day, *Investing without Borders* (Alexandria House Books); Paul Einzig, *A Textbook on Foreign Exchange* (St. Martin's); Mark Skousen, *High Finance on a Low Budget* (Bantam Books [paperback]); *Young's World Money Forecast,* 366 Thames Street, Newport, RI, 02840 (monthly).

Money Market Funds

"The rich get richer and the poor get children." And when it comes to interest on money market vehicles, the rich have always been able to get high yields with their big deposits while the average investor has always had to settle for his 5¼% from a simple savings account. That is, until some financial entrepreneur figured out that if you got enough people with small amounts of money together, they would then have as much cash as one rich investor, and they, or their representative, could go to any bank or corporation or Treasury office and get the highest yield available on that money. That's what money market funds do. They pool lots of little guys' money, invest it in short-term money market instruments, take a small percentage of the total portfolio yield as a service charge, then return the rest to the individual investor in proportion to the amount of money he has invested. In early 1982, there were over 100 such money market funds, with their number increasing weekly. Two dozen or so invested solely in government securities for safety's sake. The others had their portfolios apportioned thus: 38.6% commercial paper (short-term, unsecured corporate promissory notes); 15.2%, short-term repurchase agreements (usually governmental); 12.2%, bank certificates of deposit; 11.2%, European and Yankee dollar investments (foreign bank certificates of deposit); 9.2%, bankers' acceptances (used to finance foreign trade); 7.7%, federal agency securities; and 7.1%, U.S. Treasury bills.

With demands persisting for credit from corporations and the government alike, money market fund yields ranged between 15% and 17% throughout 1981 and into 1982. Of course, the big investor with more than $100,000 to plunk down in a bank certificate of deposit or a piece of short-term commercial paper could still negotiate with a bank or broker a rate of interest a point or so higher than any a money market fund could provide. But at least the spread between the yields millionaires could command and those available to the average investor had narrowed to a palatable range through this most popular investment innovation of the seventies.

All major brokerage houses now include a money market fund among the products they offer to their customers.

Further reading: William E. Donoghue, *Complete Money Market Guide* (Bantam Books [paperback]); *Donoghue's Moneyletter*, P.O. Box 401, Holliston, MA, 01746 (24 issues);

Money Fund Safety Ratings, 3471 N. Federal Highway, Fort Lauderdale, FL (monthly); Paul Sarnoff, *The Smart Investor's Guide to the Money Market* (Signet Books [paperback]).

Tax Shelters

Of course, the best investment plan in the world won't do you any good if you don't get to keep any of the money you make by following it. And the biggest guarantor to your keeping as little of your investment income as seems possible has always been the taxing arm of the federal government. Still, just as the tax man taketh away, he also giveth, because the government has discovered that if it taxes too heavily the profits every investor has to take some risk to make, pretty soon there won't be any investors willing to take such risks. And no risk capital means no business expansion. And no business expansion means no jobs, no taxes, no government, and, ultimately, no country.

So the government has made statutory additions to the federal tax code that allow investors to shelter a certain amount of income and gains from specific investments — either in the form of deductions, exclusions, or deferred payments. And various tax experts and economic entrepreneurs have set up a wide assortment of programs designed to help investors in all income brackets take advantage of these shelter opportunities. In earlier chapters we have discussed two of the most common investment tax shelters: the long-term capital gains tax, which shelters from federal taxes 75% of all profits on stocks held for one year or longer, and the exclusion from all federal taxes of interest on municipal bonds.

But in recent years many large brokerage houses have formed tax shelter departments of their own — to help their customers pick the appropriate shelter opportunity for their fiscal and family situation from among the many confusing and constantly changing opportunities available. Investors can now shelter income by investing in certain areas of real estate, oil and gas exploration, equipment leasing, livestock raising, movies, and an exotic assortment of other specifically structured shelters. These tax shelter programs are not for the beginning investor, nor even for the average wage earner paying less than 30% of his income in taxes. But as income increases tax shelters begin to make more sense. As long as they show promise of making money eventually as well as sheltering it from taxes now, as long as you are in a high enough tax bracket so that the expenditures and illiquidity inherent in any tax shelter make sense, and as long as you pick a trustworthy and competent specialist to pick the right shelter for you from the maze of endlessly changing options available. Your broker can either recommend someone to you or choose for you someone from the tax shelter section of his own firm.

Retirement Plans

Most specialized tax shelters may just be for investors in the upper income brackets. But there is one long-term tax shelter opportunity that is for *everyone*. It is the tax-deferred retirement program in the form of Individual Retirement Accounts, Keogh Plans, and annuities. Every American should take advantage of the many saving features these plans offer.

Beginning in 1982 everyone with earned income, whether covered by an existing pension plan or not, can contribute up to $2,000 of that earned income ($4,000 for joint return, $2,250 for couples with one nonworking spouse) to an *Individual Retirement Account (IRA)*. This money is automatically sheltered from federal taxes until the individual starts taking it out of the plan at age 59½, at which time he will probably be in a lower tax bracket. In addition, all the money this money earns while it is in the IRA is exempt from taxes. However, stiff financial penalties apply to those who remove funds from their IRAs.

The individual IRA holder has a wide variety of choices of how to invest his IRA money, but except in the case of government retirement bonds, the money has to be invested through a custodian or trustee who's been approved by the IRS. Such trustees include banks, credit unions, mutual funds, insurance companies, and brokerage firms. You can have as many IRA accounts as you wish as long as the total annual contributions don't exceed $2,000. Annual administrative fees charged by trustees may make it impractical to have too many IRAs, however. And you can move your money between your accounts only once a year, although if you invest in a so called *fund family* — a mutual fund like Dreyfus or Fidelity, which has many different types of funds (money market, stock, bond, and others) — you can move your money around among as many different component funds of the fund family as you wish as often as you want. You should ask your broker which IRA investment plan he recommends for you.

Should you try to lock in high-current-interest yields with a fixed-rate certificate of deposit? Should you invest in a fund family? Or should you establish a self-directed IRA account at your brokerage house, which allows you to pick your own stocks for your IRA portfolio? Whichever way you go, the advantages to establishing and maintaining an IRA to its full limits are staggering: if you put in $2,000 annually beginning at age 29½, and it grows at only 10% a year, you'll have over $360,000 at age 59½.

Keogh Plans are IRAs for the self-employed. They work in very much the same way as IRAs except that individuals with Keogh Plans can contribute up to 15% of their annual income, or $15,000 a year, whichever is less. Keogh Plan holders can also have an IRA.

A wide variety of annuities, some of them tax sheltered, are also available from various fund families, brokerage houses, and insurance companies. These are self-imposed long-term savings programs with no maximum limits on their contributions.

Whichever form of retirement account you choose, you should definitely choose one, with the help of your banker or broker. Not only are they a painless way to save for your retirement, but they offer an unprecedented opportunity to shelter part of your present income, and all of that money's future yields, from federal taxes.

Further reading on tax shelters and retirement plans: William Drollinger, *Tax Shelters and Tax Free Income for Everyone* (Epic); Robert and Carol Tannenburg, *Tax Shelters: A Complete Guide* (Harmony Books); *The Retirement Letter*, 7315 Wisconsin Avenue, 1200 N. Bethesda, MD 20014 (monthly); *Tax Shelter Digest*, Suite 604, 9550 Forest Lane, Dallas, TX, 75243 (monthly).

Cash Management Accounts

In the early 1980s many large brokerage houses and other financial institutions began to develop programs for "umbrella-ing" all their services in one account. Merrill Lynch's Cash Management Account was the pioneer in this field. It allows customers who start with a $20,000 balance in their account to write checks against it, use a special Visa credit card against it, buy stocks, bonds, gold, or any of Merrill Lynch's numerous other investment products with it, either in cash or on margin, all transactions to be recorded in one monthy statement and all of the spare cash in the account to be yielding competitive current money market fund rates. The CMA and its numerous competitors are an extremely useful new tool the American brokerage community is developing to help clear away the confusion surrounding, and consolidate the activity in, the staggering number of varied investment possibilities that have been developed for the average investor in the past few years. Surely even more new investment possibilities, and ways of making them more understandable and accessible to the public, are on the way.

CHAPTER *38*

Further Reading

NOW that you have familiarized yourself with the basics of investing in common stocks you can begin to deepen your knowledge of specialized areas and techniques. What follows is a list of books to help you do just that. They are the books most often recommended by investment authorities. Some are old. Some are new. Some are dispassionately restrained. Some are passionately strident. But all are eminently approachable by the average reader. And all should be read with careful attention to the individual prejudices and idiosyncrasies of the authors and a clear eye to how the information and techniques outlined in them can best be applied to your own individual investment program.

Basics

Kiril Sokoloff, *The Thinking Investors Guide to the Stock Market.* The editor of the *Personal Finance Letter* explains why stock prices move the way they do in simple, understandable language.

Paul H. Cootner, ed., *The Random Character of Stock Market Prices.* A scholarly examination of market forces in 22 essays written by 22 different specialists.

Gerald Loeb, *The Battle for Investment Survival* and *The Battle for Stock Market Profits.* The "Dean of Wall Street" outlines his practical stock investment theories, based on 35 years' experience as a broker.

David Darst, *The Complete Bond Book* and *The Handbook of the Bond and Money Markets.* Everything you need to know about bonds and how and when to buy them.

C. Colbrun Hardy, ed., *Dun and Bradstreet's Guide to Your Investments.* A simplified guide to all investment markets and how to participate in them. Revised annually.

Andrew Tobias, *The Only Investment Guide You'll Ever Need.* A brief, witty and extremely lucid disentangling of the sometimes overpowering money puzzle.

Burton Crane, *The Sophisticated Investor.* A former *New York Times* financial reporter distills his lengthy experience to outline the basic happenings on Wall Street.

United Business Service, *Successful Investing: A Complete Guide to Your Financial Future.* A complete guide to sensible, long term investing.

Technical Analysis

Robert D. Edwards and John Magee, *The Technical Analysis of Stock Trends.* The Bible of the Chartists. The essential work on technical effects on stock prices.

William D. Gann, *Forty-five Years in Wall Street.* One of Wall Street's most successful veteran technicians explains his 24 rules for profitable trading.

Joseph Granville, *Granville's New Strategy of Daily Stock Market Timing for Maximum Profit.* Wall Street's most flamboyant technician reveals his trading secrets.

William Jiler, *How Charts Can Help You in the Stock Market.* The most basic primer on technical strategy. Clear. Concise. Comprehensive.

Jesse Livermore, *How to Trade in Stocks.* The legendary speculator summarizes his trading philosophy.

Thomas Noddings, *Advanced Investment Strategies.* The most accessible explanation of "hedging" techniques ever written.

Alexander Paris, *A Complete Guide to Trading Profits.* A short course in technical analysis, mixed with a brief distillation of fundamental strategies.

Richard Russell, *The Dow Theory Today*. The most famous and reliable technical theory thoroughly examined, simply explained, and totally updated.

William X. Scheinman, *Why Most Investors Are Wrong Most of the Time*. A relatively new concept — a blending of technical and fundamental analysis with psychological factors called divergent analysis.

Harry Schultz, *Bear Markets: How to Survive and Make Money in Them*. Explains how to prosper during the 33⅓% of the time the general market is tumbling.

Kenneth Smilen and Kenneth Safian, *Investment Profits Through Market Timing. A Professional Approach*. When to buy and sell is as important as *what* to buy and sell. Two professional money managers explain their timing tips.

Ernest Staby, *Stock Market Trading: Point and Figure Investing Made Easy*. Explains the technician's most popular technique clearly and thoroughly.

Conrad Thomas, *How to Sell Short and Perform Other Wondrous Feats*. A breezy distillation of all the technicians' many tools.

Jerome Tuccille, *Everything the Beginner Needs to Know to Invest Shrewdly*. A successful broker outlines the basic theories and techniques.

Fundamental Analysis

Benjamin Graham and David Dodd, *Security Analysis: Principles and Techniques*. The fundamentalist Bible. Explains how to recognize underlying value in a stock and the company it represents.

Benjamin Graham, *The Intelligent Investor*. The "Father of fundamental analysis" outlines the sound principles he's devised in his half-century of stock market experience.

Douglas Bellemore, *The Strategic Investor.* A guideline to a prudent lifelong stock-accumulation program.

Richard Blackman, *Follow the Leaders.* A practical self-help book for everyone who seeks to build a profitable long-term investment program.

Roger Bridwell, *The Battle for Financial Security: How to Invest in the Runaway 80's.* A guide for middle-income investors to inflation-resistant stocks.

Peter L. Bernstein, *Economist on Wall Street.* A literate contrarian and former money manager delivers a dispassionate overview on both economic theory and sound practical investing.

Ira Cobleigh, *The Dowbeaters.* Outlines techniques used by Wall Street's most successful minds to identify potential capital gains candidates.

David Dreman, *Contrarian Investment Strategy.* The basic explanation of contrarian thinking. Explains why experts are mostly wrong and how to profit from this fact.

Philip Fischer, *Common Stocks and Uncommon Profits.* A successful investment counselor explains how he picks winners for his wealthy clients.

Norman Fosback, *Stock Market Logic.* The results of a five-year study applies mathematics to the study of financial data to produce stock market profits.

Jacob O. Kamm, *Making Profits in the Stock Market.* A sound long-term stock buying plan based on an intelligent and unified overall game plan.

Winthrop Knowlton, *Growth Opportunities in Common Stocks.* An experienced analyst tells how to recognize the most dynamic growth stocks.

Lin Tso, *The Investor's Guide to Stock Market Profits in Seasoned and Emerging Industries.* A respected veteran analyst tells how to pick the right industries to invest in at the right time.

Burton Malkiel, *The Inflation Beater's Investment Guide.* A Princeton professor explains why, and *which*, stocks are the best inflation hedges for the eighties.

Justin Mamis and Robert Mamis, *When to Sell.* First-rate advice on the critical issue of market timing.

Sam Shulsky, *Sam Shulsky on Investing.* The veteran financial journalist sums up his own practical investment philosophy.

Kiril Sokoloff, *The Paine Webber Handbook of Stock and Bond Analysis.* An industry-by-industry analysis of portfolio design and proper diversification.

John Touhey, *Stock Market Forecasting for Alert Investors.* A perceptive analysis of the 11 economic indicators the author feels most influence the market.

John Train, *The Money Masters.* An in-depth analysis of the techniques used by the great portfolio managers. Indispensable.

James Nisbet, *The Dow is Dead.* How to find, and when to buy and sell, stocks in undiscovered growth companies.

Anthologies

Bill Adler, ed., *The Wall Street Reader.* Selections from all the prominent theorists: Loeb, Cobleigh, Crane, et cetera.

Harry D. Schultz, ed., *A Treasury of Wall Street Wisdom.* More of the same.

Special Interests

Leonard Silk, *Economics in Plain English.*

Colleen Moore, *How Women Can Make Money in the Stock Market.*

John Tracy, *How to Read a Financial Report.*

Peter Wyckoff, *The Language of Wall Street.*

George Selden, *The Psychology of the Stock Market.*

David Markstein, *How to Make Money with Mutual Funds.*

Paul Sarnoff, *Puts and Calls: The Complete Guide.*

Sidney Fried, *Investing and Speculating with Convertibles.*

Edwin O. Thorp, *Beat the Market: A Scientific Stock Market System.*

Adam Smith, *The Money Game.*
Victor Harper, *Handbook of Investment Products and Services.*
Charles Mackey, *Extraordinary Popular Delusions and the Madness of Crowds.*

Behind The Scenes

"Brutus" (John Spooner), *Confessions of a Stockholder.*
T. A. Wise and the Editors of *Fortune, The Insiders, A Stockholder's Guide to Wall Street.*
Martin Mayer, *Wall Street, Men and Money.*
Murray Teigh Bloom, *Rogues to Riches.*
John Sprizer, *If They're So Smart, How Come You're Not Rich.*
Leonard Sloane, *The Anatomy of the Floor.*
Robert Sobel, *Inside Wall Street.*

History

John Brooks, *Once in Golconda. The Seven Fat Years.*
Charles Collman, *Our Mysterious Panics.*
Stewart Holbrook, *The Age of the Moguls.*
John Kenneth Galbraith, *The Great Crash.*
Matthew Josephson, *The Robber Barons.*
Donald Rogers, *The Day the Market Crashed.*
Robert Sobel, *NYSE. AMEX. The Last Bull Market. The Big Board. Panic on Wall Street. The Great Bull Market.*
Dan Thomas, *The Plungers and the Peacocks.*

Biography

Bernard Baruch, *My Story.*
Ralph G. Martin, *The Wizard of Wall Street: The Story of Gerald M. Loeb.*
Sidney Rheinstein, *Trade Whims.*
Paul Sarnoff, *Jesse Livermore, Speculator King.*

Bibliographies

Sheldon Zerden, *Best Books on the Stock Market.*

James B. Woy, *Investment Methods: A Bibliographic Guide.*

Sylvia Mechanic, *Investment Bibliography* (Brooklyn Public Library).

Index